QUEEN

OF THE

AIR

DEAN JENSEN

QUEEN

OF THE

AIR

A TRUE STORY OF LOVE
AND TRAGEDY AT THE CIRCUS

CROWN PUBLISHERS
NEW YORK

Copyright © 2013 by Dean N. Jensen

Published in the United States by Crown Publishers, an imprint of the Crown
Publishing Group, a division of Random House, Inc., New York.
www.crownpublishing.com

Library of Congress Cataloging-in-Publication Data
Jensen, Dean.
Queen of the air: a true story of love and tragedy at the circus/Dean Jensen.
     p.   cm.
1. Leitzel, Lillian. 2. Aerialists—United States—Biography. 3. Woman circus
performers—United States—Biography. I. Title.
GV1811.L424J46 2012
791.3'4092—dc23
[B]   2012018066

ISBN 978-0-307-98656-6
eISBN 978-0-307-98658-0

Printed in the United States of America

BOOK DESIGN BY ELINA D. NUDELMAN
JACKET DESIGN BY BEN WISEMAN
JACKET PHOTOGRAPHY: COURTESY OF CIRCUS WORLD MUSEUM, BARABOO, WISCONSIN

10 9 8 7 6 5 4 3 2 1

First Edition

for my wife, rosemary, still and forever the center ring star in my life;
my daughters, jennifer anne loew and jessica jensen maxwell;
my son, dane marco antonio jensen; and
my grandchildren, lucas, kyle, and brendan.

and in memory of the late charles philip (chappie) fox, the circus's
greatest champion of the twentieth century, and the man who opened
my eyes and heart to what its excitement is all about.

PROLOGUE

$\mathcal{A}$ soaking rain had fallen much of the day, turning the circus lot into a quagmire. By sundown, though, the downpour finally had stopped, and now, on this mid-June night in Boston in 1919, a canary-colored moon hung over the Ringling Bros. and Barnum & Bailey tents like a blessing.

A show had been under way in the big top for more than an hour. It was a little beyond eight o'clock when two women, one of them in a costume of white and spangled chiffon, plodded to the great tent from the circus's train, idled on a railroad siding a quarter mile away.

From a little distance, the costumed woman looked like a child. She was delicate of face and frame, and so tiny, just four foot nine. She walked with her eyes cast to the ground, careful to avoid placing her kid slippers into the puddles and the depressions left in the mud by the circus's elephants and horses. The woman at her side was her lady-in-waiting and constant companion. She was over six feet tall and wore a charwoman's bonnet and a dowdy, ankle-length, cinder-colored dress. Her expression was unchanging in its dolefulness, and she had teeth that leaned every which way like gravestones in an unattended cemetery.

A hundred or more of the circus's other attachés were already bunched up at the big top's back door by the time the costumed woman and her consort arrived there. The gathering included wire walkers, clowns, the trainers of the big cats, and even some of the sideshow's freaks. Such back-door groupings always formed when it was close to the time she was about to perform. It was a way for the other troupers to pay regular homage to her. She was queen to the circus's thirteen hundred performers and laborers, and by far its greatest star.

A brassy, Napoleonic-sounding composition started playing inside the big top, the "Crimson Cradle March," a work expressly written for the Queen of the Air, as she was known. The music's sounding was a cue for those gathered at the door. A seam opened midway in the swarm, through which she and her maid advanced.

A diagonal column of white light aimed from above located her the instant she appeared in the tent, and the roaring that erupted from the crowd was almost fearful. The big top shuddered as though it were housing a great cataract like Niagara Falls. There were fifteen thousand people in attendance this night, a full house.

Your great-grandparents or great-great-grandparents could have seen her that night in Boston, or, if not there, maybe in Chicago, San Francisco, Biloxi, or some other town. The Ringling circus, the most gigantic ever assembled, traveled by train to about 125 towns each year, staying three, four, or more days in some of them. The circus put on two shows daily, a matinee and evening performance, and often played to two and a half million people in a season. Its queen was almost certainly seen live by more people of her time than any other single figure in America, whether a prima ballerina, a sports hero, or even the president.

With the crowd still cheering, she skipped to the center ring, throwing kisses to every corner of the canvas cathedral. Her attendant was eight or ten feet behind her, outside the spotlight, holding a train of white tulle that streamed from her employer.

Inside the ring, after taking more bows, she moved to her web, a thick, white, velvet-wrapped rope that served as her transit way to the big top's stratosphere. She started moving upward, hand over hand. Her ascent was made easily, without strain, as if she had simply entered an elevator and pushed a button to the fifth or sixth floor.

Then she was in the big top's heavens, and now even the spectators in the highest seats had to tilt back their heads to see her. Her expression was one of pure rapture, and she appeared to have instantly transformed into a state more Icarus-like than human.

And then she was flying.

Flying.

Sailing, soaring, swooping.

She weighed fewer than one hundred pounds on the ground, but up here, she seemed to be incorporeal, as heftless as a butterfly. The air embraced her, held her protectively, loved her.

She was now aboard a trapeze and moving ever higher in the ether—so high that in her upward swings it appeared she might burst through the canvas ceiling and keep rising until vanishing in the sky.

"Mother of god," the people in the seats cried at the wonder of her.

She might have been inside a dream, one of those glorious reveries that maybe everyone has, in which the dreamer discovers that by simply willing it, she or he can lift and fly over church steeples, above mountains, above the clouds.

She clung to the trapeze's bar by just a single hand as it moved pendulously in a great arc. She did hand and headstands on the widely sweeping bar. Then, changing her position, she dangled from it upside down, with one of her legs crooked at the knee over the bar. Finally she journeyed in space with her arms and legs akimbo, secured to the conveyance by nothing more than the nape of her neck.

"Mother of god."

After minutes of such cavorting, she left the trapeze for another appurtenance in her playground, a rope hanging down from above with a silver hand ring at its bottom. She pushed her right hand through the ring and then gripped the rope. She was now hanging loosely fifty or sixty feet in the air, without a net anywhere between her and the earthen hippodrome floor.

Her back-and-forth movements were slight, almost imperceptible, at first. In not many seconds, though, her body started describing half circles in the air. She continued to rise, her feet moving higher than her head in her forward and backward swings. In seconds more, she started turning full heels-over-head circles in the big top's sky. With each of the turnovers, her arm dislocated from her shoulder, and then clicked back in place.

Some in the crowd started tolling off the numbers of each of her revolutions: "One . . . Five . . . Fifteen . . . Twenty . . ." But then, her throw-overs started coming so fast that she changed into a white blur, and it became harder for most of the spectators to continue their counts.

The tresses atop her head that her lady-in-waiting had earlier bobby-pinned in place started to become undone and fall. They banged softly at her beaming face in golden corkscrews.

"Oh, mother of god," the crowd gasped.

Typically, the little queen essayed about a hundred of the revolutions in her performances. But the pain in her shoulder may have bothered her more this night than most others. She ended her turns somewhere short of her usual number and descended her web to harvest her applause.

The rushing sound of a mighty cataract returned to the tent. Almost everybody in the tent was standing, and applauding, and cheering.

"Leitzel . . . Leitzel . . . Leitzel . . ."

She bowed and bowed, and flung kisses in every direction. Then, with her maid following, she made her way to the tent's back door. The crowd was not willing to yield her to the night so easily, though. Leitzel was called back a second time to say good night, and then a third and a fourth.

Many of the circus queen's subjects were still outside the back door when she left the tent a final time. Among them were three midgets.

"How splendid you were tonight, Mademoiselle," one of them said to her. "It was seventy-nine, wasn't it?"

One of the other dwarves was carrying a flashlight. He laid down a carpet of light before her.

"Look out for the mud," he cautioned.

Leitzel, her maid, and the three little men then started poking over the puddled and miry ground to the siding where the train gleamed in the moonlight. There, they came upon two teenage boys who were leaning against the queen's wheeled apartment, smoking cigarettes.

They were members of a Japanese acrobatic troupe. One of the young men lifted the queen to the foot ledge just outside the door to her quarters. Next, he offered her a wish just before she closed the door behind her.

"Beautiful dreams for honorable little lady," he said.

PART ONE

Nellie Pelikan, age fourteen, mother of Leitzel
(author's collection)

CHAPTER 1

Firelight was entering the circus wagon through a narrow open door when Nellie woke. The orange light was jumpy, flickering. It played over the walls of the roofed wagon and its collection of costumes, trunks, hoops, juggling balls, and other props. The air in the wheeled cabin was scented with woodsmoke and meadow grass.

She lay on a straw-filled ticking spread on the plank flooring. At her side, sharing the thin mattress with her, were an eight-year-old boy and nine-year-old girl, a brother and sister. Nellie was unable to communicate with them. They were Czech. She understood only German and a little Polish.

Always, though, Nellie and the children held hands as they lay together as the wagon rolled through the nights, with the brother and sister whimpering, "Matka . . . Matka . . ." over and over before falling asleep, and Nellie crying, "Mutter . . . Mutter . . ."

It was the spring of 1890, April or May.

Nellie Pelikan was twelve, and doll-like. She was small for her age, maybe four foot four or five. Her head bore a large corona of soft curls that were exactly the chestnut brown of her sad eyes.

She along with the brother and sister were wards of Willy Dosta, the operator of a one-wagon, one-horse circus. The show was one of hundreds of such gypsy affairs that toured Europe in the second half of the nineteenth century. Mostly the Willy Dosta Circus rolled over the rutty roads veining the dark, thickly forested wilderness of the Carpathian Mountains along the boundary between Poland and Czechoslovakia. The circus depended on free-will offerings and seldom played to audiences of more than a dozen or so.

This night, as every night, Nellie and her companions had fallen asleep while Dosta was at the reins, searching for another hamlet where he could put down the show. At the time Nellie awoke, though, the wagon was off the road and stopped in a clearing. It was dark outside except for the flaring of a fire. It might have been in the dead of night or an hour or two before dawn.

She had awakened with an urge to empty her bladder. She squirmed this way and that on the mattress, hoping that she could hold off leaving the wagon until daylight.

Her discomfort grew and finally she rose from the bedding. The floor creaked beneath her bare feet. She tried to step more lightly. She did not want to disturb the sleep of the brother and sister.

She froze when she had padded to the open door, startled at the sight before her. Thirty or forty steps outside was Reiter, the Percheron horse that not only towed the wagon from place to place but also appeared in the ring of the Willy Dosta Circus. Reiter was a gentle horse, but freakishly massive, twenty hands, almost seven feet, and with the inky air blanking all details of the landscape around him, he appeared to Nellie to have grown to an even greater size. Not only that, but Reiter was glowing. His white-gray coat was fluorescing with crimson light. The great horse was tethered near a campfire, munching grass.

Closer to the fire, lying on a scrap of canvas, was Willy Dosta. His boots were on one side of him and his rifle on the other, and he appeared to be sleeping. Dosta, a Scotsman, was a man in his late thirties, with a broad chest, muscular arms, and the neck of a bull. His red mustache was so bushy it masked the entire lower third of his face like a bandanna covering the mouth of a stagecoach bandit.

Nellie shivered. She cowered at every sight of him. Even in sleep, his expression was one of sullenness. It had been that way since that spring night a month or two earlier when, as she cried and screamed and begged to be released, he penned her inside the circus wagon, latched the door with a lock, and then, with a shake of Reiter's reins, took her from her family in Breslau, Silesia.

Nellie leaped the three feet from the wagon floor to the ground and struck out in a direction opposite from where Dosta lay, wading through a field of hip-high grass. When she had moved a hundred steps or so, she stopped, drew the hem of her nightshirt to her waist, and squatted to pee.

Her head had vanished beneath the top of the grasses when she heard a swishing in the field. Her heart started drumming. She remained crouched, trying to make herself smaller. Brown bears, lynxes, and wolves were everywhere in the Carpathians, but in an instant, she would see an even more frightful animal.

Dosta was at her side, towering over her. He had found her easily by following in the wake she had cut through the grasses.

With a single hand clenching her shoulder, he drew her up and then led her deeper into the grasses. Next, he pushed her to the ground, then dropped down himself and threw one of his heavy muscular legs over hers. He clamped his furry mouth over her lips. She could not scream. She could barely breathe. He slipped a hand under her nightshirt and moved it to her chest. He discovered only small, boyish buds there, and moved his hand down beneath her underwear. His fingers were scratchy and hard with calluses from gripping Reiter's reins for hours each day. With his free hand, he slipped the suspenders from his shoulders and pushed down his trousers so the pants legs gathered around his boots.

He was gone when she awoke. She lay in the grass for a moment, looking up at the moon and stars, and then got onto her feet. From afar, as she was approaching the wagon, she saw that Willy was again sprawled out on his patch of canvas near the campfire. She reentered the wagon, and, waiting for daybreak, took her place on the mattress between the sleeping boy and girl.

She must have thought about escaping. But how? Every day the wagon penetrated deeper and higher into the wilds of the Carpathians. Was she a hundred miles from the family home in Breslau or a thousand? She could not have had any idea. She was never even sure of the country she was in. During their meanderings, Dosta and his charges continually wove in and out of regions in Poland, Slovakia, the Ukraine, and Romania.

◆ ◆ ◆

Dosta had rarely spoken to Nellie before, except to issue commands. His relationship toward her became even more remote after the assault. He showed no signs of remorse and seemed to view the molestation as another demonstration that she was fully his chattel.

Nellie ached with homesickness for her mother and four brothers and sisters. But she sank into even deeper despair after the attack. She became preoccupied with one thought: she was going to burn eternally in hell.

Almost from the time Nellie Pelikan started walking, she had lived the life of a nomad. She had been an equestrienne and acrobat in Eduard Pelikan's Family Circus, a show operated by her father. Because she was on the move seven or eight months a year, her schooling was irregular. But winters, when the Pelikans were back in Breslau, she was enrolled in a school operated by Polish nuns. Because her native language was not Polish but German, she had trouble absorbing the lessons of arithmetic and history. Often the nun placed the dunce cap on her head and ordered her to sit on a stool in front of the class.

If Nellie had trouble concentrating on the secular subjects, though, she was attentive when the sister cleared the classroom of the boys and preached to the girls about the evils of fornication. A girl could commit no greater sin than to allow herself to be touched by another in her private areas, the nun would lecture. The sister would then open an oversize copy of Dante's *The Divine Comedy* and, standing before the classroom desks, turn the pages to the illustrations showing wailing sinners in the fiery pits of hell. Some of the children in the pictures seemed to Nellie to be no older than she was.

"This will be your forever if you disobey God's commandment to remain chaste," the nun would warn. "The sinners you see here are still in hell today, and they will be there tomorrow and when all of you are old and gray. Once you enter hell, there is no escape. These sinners are there for the eternities."

The pictures of the sinners stayed in Nellie's mind. She recalled them in all their vivid details after Dosta's attack.

◆ ◆ ◆

Nellie was five when she had started appearing in the circus ring. She was, from the start, the star of Eduard Pelikan's Family Circus. She was also Eduard's great pride. With her legs and arms akimbo, she balanced head-to-head atop her father. And as he rode a galloping horse Roman-style around and around the outdoor ring, she was perched on his shoulders, juggling oranges.

Each year, as Nellie grew older, she became more accomplished. By the time she was eight or nine, her performances were dazzling to behold. Her platform was the broad back of a loping white horse that endlessly circumscribed great rings in grassy fields and the squares of towns where Eduard Pelikan's Family Circus appeared. She threw cartwheels and forward and backward somersaults on the back of the smoothly cantering horse. She finished her turn in the manner of a prima ballerina, posing *en pointe* and seemingly defying all laws of gravity as her four-legged stage continued on and on in its rounds.

Nellie was joined by other siblings in the shows. Her younger sisters, Toni and Tina, appeared in the ring with Eduard, who juggled the pair with his feet. Adolph, the youngest of the Pelikan children, bounded high into the air from a springboard and then tossed somersaults before alighting on his feet. Julia Pelikan, matriarch of the family, had been a trapeze artist in her girlhood in Bohemia. But because there seemed never a time when she was not either nursing a baby or about to give birth to a new one, her appearances in the ring were limited now to singing and clowning.

Once the circus came upon a hamlet where Eduard sensed it could attract even a small audience, he would seek out a playing area. Adolph and his brother, Horace, would unhitch the horse from the wagon and brush away the animal's road dust. Next, as Nellie and the other children were changing into their costumes, the boys walked around the village, banging on drums to let everyone know a circus was about to begin its show. At the conclusion of the performances, Julia and the children would weave among the spectators with tins in their hands, seeking donations. Not all of the proceeds came in the form of coins. Some villagers paid with loaves of bread or live chickens and rabbits. Because the countryside through which the circus traveled was sparsely populated, the family was never rewarded with big purses.

Still, the summers of trouping were happy times. The family enjoyed the adventure of traveling to new places. There was fishing and swimming in the streams almost every day. Most of all, the Pelikans considered themselves richly blessed because they were always together. Nights, after they were at rest from their travels and performances, they would all gather around a fire. Eduard would then dream out loud about someday when the family circus would have its own big tent, travel by train, and play only the bigger cities. His ambition would never be realized.

Eduard had been troubled for years with arthritis, a condition aggravated not just by the sprains and broken bones he had suffered over thirty years as a gymnast and professional strongman but also from decades of working and sleeping outdoors in weather that sometimes was icy and rainy. The arthritis worsened each year, and, in time, he also began suffering from rheumatic fever. There were days when he felt that a red-hot coal was glowing inside his chest, and, after the 1889 touring season, he was forced to quit trouping.

No one was sadder than Nellie. Although quiet and shy in most situations, she reveled in performing and hearing the cheers and applause of the always amazed audiences. She also exulted in the visible signs of pride her father had shown after each of her performances. What troubled her most about the collapse of Eduard Pelikan's Family Circus, though, was how its demise changed her father. He sank into depression and became snappish to her and the other children, and even to Julia.

When the family returned to its quarters in a tenement in Breslau in the fall of 1889, Eduard rolled the circus wagon into the backyard, removed its spoked wheels, and painted over the lettering on its side advertising EDUARD PELIKAN's FAMILY CIRCUS. The wagon that had been the family's summer home was converted into the quarters for a small cabinetmaking shop. Eduard sold the horse that had been in service to the family for dray and ring performances.

◆ ◆ ◆

Willy Dosta must have been surprised at the condition in which he found Eduard in early 1890 when he paid a call at the Pelikan home and saw him in the cabinet shop. By then, Pelikan was bent forward at the waist like a burned matchstick. He needed a cane in each hand to walk.

From the time he was a boy, Eduard had been a *saltimbanque*, a member of a nameless tribe of eternally wandering vagabonds without nationality who lived under the sun and stars, and roved everywhere with trained bears and satchels filled with magic props, or maybe no possessions at all except for an ability to eat fire, swallow swords, or walk ropes.

Spring was just starting its greening. As always at that time, Pelikan was stirred by some unappeasable, almost instinctive urge to again take flight with the family circus. He would not be going out this year, though. He felt like a bird whose wings had been clipped.

He held his hands out for Dosta to see. They were curled into ugly claws.

"I used to be able to throw down an ox with these," he declared. "Now look at them. I can hardly lift a soup spoon to my mouth. How does a man feed a family with hands like these?"

Because his earnings as a cabinetmaker were skimpy, Julia helped out by taking in laundry, including the bloody aprons of a neighborhood butcher. Late at night, while their children slept, she and her husband talked about the need to place the youngest of them in an orphanage.

Dosta recruited the children for his circus by approaching large families that were having trouble feeding their broods. He and Eduard had never been anything more than acquaintances, but as the operators of wagon circuses that snaked through the forests and rural arcadias, their paths had crossed over the years. Dosta regarded Nellie as the most naturally talented child performer he had ever seen. When he learned that Eduard's failing health had forced him to retire the family show, he saw an opportunity.

The air inside the wood shop was sweet with the scent of wood shavings. Dosta placed a small leather pouch on the workbench where, with great pain, Eduard was moving a plane over a cabinet door. Dosta took a seat on a stool.

"I'd like Nellie in my circus this year," he said. He nodded at the pouch on the bench. "It's payment in advance. Enough pay for the entire season. In the fall, when I bring her back, there'll be more money."

Eduard did not look up from his work.

"Nellie's too young," he said. "She needs to be with her mother and father. Who knows what could happen to her out there?"

"I'd look after her good," Dosta said. "I'd look after her like she was my own. She'd never be out of my sight."

Eduard may have stolen a sidewise glance at the money pouch. Pay for an entire circus season. Certainly that would help ease the family's burden. And with Nellie away trouping for the spring and summer, there would be one fewer mouth to feed. Dosta's offer must have sounded tempting. And he may have reasoned that there could be an even more important consideration why Dosta's offer would be good not just for the family, but also for Nellie herself.

Eduard had been around circus people all his life. He saw that, more than any of his other children, Nellie had the potential for greatness, and might someday even monumentalize the Pelikan name in the circus world. When she was performing her lofty springs and graceful pirouettes on the back of a cantering horse, she did not so much resemble a human being as a sylphid, a spirit who, along with the fairies, was most comfortable inhabiting the air. What had hurt Pelikan more than anything else about dismantling the family circus was the disassembling of his ambitions for Nellie. Were he to apprentice her to Dosta, she could continue to burnish her talents as a performer.

Dosta and Eduard talked from the afternoon into the night about

Dosta's proposal to take in Nellie as an apprentice. Eduard finally agreed to Willy's request.

✦ ✦ ✦

Nellie was sobbing and gasping for breath.

Eduard and Julia had just revealed the plan to her. They were apprenticing her to another show, Willy Dosta's Circus. There was no other way. It would mean she would be separated from the family for months, but maybe by the time she returned home, Eduard's health would be improved, and everything would be easier. Maybe, even, the old family circus could be put back together and roll out again the following spring. Julia was weeping herself. She told Nellie that because things had grown so desperate, she was the only hope of keeping the family together.

Julia tried putting her arms around Nellie, but she wriggled free. Her eyes were so welled with tears that the man and woman at the table appeared to her as blurred figures, strangers. She had stopped hearing anything they said.

"No. No. No," she pleaded.

In his frustration at trying to make Nellie understand the gravity of the family's situation, Eduard tried at one point to strike her. His arm, crippled with arthritis and slow moving, was easy to dodge.

Three days later, toward evening, Willy Dosta returned to the Pelikan home. Carrying a small suitcase with Nellie's costumes, Julia led Nellie to the wagon. Eduard was unable to watch Nellie's departure and remained in the house. Nellie was quiet until Dosta opened the door at the back of his wagon. She peered into the half light and saw two other children, a boy and a girl. They were huddling in a far corner, quivering like rabbits. Nellie began crying again, promising her mother she would do anything if she did not have to leave home. Dosta placed her suitcase into the wagon. Next, he lifted Nellie, pushed her into the wagon, and locked the door against her.

She was caged and engulfed in complete darkness. In a moment, the wagon started moving, its creaking wheels crunching over cobblestone streets and then, after it had left Breslau, dirt roads. She sat with her back to a wall, never moving. Everything that had been fixed and familiar in her world was gone. She no longer had a home. Even harder to bear was her father's betrayal, and his casting her from the family. She lay on the wagon's floor, trying to fall asleep, but she was used to sharing a bed with her younger sisters, Tina and Toni. Hours may have passed. She became groggy, and then drifted off.

Upon awakening, Nellie discovered that there were two small bodies bunched up against her. With her eyes not yet opened, she reached to the faces of her sleep-mates, but they were not those of Toni and Tina. They were those of the young boy and girl she had seen in the moment before Dosta had shut the wagon door on her.

Within days, the captive children were roving the lowlands of Poland's Carpathians. The ground was still patched with snow, and the trees were only just starting to become lacy with budding leaves, but Willy Dosta was ready to begin a new circus season wherever ten or twenty people could be gathered.

✦ ✦ ✦

Always the productions began the same way. Dosta, outfitted in red tights and white trunks, was first to appear in the ring. He was a Scot but knew enough Polish, Czech, German, and Romanian to extend welcomes to the spectators, whatever they were. The sister and brother entered in the ring next. Dosta introduced them as his own children. Finally Nellie stepped into the sawdust ring, leading Reiter by a halter.

Few of the spectators had ever seen a horse of such titanic size. Many of them shrank back several steps from the wooden curbing of the circus ring. Others, mostly farmers, moved closer, intrigued.

Dosta, his three wards, and Reiter paraded around the ring three or four times. Then the children and Reiter exited, leaving Dosta alone in the sawdust circle. He searched the crowd, picking out a couple of strapping young men. Just outside the ring, near its entranceway, was a log four or five feet long and a foot in diameter. Dosta directed his enlistees to carry it into the ring. Next, he lay on his back in the center of the ring and signaled his helpers to lay the log across his slippered feet.

Groaning and grunting all the time, he pumped the log with his powerful legs, causing it to twirl horizontally over him like a giant baton.

"Arghrr . . . Arghrr . . . Arghrr. . . ."

After some moments, he stopped the tree-trunk propeller and then restarted it, sending it whirling in the opposite direction.

"Arghrr . . . Arghrr . . . Arghrr. . . ."

Dosta's face was the color of raw meat, and so great was the strain on his legs that the lineaments of his muscles showed through his tights.

Next he repeatedly thrust the log two or three feet into the air, catching it again with his feet. Finally, first with one foot and then the other, he balanced the thick pole upright on his soles.

Dosta was always a little woozy and wobbly when he got back on his feet.

The Czech sister and brother began their turn in the ring with a juggling display, sending wooden balls, hoops, and chicken and goose eggs arcing into the air between them. Next, they walked on their hands and threw cartwheels and forward and backward flip-flops.

To Dosta, the girl and boy were less valuable as performers than as human props in his own shows as a strongman. After they finished their juggling and acrobatic routines, he reentered the ring and, once again, lay on his back at its center. The act started with the brother and sister performing handstands on Dosta's upraised feet and hands. By turns, the routine became more and more complicated. At one point, the girl stood slippers-to-slippers on Dosta's feet while her brother balanced on her shoulders. It was, though, the close of the trio's act that drew the loudest cheering. The boy perched on Dosta's feet and tucked his body into a ball while his sister assumed a similar posture on Dosta's hands. Over and over again, Dosta juggled the pair back and forth from his feet to his hands, thrusting the children ever higher into the air as he did so. As spectacular as the feat was, it was punishing for the children. The bodies of each bore bruises from occasional midair collisions.

It was Nellie, though, who was always the favorite of the mountain dwellers wherever the Willy Dosta Circus rolled. It had been that way from the first of her appearances with the show. To these woods people whose days were mostly drab and numbingly the same from sunup to sundown, she must have appeared almost otherworldly, a tiny, curly-haired moppet in a tutu who leaped and somersaulted atop the back of a gigantic horse that just kept cantering around and around in a circle.

◆ ◆ ◆

Dosta's assaults on Nellie continued almost daily after that night in the field. Some afternoons, when the circus was at rest, he would sharply scold the eight-year-old boy and nine-year-old girl for not working harder to become better performers, and send them into a field to rehearse their juggling and tumbling. He would then lead Nellie into the wagon, latch the door from the inside, and force her down on the mattress where she and the two other children slept. Other times, late at night, he would creep into the wagon, rouse her from sleep, and lead her outside to have his way.

In his drive to take his show ever higher into the Carpathians, Dosta seemed drunk with a belief that somewhere in the timberland, he was going to discover a Shambhala, a kingdom unknown to the rest of the world with hundreds of thousands of free-spending inhabitants. In such a place, he dreamed, he would be able to put on three or four shows a day. Why, when the summer was over, his fantasy continued, there would be so many sacks of copper, silver, and gold coins in his wagon that he could begin assembling a new Willy Dosta Circus, one twenty or forty times bigger than his one-horse operation.

Nowhere did Dosta find any great cities, though. Mostly the circus put on its performances in villages of fifty or a hundred inhabitants. Now and then, when the circus had traveled for two or three days without happening upon a town, he and the children would present shows for a single large farming or lumbering family. Dosta seldom collected any income from these performances. Instead, he and his charges might be rewarded with some venison stew at a table with people speaking in languages that Nellie could not understand.

In its meanderings in 1890, the circus had woven in and out of Czechoslovakia, Hungary, Romania, and Transylvania. There were already spits of snow in the air when, after being gone for eight months, the Willy Dosta Circus began journeying home.

Nellie was changed when Willy led her to the door of the Pelikan house in Breslau and re-presented her to her father and mother and four younger brothers and sisters. She was still tiny and delicate, but her belly was rounded out to there.

A few months later, on January 2, 1891, a daughter was born in the Pelikan household to her. The birth certificate, filed in Breslau, listed the mother as an "artiste." The space on the form for the father was left blank.

The baby, with green eyes and a fluff of red hair from her Scottish father, was christened Leopoldina Alitza Pelikan. Almost immediately, Nellie started calling her "Litza," a diminutive meaning "Little Alice." In time, that would change to Lietzel and then to Leitzel.

Nellie was a month and a half short of her thirteenth birthday on the day she gave birth to Leitzel. What she did not know, what no one in the Pelikan household knew, was that a genuine princess had been born to her, one who someday would move through thin air with the ease of angels, one who would be adored around the world.

CHAPTER 2

At day's end, when the sun was sinking and bleeding oranges and reds into the sky, Edward and Hortense Codona liked to sit outside with Victoria, their two-year-old daughter, and watch the hummingbirds. By then, the frying-pan heat was beginning to rise, as though returning to the sun, but it always came back the next day, as fierce as ever.

The three were in Hermosillo in northwestern Mexico, two hundred miles from the United States border. In fact, they had been marooned in the desert town for weeks, living in a boardinghouse, and waiting, waiting.

Hortense was well along in her pregnancy. She and Edward had made a decision to stay put in Hermosillo until the baby was born.

Hummingbirds were everywhere in this place, more than were to be found anywhere else in the world, or so the locals boasted. That was especially true in the fall, and it was the fall now. Wherever in the town there were patches of flowers, there were also hummingbirds. They were all the colors of a jewelry maker's stones and metals: lapis lazuli, sapphire, ruby, opal, turquoise, platinum, silver, and gold.

Edward marveled at how, as though they were fastened to invisible strings, the birds could hover in one place in thin air for what seemed just as long as they pleased. He could not believe his eyes as the birds sipped nectar from the blossoms with their long beaks, then backed out of the flowers and flew away backward. Backward!

The locals did not call the tiny birds hummingbirds. They called them by their Spanish name, *colibríes*. Edward and Hortense called them *colibríes*, too, though neither was of Mexican descent. Both had been born in Mexico, but Edward's forebears were from Scotland; Hortense's were from France.

Always when Edward watched the hummingbirds, Victoria was on his lap. She had auburn hair and eyes the color of violets.

"Oh, if any man could do what these birds can do," Edward would say to little Victoria, "there would be no place on earth where his name was not revered."

But, of course, no man had ever been born that could defy gravity the way the *colibríes* did. Not yet anyway.

The spectacles the hummingbirds staged at dusk may have put Edward in mind of a circus where all the performers were costumed in richly colored satins and sequins. Circuses were something he knew about. He himself was the operator of a traveling, tented show.

Like a mother who buys an oversize suit for a young son in a belief the boy will get two or three years of churchgoing out of it, Edward, from the start, gave his circus a title that he was sure it would eventually grow into: "Gran Circo Codona—*Primero en Su Clase.*"

It was a fine circus. It really was. But at its start, the Gran Circo Codona—*Primero en Su Clase* had just three performers: Edward, Hortense, and a horse. The circus just never grew, though. After rolling up and down through Mexico for six or eight years, it was still just Edward, Hortense, and a horse. The Gran Circo honorific that Edward had given the tiny show hung on it as baggily as a fat man's suit drapes on a schoolboy.

Edward arranged with the operators of small freight trains to move his circus from one stand to another. The entire show—the tent, its props and bench seating, the horse, and Edward and Hortense, along with Victoria—could easily be packed in a single, small railroad-baggage car.

Though the show had no printed programs to sell or hand out to its patrons, this is the lineup that the audience saw after taking their seats on the benches inside the tent:

Horizontal Bars. Senor Eduardo Codona

Wire Walking. Senora Hortense Buislay

Single Trapeze. Senor Eduardo Codona

Trick Horseback Riding. Senor Eduardo Codona

"Los Cometas" (The Comets), flying trapeze act.
Senor Eduardo Codona and Senora Hortense Buislay

"Equilibrium Act" (ground acrobatics). Senora Hortense Buislay

Horizontal Bars. Senor Eduardo Codona

"Spiral Mountain." Senor Eduardo Codona

The Spiral Mountain was by far the most spectacular of the Gran Circo Codona's attractions. Edward performed the act on an ascending wooden ramp that curled like a corkscrew from the bottom to the top of a towering wooden pole that was at its center. Wearing slippers, he balanced himself atop a large wooden globe that was positioned at the bottom of the ramp. Then, by moving his feet in a shuffling motion over the globe, he started making his slow ascent. It took him minutes to reach the "mountain's" summit. Then, by resuming the shuffling motion of his feet atop the globe, he made his way back to the ground.

Victoria Codona would remember the Spiral Mountain as being "as high as a church steeple, one hundred feet, at least." But the eyes of children have magnifiers, and she was very young when she saw her father perform on the queer-looking wooden Matterhorn. Probably the Spiral Mountain was not more than thirty or thirty-five feet high. It was, though, far too towering to be installed inside the small tent of the Gran Circo Codona. Edward always presented the act outside as the finale of the little circus that, at least in his view, was *primero en su clase*.

Edward may have acquired the Spiral Mountain from Etienne Buislay, an uncle to Hortense. Etienne was a member of The Buislays, a large family of French circus daredevils. The troupe immigrated to the United States in 1865 when Hortense was eight. There were a dozen or fourteen performers in The Buislays—wire walkers, trapeze flyers, bareback riders—and the Spiral Mountain act was always a feature of the spectacles the troupe presented. Usually it was Etienne, the originator of the Spiral Mountain act, or Stephan Buislay, Hortense's father, who made the trips up and down the mountain.

The Buislays appeared with numerous large circuses in America and were a sensation with all of them. In time, the troupe started its own circus, one that toured year after year in Cuba, South and Central America, and Mexico. The Buislay Family Circus eventually combined with another gypsy show meandering in the same territory, a one-ring enterprise operated by Edward's father, Edward Codona Sr., a former shipyard worker in Glasgow. Edward and Hortense began appearing in the newly merged Buislay-Codona circus as a flying trapeze duo, Los Cometas. They married in 1878 when the circus traveled to Colon, Panama. He was twenty-four, she fourteen.

Not long after, the newlyweds broke from their families to start their own show, the Gran Circo Codona. Edward proudly had handbills printed up to advertise the new circus. The small posters, in black ink and printed from wooden type, were illustrated with features from the new circus—a horse galloping around a ring, a woman on a tightrope, the Spiral Mountain. The posters also bore a small portrait of Edward, although he had altered his name to "Eduardo" on the advertisements. He must have believed that the circus would draw greater patronage in Latin America if the people thought the show was operated by one of their countrymen.

The babies started coming along fast after Edward and Hortense married, the first of them when she was fifteen, and others every year or two. All of the first children were stillborn or died in the sand and rocks of Mexico's desert early in infancy. Hortense was half the Gran Circo Codona, and without her there could be no show, so she continued to perform on the trapeze and tightrope until the seventh or eighth month of each pregnancy.

Victoria was the first of Edward and Hortense's children to survive. She was born in Veracruz, Mexico, on March 6, 1891.

✦ ✦ ✦

Weeks went by in Hermosillo for Edward, Hortense, and Victoria, and then a month, and then almost two months. As a circus nomad, there had hardly been a day in Edward's life when he was not moving on to some new place somewhere. Now he felt like a butterfly that a child places inside a lidded glass jar. He knew the freedom of the world out there, but now he could only move a little way before being stopped. He had never been immobilized anywhere for so long, but he made the decision to rest his circus from its travels for a while. This would be best for Hortense, and maybe it would be for the baby, too.

Did Edward, though, maybe for the first time in his life, now start dreaming in reverse? He was thirty-three. In its six or eight years, his Gran Circo Codona traveled north and south and east and west in Mexico, but it still remained where it started, with just him, Hortense, and a single horse. Did he now start wondering whether there might be some other life for him, for Hortense? She had been born a circus gypsy, too. She was never complaining. But their life had been harsh and, way too often for both of them, so heartbreaking.

When they started the Gran Circo Codona—*Primero en Su Clase*, he and Hortense had dreamed that there would be a lot of Codonas, more than enough so that the show would live up to its advertised promise as a grand circus, one that was first in its class. The children came but did not stay long. Until Victoria arrived, he and Hortense themselves buried them one after another in places that had never been given names because they were nothing more than rocks, dust, tumbleweeds, and scattered cattle bones. Certainly Edward must have wondered whether those babies might have lived if they had been born into some life other than that of a tiny, traveling desert circus.

And what about little Victoria? Edward must have asked himself. Because he had a crazy dream that year after year he could not, or just would not, give up, was he being fair to her? He could not have failed to see the yearning in her light blue, almost purple eyes when, after each of the performances, she watched other children leaving the tent with their mothers and fathers to go to real homes. She was still a toddler.

She did not have the words then to wrap around her feelings, but they would come.

"I only wanted a home," she would say later. "I used to look at the lighted windows of houses in every new town, and wonder why those people would ever leave their homes to go to the circus."

+ + +

The event for which Edward and Hortense had been waiting finally occurred. It took place in the Hermosillo boardinghouse on October 7, 1893. That is when she delivered another child, a boy.

Not long after, maybe another month, maybe two, the Gran Circo Codona was rolling again. When the show stopped now, it was again to raise its tent.

The newest member of the family—he was christened Alfredo Codona—made his professional debut at seven months. At every show, Papa Codona held him aloft in his right hand and paraded around and around the sawdust ring as though his new son was some grand prize, which, of course, he was.

By the time Alfredo was a year and a half, Edward started placing him into a leather pouch that was belted around his waist. Papa Codona then climbed a rope ladder to the trapeze. While sitting on the bar of his trapeze or hanging from it with his muscular arms, he glided back and forth in space, and young Alfredo did, too.

The people on the benches below applauded and laughed and laughed. Only the small, curly-topped head of Alfredo appeared outside the pouch. He looked like a young kangaroo peering out of its mother's marsupium. There was not a trace of fear on Alfredo's face, only wonder, only curiosity.

Edward Codona was pretty sure even then that his boy would amount to somebody in the circus someday, maybe even do things like those hummingbirds of Hermosillo could do, things that no man had ever done before.

The impresario of the Gran Circo Codona—*Primero en Su Clase*—was no longer dreaming backward. Papa Codona's dreams again were only of tomorrows.

CHAPTER 3

Eduard Pelikan must have known Nellie would hate him for it, hate him until the day clumps of dirt were shoveled over his coffin.

He did not feel that he had any other choice, though.

His arthritis and rheumatic fever were becoming more and more debilitating. He was broken, unable to turn out enough work in the wood shop anymore to support his family. The only chance of keeping it together was his thirteen-year-old daughter and whatever meager earnings she could gather as a circus performer.

So when Willy Dosta again came to the Pelikan apartment in Breslau in January 1891, just a week or two after Nellie gave birth to the baby, Eduard said yes. Yes, he would apprentice Nellie to him for a second time, he said, but this time things would have to be different.

Eduard gave his assent after Willy placed a sack of money before him on the kitchen table, after he said he would swear on a stack of Bibles he would never assault Nellie again.

A smile likely formed on Willy's lips upon winning Eduard's agreement. If so, Eduard could not have seen it. Dosta's mouth had not been visible for years. It was still hidden somewhere beneath the bushy, wide-spreading, tomato-colored mustache that covered his lower face.

Before Dosta left the apartment, he had another request. Because of Eduard's skills as a woodworker, he wanted him to help design and build a structure for a portable trapeze, one he could carry atop his horse-drawn wagon, one that could be quickly assembled and disassembled as the Willy Dosta Circus again moved through the Carpa-thian Mountains.

He was going to turn his daughter into a trapeze artist, Willy told Eduard. Just you wait, he said. She would rise and fall like an eagle rid-ing the wind, he promised. He would train her himself.

◆ ◆ ◆

Even though Eduard and Nellie lived in the same cramped apartment and sat at the same table, they never looked at each other anymore. Both made sure their gazes were always zoned inches to one side of the other. They no longer spoke to each other either.

It was left to Julia to tell Nellie of the arrangements that had been made for her to be indentured once again with Willy Dosta's circus when spring arrived. It may have been the hardest thing she ever had to do.

There had been nights when she had to go to her daughter's bed to calm her after Nellie woke up shrieking from nightmares that were inhabited by Willy Dosta. Nellie was as much in terror of him as she was of Beelzebub, whom the nuns in school had also told her about.

Julia tried to make Nellie understand just how desperate things had become in the family. Because of Eduard's patchy work in his wood shop, there was no longer enough money to feed and clothe every-body. Without her earnings as a performer in Willy Dosta's circus, baby Leitzel, along with the youngest of Nellie's brothers and sisters, would have to be placed into poorhouses.

She told Nellie that Willy had promised her father that he would never again be cruel to her. "Willy assured him he will treat you only with respect and kindness, as though you were a daughter of his own," Julia said. "He said he would swear this to God."

Nellie sobbed uncontrollably and quivered like a rabbit cornered by a fox. Julia held her daughter's hand and told her how sorry she was for her fright. She was a gentle woman. She was crying, too, and asked Nellie to be brave. But Julia was so ashamed. How could she hurt her own child so deeply? She may have wondered not only whether Nellie would ever forgive her, but also whether God would.

Nellie's trapeze training with Dosta started just days after he and Eduard had come to an agreement. The sessions were carried out in a barn in Breslau in which Willy had strung up a swing bar, Roman rings, and a net. Nellie took Leitzel to the barn in a basket each day so she could continue nursing her.

Dosta showed little sympathy for his pupil when she complained of aching muscles and the scrapes and burns she suffered when she tumbled from her rigging into the net. He was a demanding coach, but he was also an able teacher. A quarter century earlier, while traveling with wagon shows in Scotland, he himself had performed as a boy trapeze artist.

Within just weeks after she began her training with Dosta on the swinging bar and trapeze, Nellie was already moving through the air like a swallow, rising and falling, and pinwheeling. She so loved soaring in the barn's heavens that sometimes it was hard for Dosta to get her to return to the ground. She had never felt as free. By the time the new spring arrived and Dosta was making final plans to return to the road, Nellie's performances were as polished as those of the artists appearing with the big circuses.

◆ ◆ ◆

When Willy Dosta called at the Pelikan apartment on an early evening in March or April of 1891, Nellie was already waiting for him. Her coat and mittens were nearby, and a small trunk was at the door. She was rocking Leitzel in her arms, and huddled around her were her sisters and brothers. Julia was close by, too. She was holding a ragdoll that she had made from scraps and ends. The doll, fashioned in the likeness of a baby girl, was a good-bye present for Nellie.

Dosta took no notice of the infant in Nellie's arms. He was fidgety. He kept his coat and cap on and had seemed to be anxious to leave the apartment from the moment he stepped into it.

Eduard Pelikan appeared to be emotionally adrift, disengaged from the drama playing out near the door. He sat in a chair, smoking his pipe, and staring blankly into space.

Tears were rolling down Nellie's cheeks and drizzling onto her baby's face. Finally she gave Leitzel a last kiss on the forehead and placed her into Julia's arms. Nellie kissed each of her siblings, and then she and her mother embraced for a long time, both of them crying. Without saying anything to her father, or even looking back at him, Nellie walked out of the apartment and, with Willy, descended the tenement's stairs. He was carrying a trunk with her clothes and costumes, and she was clutching the doll her mother had presented to her. Clearly Julia had intended for the humble gift to signify love, but it seemed a strange present nonetheless. Nellie was leaving her baby behind. In exchange, she received a doll.

Lashed to the roof of Willy's wagon and extending beyond its back end a few feet into the air was a stack of large wooden beams, the components of the portable trapeze that, with Willy's help, Eduard had cobbled together in his wood shop.

When Nellie moved to the wagon's front to see Reiter and nuzzle the massive white horse, she was momentarily startled. Cocooned in a quilt against the cold, seated atop the wagon on its driver's bench, was a woman whom Nellie had never seen before. It was then she learned that Willy had a wife. Some of her anxiety about starting a new tour with him may have eased. Because Willy's wife would be traveling with the circus this time, maybe Willy would not resume his attacks on her.

Nellie opened the door at the rear of the wagon, and this time, without any shoving from Willy, entered the wooden cabin on her own. There were two boys inside, both of whom appeared to be two or three years younger than she was. They sat on the wagon's plank flooring before a small iron stove through whose grate a fire glowed.

In a moment, the wagon started rolling. It moved between block after block of dour and decaying tenements that, like drunkards, leaned on one another this way and that, as if to stay upright. It would be at least two or three days before the Willy Dosta Circus reached the foothills of the Carpathian Mountains, 125 miles away.

✦ ✦ ✦

Leitzel was but a babe in arms that early spring night of 1891 when her mother abandoned her for the first time. Because of her freshness in life, she could not have felt any of the heartache that Nellie suffered.

Within just an hour or two after her mother left her, though, perhaps even in as little time as minutes, Leitzel may have sensed dimly that a critical matter had changed in her life. Julia, her grandmother, had replaced Nellie as her feeding station.

Julia, around forty, had been nursing children of her own almost continuously for the last dozen years or so and was still nursing when Leitzel was born to Nellie. Leitzel may not have discerned any differences in the tastes of the milks of her mother and grandmother, but she may have happily sensed a difference in the quantity of nourishment that was now available to her. Nellie was small and barely nubile when she brought Leitzel into the world. Julia was a large woman whose body seemed to have taken form by stacking great spheroids on top of one another. Her breasts, which she took out of her dresses several times a day for feedings, were milk swollen and as fat as pigeons.

Years later, when Leitzel was widely proclaimed as the greatest performer ever to be produced in her medium, some members of her family would ascribe her preeminence to the diet she had as an infant. And could it be otherwise? Her development might have been quite like that of the goddesses of Greek mythology who took on the attributes of the noble birds and beasts on whose teats their lips had pulled as babies. Not only had Leitzel been suckled by a mother who was a circus artist, but also by a grandmother who had been a circus strongwoman and trapeze performer before largely devoting her life to baby making.

◆ ◆ ◆

The gypsy circuses that meandered the Carpathian Mountains, by and large, were different from one another by name only. They were all one- or two-horse, one-wagon enterprises, and almost all of them offered a bareback riding act, along with a tumbler or a juggler or two, and maybe a clown or a dancing dog or plank-walking pig. Dosta's circus was still a one-wagon affair in 1891, but now it had an attraction that set it apart from all the other roving aggregations. It had a genuine trapeze artist, something only the bigger circuses in the cities featured.

Town-wide holidays seemed to occur instantly in just about every mountain hamlet where the mud-spattered wagon of the Willy Dosta Circus appeared, drawn by its elephantine white horse. Houses, stores, and even the saloons emptied out, and everyone streamed to the town square, where, immediately upon the show's arrival, Dosta and the two boys started erecting Nellie's portable trapeze. There were a lot of kids, of course, but also mothers and fathers, and some grandparents who were so ancient they had to be rolled to the squares on hand-pulled carts.

"They say they got a trapeze artist just like them shows in the cities," the townspeople hummed to one another "That's her over there. So pretty, and they say she flies like a bird. Imagine."

As in her tour the season earlier, Nellie appeared first in the shows as an equestrienne. She threw backward somersaults on Reiter's wide back as the old white horse cantered around and around in a circle. She pirouetted like a prima ballerina on her moving stage. Dosta, standing on the wooden curbing of the ring, held hoops in the air as Reiter circled around and around. Nellie leaped from the horse's back through the hoops and then realighted on the loping behemoth.

Willy continued in his role as a strongman, lying on his back and, with his feet, twirling heavy logs like batons, and juggling the show's two boys in the air.

There were times during the show when the two young boys also had the ring to themselves. Facing each other from afar inside the sawdust circle, they sent goose eggs and then flaming pine sticks arcing back and forth between themselves. In another of their turns, they chased each other around the sawdust ring in circles while throwing flip-flops and cartwheels.

But it was always the bird girl that the rustics were most anxious to see. Knowing this, before Dosta permitted her to appear, he sent his wife weaving through the crowds with a pie dish. The coins and bills accumulated more rapidly and richly in the tin than they ever had before at his circus.

Then Nellie appeared from the wagon, her costume changed from the rose-colored tutu and leotard she wore in her bareback riding act to one of white. She walked to the tower of bolted-together wood beams, and then climbed its rope ladder to the trapeze.

She gripped the trapeze bar by nothing more than the backs of her ankles, and then, for the longest of moments, hung upside down in the air magically, motionlessly, like a tiny fluff of cloud on a still day. Then she was flying, sailing over the heads of the families of farmers, timber men, and stone masons below. She performed handstands and then a headstand on the bar of the widely arcing trapeze. Sometimes she soared so high that the trapeze turned full circles in the air.

Finally, at the trapeze's farthermost forward thrusts, she left the conveyance, and then, after being catapulted twenty or twenty-five feet through the air, landed in Willy's muscular arms with the lightness of a mother robin returning with a worm to her nest of days-old chicks.

In many of the towns where the Willy Dosta Circus appeared, the performances ran continuously from early afternoon until the moon nudged the sun out of the sky. Willy's wife kept passing through the crowds with the tin. When it filled almost to the point of overflowing, she carried it into the wagon, poured the coins and bills into money sacks, and then, like a church usher, returned again to the gatherings.

Willy, of course, was thrilled at the patronage Nellie's trapeze performances drew, and what was especially gratifying to him was that he had been able to add the new feature without adding to his payroll.

Oddly, as bestial and hideous as Nellie had always found Willy, she started to feel some softening of her detestation toward him as the circus continued its push through the mountains. Her own father, she believed, had discarded her. Willy was now the most dominant adult in her life. Her survival, and that of her baby and the rest of her family, were dependent on him. There may have been another reason for the growing closeness Nellie began to feel toward Willy.

"My mother had been born into the circus world, and it was in her blood," her son, Alfred Pelikan, would observe years later. "She loved everything about life on a traveling circus—the freedom, the strangeness of the places and the people she encountered every new day, the approval she received from audiences, even the brushes with danger she experienced when she was doing her bareback riding act or performing on the trapeze."

For the first time in all the years the Willy Dosta Circus had toured the Carpathians, the show now had a genuine star—and Willy had created her. He decided it was time to descend the mountains to start playing the bigger cities.

Possibly because his wife was with him everywhere, Willy seems not to have resumed his assaults on Nellie at any time during her second tour with his circus. He was still quick to anger, though, and there were still occasions when he whipped her and the two boys. Dosta's wife did nothing to discourage the attacks. She was, according to Nellie, a "poor, timid" woman who was as much in terror of her husband as were his apprentices. Dosta was so open about flogging Nellie while the circus was appearing in Königsberg, Germany, that his attack drew the attention of passersby who reported it to authorities.

"His methods were so cruel that the police got after him," Nellie said. The police placed her on a train and sent her back to her home in Breslau, 325 miles away.

But Nellie was not reunited with her family, including her baby daughter, Leitzel, for long. Dosta also boarded a train for Breslau and, in a day or two, was pounding at the door of the Pelikan apartment. He again placed a sack of money before Eduard and told him the money was only a down payment for what he would earn if he ordered Nellie to return to his circus to finish out the season. Dosta and Nellie were together on the next Königsberg-bound train.

✦ ✦ ✦

Leitzel was nearly a year old when, late in the year, her old mother, not quite fourteen, returned home from her 1891 circus tour. Nellie was surprised at how much her daughter had changed in the time she was gone. Her head bore a cloud of frizz the same orange-red as Dosta's hair. She had started walking and had learned her first word—not *mutter*, but *großmutter*. And clearly she had thrived through her grandmother's nursing. She was plump and round.

During her mother's absence, Leitzel had been doted on not only by her grandmother but also by her four aunts and uncles. She appeared to be at perfect peace in the crowded Pelikan household and regarded her mother as a stranger and an intruder after she returned home. When Nellie tried to hold her, she squirmed and cried until she was freed. She would then toddle over to her grandmother, or another family member, to be picked up. Julia told Nellie it would take a little time for her child to know her and realize she was her mother, but Nellie was desolate.

What hurt Nellie most was watching her mother unbutton the front of her dress several times a day to bring out her breasts and nurse Leitzel. Nellie was left with no role in the nurturing of her daughter.

✦ ✦ ✦

Nellie went on the road with the Willy Dosta Circus yet again in 1892, a third tour. Willy's wife apparently did not travel with the show this time.

When Nellie returned to her family later in the year, she was in the same condition she had been in when Willy returned with her two years earlier.

On March 15, 1893, Nellie, now barely fourteen, gave birth to a second child. The baby, delivered by Julia in the Pelikan household, was christened Alfred George Pelikan.

✦ ✦ ✦

Nellie had become a much-changed young woman during her last tour. Her days of performing in weedy fields and backwoods villages before sprinklings of peasants were behind her. Throughout much of 1892, Dosta had arranged for her to make appearances with such popular big top institutions as the Zirkus Althoff in Berlin, the Zirkus Schumann of Denmark, and the Zirkus Renz, which had not only a permanently operating amphitheater in her hometown of Breslau but also others in Hamburg, Berlin, and Bremen, Germany, and Vienna, Austria. Nellie—now more commonly known to her public as "La

Belle Nellie"—was beginning to gather recognition as a true circus sensation.

Dosta spent the winter of 1892 to 1893 counting and recounting his earnings from contracting out La Belle Nellie to the big circuses, those that played in the amphitheaters and beneath big tops that commonly drew audiences of a thousand or more. In all the years he had been taking out his one-wagon show, he had barely earned enough to survive the winters. Now he had more money than ever. He was sure that with just one more season of contracting out appearances by his girl wonder, he would amass enough riches to assemble a truly first-class circus, one with a big top, maybe even a small train with WILLY DOSTA'S GREAT RAILROAD SHOWS emblazoned in gold on all its cars.

He could not wait for the new circus season to begin.

CHAPTER 4

The man Julia admitted into the Pelikan apartment was tall and wispy. He had just ascended three flights and was puffing slightly.

The younger children in the household drew up to the stranger, Leitzel among them. It was January or February of 1893, and she had just passed her third birthday.

The visitor to the Pelikans' apartment reached down to ruffle the hair of the children nearest him.

"Hallo, hallo," he said

He was fifty, but his face was unlined, soft, almost feminine.

The children just stared. He did not have the appearance of anyone they could ever have expected to see in their drab and crowded apartment. Indeed, in the whole of the gray and decaying section of Breslau where the family lived, it was unlikely that so elegant and dignified a man had ever before appeared in their neighborhood.

He carried a valise embossed with the initials *E. J. L.* and wore a three-piece suit. White cuffs fastened with diamond buttons poked out from the sleeves of his coat. His hair, including a luxuriant mustache with its ends curled upward in backward *c*'s, was of the purest white. It glinted like new-fallen snow brushed in morning sunlight. It was because of his striking hair that those who knew him well—theater managers, the owners of the bigger circuses—affectionately referred to E.J.L. as "The Silver King." As imposing a figure as E.J.L. was, though, what always first drew the attention of strangers to him, and what drew the attention of the Pelikan children that day, was an article of jewelry. It was a large Christian cross, two or three inches high, that he wore on a silver neck choker. The cross was studded with about twenty large diamonds. He wore it whenever he was in public.

The caller had come to see Eduard. He had handed Julia his card before she let him into the apartment.

Prof. Edward J. Leamy, Mgr.
Vaidis Sisters, Aero Artistes
New York, San Francisco, London & Berlin

Julia waved her arms and shooed the children like ducklings as she led the professor to the kitchen, where her husband was seated at a table. They scattered, but in not much time, most of them had taken places in the kitchen, where they resumed their mute inspection of the caller. Among the children was Toni Pelikan, at twelve or thirteen, a year or two younger than Nellie, and the second oldest in the Pelikan brood.

"The cross at his neck was the most beautiful thing I had ever seen," Toni would remember. "It flashed with light. I was sure it had magical powers. I thought it must be a talisman of some kind."

After taking a seat at the kitchen table, Leamy opened his valise and brought out a roll of large drawings. Slowly, one after another, he pushed the sheets before Eduard. In big block letters, each of the papers bore the puzzling title "TRAPEZONE ROTAIRE." The drawings, the works of a mechanical engineer, were also stamped with the name Bown Company, Birmingham, England, a manufacturer of sewing machines, bicycles, and roller skates.

Each of the pages was illustrated with various details of a massive mechanical contrivance that was illuminated with dozens of electric lightbulbs, at the time still a new invention. The outer part of the apparatus was formed by four lengths of steel that, as joined together, formed a large trapezoid. The inner part of its frame was filled with a maze of crisscrossing polished steel elements that gave the creation the appearance of a partially complete "giant spider's web." As peculiar as the creation must have appeared to Eduard, there was, at its center, a familiar conveyance: a bicycle.

Leamy addressed Eduard in German, although he himself was American. He had grown up in Syracuse, New York, and, at sixteen, traveled to Europe on a steamer. There he found work as a circus property boy for a trapeze troupe, and then, after some years, started managing trapeze acts on his own.

Leamy continued pushing the large sheets before Eduard and then finally showed him the largest and most richly detailed of the conceptions. It presented an interior view of an opulent theater, along with an audience that appeared to be in the thousands. The trapezone rotaire was shown high in the air of the theater, the trapezoid oriented in a horizontal position and guyed by cables to the theater's ceiling. Because lights were glowing from it everywhere, it looked like it might have been the largest chandelier ever assembled. Dangling in the air beneath the contrivance's undercarriage were two women aerialists, one of them on a trapeze, the other hanging at the end of a rope by her teeth in what circuses called an "iron jaw act." Atop the trapezone rotaire, shown astride the bicycle, was yet another woman in a leotard.

Leamy explained to Eduard that the bicycle was connected to the trapezone rotaire through a complex assembly of gears and chains, and, thus, when the bicycle was pedaled, the entire contrivance was set into motion, revolving in space. He pointed an index finger upward and moved it around and around in the air in front of him, tracing an imaginary circle.

Eduard looked at Leamy, looked at the drawing again, and then exactly mimicked Leamy's tracing motion. His head was nodding up and down and he was smiling broadly. His expression was one of wonderment. He called Julia to the table. He called Nellie, who had rejoined her family in the fall of 1892, when, at the end of his circus tour, Willy Dosta had returned her.

The trapezone rotaire was entirely Leamy's invention. He had unveiled a simpler, far smaller version of the creation as early as 1884, a few years after he began representing Louise and Lizzie Vaidis, a sister trapeze act that he was to make famous. He had presented the

Vaidis Sisters on the trapezone rotaire at venues as scattered as the Royal Aquarium in Westminster, central London; the National Theatre in Washington, D.C.; the California Theatre in San Francisco; and, perhaps most surprising, the Gem Saloon and Theater in Deadwood, South Dakota, a miners' hangout storied for its gunfights and indentured prostitutes.

Leamy finally came to the point of his call. The Vaidis Sisters, whom he had been managing for more than twenty years, were retiring. He was preparing now to produce an even more spectacular trapeze act, one employing a trapezone rotaire that would be more than twice as big as the one on which the Vaidis sisters performed, one with more electric lights, one that was already in production at the Bown plant in England. For much of the last year, he said, he had been scouring the major circus houses of Europe, searching for a trapeze artist who would be the star of the new attraction he was already referring to as the Leamy Sisters.

He wanted La Belle Nellie, Leamy said. He revealed that he had seen her perform under Willy Dosta's management in several European capitals, including the Zirkus Renz in Breslau. It seemed to him, he said, that she was born with avian instincts. She seemed as much at ease in the air as on the earth. She had grace and flew with lightness. Further, she had an ability to make a connection with the spectators in the most distant seats. Under his management, Leamy assured Eduard and Julia, their daughter would become an international star.

The financial terms that Leamy proposed are not known, but clearly they must have been more attractive than any Dosta had ever proffered to Eduard. Willy could . . . well, Willy could just go to hell, Eduard decided. He did not care. He took the pen Leamy held before him and signed a contract right there on the kitchen table.

◆ ◆ ◆

Leamy returned to the Pelikan apartment for Nellie a few weeks later. He was taking her to England. There she would help in selecting and training two other young women for the revolving trapeze.

Nellie was again tearful at leaving behind Leitzel, three at the time, and now also Alfred, an infant, two or three months old. She did not, though, feel any of the dread that gnawed at her when she was touring with Dosta. Mr. Leamy appeared to worship her, and Nellie, in fact, was brimming with excitement at what might lie ahead with him. She knew of the Vaidis Sisters. They had been famous throughout Europe. Now she was under the management of the courtly, silver-haired impresario who guided the pair to fame.

In her wanderings with Willy Dosta, Nellie had often been away from home for months at a time. Nellie probably did not know it when she kissed Leitzel and Alfred good-bye and, for the first time, left the Pelikan home with her new manager. But now, traveling with Leamy, there would be times when she would be separated from her children for years.

"I was only months old when my mother left with Edward Leamy," Alfred said. "My grandmother had a few photographs of my mother, but except for those pictures, I had no idea of what she looked like for the first several years of my life. I also had no real idea what my father looked like, although my grandmother was also able to show me a picture of him. The photograph showed a big, muscular man with a bushy head of hair and a mustache that covered much of his lower face. On the back of the photo, in my mother's hand, was writing that simply said, 'Willy Dosta, the man who took me away from my family.'"

◆ ◆ ◆

Soon after Professor Leamy left Breslau with Nellie and settled with her in London in the spring of 1893, he selected two other young women for places in his planned new revolving trapeze act. One was a hefty twenty-four-year-old named Lizzie, and the other was Emma, who, like Nellie, was fifteen.

Leamy's course of training for his three new apprentices was the same one he followed in schooling all of his aerialists, and was carried out in a large, high-roofed storage building. Each morning, and several times during the day, he put Nellie, Lizzie, and Emma to work lifting dumbbells and light clubs.

"Big clubs only develop a few big muscles," he explained, "but light ones bring them all into play, and make the body supple."

Leamy refused to allow his trainees to skip any parts of his classes. At first, he only permitted his charges to rehearse their poses and stunts on a trapeze that barely cleared the floor, but every few days, he drew the trapeze higher. Above all else, he wanted to ensure that his aerialists were thoroughly practiced before they ascended to the highest region of the storage building to try executing their feats below the revolving trapezone rotaire.

"The worst accident that ever happened to an artist under my control was when a girl tore her shoe," he lectured his pupils.

He had been engaged in training aerialists for twenty-five years.

Nellie, Lizzie, and Emma's schooling with Leamy continued almost every day for nine or ten months, and then their professor was sure they were ready to be seen by the world. He could not have been prouder of them.

◆ ◆ ◆

In Europe, as well as in the United States, circuses were the most popular public entertainments in the late nineteenth century. Most of the biggest American circuses presented their three-ring spectacles under great tents, called big tops, and traveled from one city to another in long trains. It was different on the Continent. With few exceptions, the circuses were presented in permanent buildings, and almost every European city boasted at least one such amphitheater, and some cities, including London and Paris, had two or three or more.

There does not seem to be a reliable record of just where the Leamy Sisters presented their premiere performance in the spring of 1894. By all accounts, though, Edward Leamy was among the most attentive and careful of entertainment producers. Because the troupe and the new trapezone rotaire had yet to be tested before a large and discerning public, it seems probable he would have scheduled the first appearances either in one of the less distinguished houses in London or perhaps in a venue somewhere in the provinces.

Wherever it was that the aerialists made their debut, though, their showing must have been auspicious. It was not long before Leamy received an invitation to present his troupe in a summer appearance in the most opulent new amphitheater anywhere in Europe, the Blackpool Tower and Circus in the seaside resort of Blackpool in Lancashire in northern England.

The Blackpool Tower and Circus, which opened to the public on May 14, 1894, after being under construction for three years, was the pride and joy of everyone living in Blackpool. It had been a brainchild of John Bickerstaffe, a hotelier and the town's mayor. He and his family had traveled to Paris in 1889 to see the Great Paris Exhibition. Bickerstaffe was so astounded by the sight of the Eiffel Tower that when he returned to Blackpool, he began rounding up local investors to erect a similar landmark in town. It would draw free-spending tourists from throughout the United Kingdom, he assured. To get things rolling, he anted up two thousand of the nearly three hundred thousand pounds the tower would ultimately cost.

Built on a stretch of beach called the Golden Mile, the Blackpool Tower turned out to be, almost girder for girder and rivet for rivet, a close clone of Gustave Eiffel's landmark, albeit one that at 519 feet was less than half the 1,063-foot elevation of La Tour Eiffel. Still, there was no need for Bickerstaffe or the other investors to suffer any embarrassment over the somewhat stunted elevation of their creation. The Blackpool Tower had something at its base that the Eiffel Tower lacked: an imposing, multistory brick entertainment complex that included a ballroom and a large performing hall for circuses and aquatic shows. The Blackpool Tower also had something else that set it apart from any other man-made work of architecture—it had an apartment near the topmost part of its spire, at the time the highest residence in the world. The space was occupied by a company of dwarfs, the Blackpool Tower Midgets.

✦ ✦ ✦

All the lights inside the Blackpool amphitheater had been extinguished, plunging the soaring, open hall into blackness, and there was much rustling in the three tiers of seating. Nellie, Lizzie, and Emma were in total darkness as, one after the other, they ascended a rope ladder to the towering ceiling of the great, open hall.

A minute or two passed, and then there was the sound of a slight, metallic, cranking noise far up above. In another instant, as the trapezone rotaire began turning, a soft breeze started fanning the faces of the three thousand spectators in the seats, and soon the ceiling, walls, and floor of the entire theater were awash in moving, twinkling light of every color.

Lizzie was seated on a bicycle fixed on top of the trapezone rotaire. With what one reviewer described as "less exertion than she would make strolling up the boulevard," she drove the bike's pedals with her tree-trunk-thick legs, keeping the steel contraption circling smoothly like a giant, midair lazy Susan.

Nellie and Emma dangled from the underside of the trapezone rotaire on trapezes and, for a time, performed a series of identical maneuvers. Then Emma, working alone, presented a flashy turn in which she hung by her teeth from a single rope and twirled like a dervish in the air at the same time that the trapezone rotaire continued to rotate. Her performance set off gales of applause.

By and large, though, Emma and Lizzie mostly served as window dressing for La Belle Nellie. She was the real star. She presented a series of feats on her swinging trapeze that had everyone in the house continually at the edge of their seats—no-arms, no-legs headstands; upside-down suspensions in which she was connected to her swing bar only by the backs of her ankles; a turn in which she hung from the trapeze only "by the back part of the neck whilst the trapeze [wheel] revolve[d]."

Finally, as the climax to her performance, La Belle Nellie took an eighty-foot swan dive from the trapezone rotaire to a net stretched eight feet above the tanbark, the bed of bark and wood shavings covering the floor. The crowd went mad, shaking the house with such loud roars of approval that its new plaster may have been close to vibrating off the walls. Everyone in the house that night must have felt exceptionally special. The spectators had been witnesses to one of the most sensational attractions seen in any circus.

Following the Blackpool engagement, the Leamy Sisters traveled to other major performing halls, including the Empire in London, Hengler's Circus in Dublin, the Tivoli Gardens in Copenhagen, and the Wintergarten in Berlin. As exciting as these engagements must have been for them, along with their manager, none could have stirred more exaltation among Leamy and his "sisters" than an opportunity that presented itself while the troupe was in Berlin.

An agent representing Oscar Hammerstein—one of ten such representatives working in Europe for the great American theater impresario—engaged the Leamy Sisters to present their act at the gala opening of what at the time was to be the world's biggest entertainment center, Hammerstein's Olympia in New York. The complex, which was in its final stages of construction, was to house three separate large performing halls. It would occupy an entire city block east of Broadway between Forty-Fourth and Forty-Fifth Streets.

✦ ✦ ✦

Opening night at the Olympia, on November 25, 1895, turned out to be one of New York's biggest social occasions in years. It appeared to some observers that nearly everyone on the famed Four Hundred register turned out for the occasion, along with another ten thousand ticket buyers.

In all, twenty-seven different attractions made opening night appearances in the Olympia's three great halls, among them opera divas, prima ballerinas, and world-famous violin prodigies. It seemed from the press accounts, though, that the most incandescent stars of the evening were those three aerial sprites on the trapezone rotaire.

The *New York World*, for example, in a pronouncement that was closely echoed by the city's other newspapers, weighed in on the appearances of La Belle Nellie, Lizzie, and Emma this way: "Quite the best feature of the evening was the revolving trapeze with the three girls who compose the Leamy Troupe. Dazzling, graceful, skillful, their act was remarkable."

Certainly Oscar Hammerstein did not have any quarrel with the *World*'s appraisal. He immediately extended the Leamy Sisters' contract to twelve weeks, far longer than that of any of the other opening-night attractions. There were no published reports of how much the Leamy Sisters were paid, but the sum was likely fabulous, especially if it was even close to the amount Hammerstein awarded to Yvette Guilbert, the French singer-reciter from the Moulin Rouge whose appearances in the Olympia started a few weeks after the massive entertainment complex opened. Guilbert received a reported four thousand dollars a week.

Edward Leamy had a reputation in every corner as an honorable man. It can be assumed he was paying a fair portion of the act's earnings to Nellie, as well as to the other young performers. However much La Belle Nellie netted as the act's *prima donna assoluta*, though, much of her pay was used to support the family back in Breslau, including her mother and father, assorted siblings, and, of course, Leitzel and Alfred.

"Our family's standard of living improved significantly once my mother started working for Professor Leamy," Alfred said. "We started enjoying chicken in the pot more often. And always my mother was sending home gifts from Spain, France, America, from everywhere in Germany—wooden trains and boats and beautiful picture books for me; Dresden dolls and expensive clothes and hair ribbons for Leitzel; pretty dresses and hats for my grandmother Julia, and suits, shirts, blouses, and dresses for my uncles and aunts." Nellie also sent home money to Julia to ensure that her children received the best tutoring that was available to them. By the time Leitzel was four, Julia was accompanying her to studios to study piano and dance. When she was five, she was also enrolled in a private elementary school that was primarily intended for the children of professors at the world-class Breslau University.

"She was in the same classrooms as children who were the sons and daughters of scientists and philosophers," said Alfred, who in a few years would also be enrolled in the same school. "She studied Latin and the classics in literature. The school was modeled after the European gymnasiums, schools intended as high schools for children who would go on to universities where they would pursue studies in medicine, science, or other subjects that would gain them professorships." To some extent, Nellie's showers of gifts on Leitzel and Alfred may have been attempts to expiate her guilt at not being a better mother. After leaving home to begin her association with the Leamy Sisters troupe, five years went by before she was reunited even briefly with Leitzel and Alfred. On that occasion, she had returned to Breslau because the Leamy Sisters had an engagement in the city's Zirkus Renz. Because she had been away since Alfred had been a babe in arms, it was the first time he ever really saw her.

"I remember how people stared at her when she walked down the street. She was dressed in the finest of clothes. She looked like someone regal. I thought she was the most beautiful woman in the world."

Everyone in the Pelikan family received gifts from Nellie upon her return visit home to Breslau. The most surprising of the presents was the one she gave Leitzel. It was a pair of silver-plated Roman rings, identical to those on which La Belle Nellie soared in circus amphitheaters everywhere, but smaller, child size. The rings were attached by their ropes to the ceiling in the Pelikans' apartment. From the time Leitzel took her first flight with the rings, she never wanted to let go of them. They were magic. They transported her somewhere she had never been before.

By the time Leitzel was five or six, she was also distinguishing herself as something of a wunderkind amid the other children in her piano classes. Not long after her aerial rings were installed in the Pelikan household, La Belle Nellie arranged to have a child's piano delivered to the home.

Leitzel and Alfred, along with Grandmother Julia and some of their aunts and uncles, were in a box at the Zirkus Renz every night during that Leamy Sisters engagement. And each day during Nellie's return home, the entire Pelikan clan visited the city zoo or went on family picnics that were organized by Edward Leamy.

"He was so good and generous with everybody, especially my sister and me," Alfred said. "For all intents and purposes, he was the only father we ever had."

After a week or two, though, the Leamy Sisters' engagement in Breslau was over.

"It was quite a scene at the train station when my mother and the rest of the party were about to depart," Alfred recalled. "Leitzel begged my mother not to leave us again, and then she begged her to take us with her. Leitzel cried so loudly that her shrieks echoed everywhere in the terminal. Her arms were locked around my mother's leg. My grandmother finally had to tear her away so my mother could catch the train."

Nellie continued to remember Leitzel and Alfred with gifts at Christmastimes, Easters, birthdays, and sometimes just out of the blue. But always she was far away somewhere, unable to be with them. Always she concluded her letters and cards to them with a promise. "Someday it will be different," she assured.

After the one return that Nellie made to Breslau to perform with the Leamy Sisters at the Zirkus Renz, Alfred said, there were a few other occasions when he and Leitzel again got to see their mother, if only fleetingly. These were times when the Leamy Sisters were playing in such cities as Berlin, Hamburg, or Copenhagen. Grandmother Julia traveled with them by train to reunite with their mother at the engagements.

"These get-togethers never lasted more than a day or two, and we always had to share our mother with her fans and the press," Alfred said. "Everyone cried when they were over, and Leitzel and Grandmother Julia and I had to get back on the train and go back to Breslau. The reunions were filled with more heartache than happiness."

Nellie never came home to stay.

CHAPTER 5

All the time that Leitzel and Alfred were growing up in Breslau, year after year, one day dawned regularly in their dreams. It was a day that loomed larger and more gloriously in their mind's eyes than all their birthdays and Christmases bunched together as one. They dreamed of a day when they would finally be reunited with their mother.

Mostly the dream visited the sister and brother at night, when they were tucked in their beds. It was then, while they were drifting close to sleep, that Grandmother Julia would reprime their imaginations with stories of La Belle Nellie.

"She has long, silky, brown-black hair, porcelain skin, and is fair and beautiful," Julia would often begin. "People come from everywhere just to see her. Even kings, even queens. She is known everywhere as La Belle Nellie.

"Oh, everyone adores her. Just everyone everywhere. She's hardly bigger than a lightning bug and she's just as glowing. She dances in the air . . ."

Grandmother Julia would go on and on with her night stories.

"Oh, and did I tell you this before?" she would ask. "Your mother is a princess. Yes, yes, La Belle Nellie is a princess, a genuine princess, and more beautiful than all the flowers in Holland."

And, of course, she had told them this before—dozens of times, maybe hundreds.

Always the woman with iron-colored hair ended her bedtime stories the same way, and by then, tears were teetering in her eyes.

"There's no two people on Earth that she would rather be with than her daughter and son. Every night when she is in her bed, she thinks only about you, and how much she misses you every minute of every day. But she is a princess, and princesses really belong to everyone, and so she must keep traveling the world."

✦ ✦ ✦

Throughout the childhoods of Leitzel and Alfred, Nellie inhabited their imaginations less as a mother than as some fabled storybook character like Snow White or Cinderella. Leitzel wanted to be like her in every way. She wanted to be prettier than all the flowers in Holland, too. She hated it that her own hair was frizzy and carrot colored. How she wished it was long, silky, and brown-black, just like La Belle Nellie's.

Leitzel and Alfred traded the dreams each had of La Belle Nellie like precious stones. Their dreams differed, of course, but mostly only in details. On one night, either of them might see La Belle Nellie floating down from the sky, her arms outstretched, like some wingless angel. On another night, one or the other might see her surrounded by a great throng in an unfamiliar city, or on the floor of a hippodrome inside a great circus amphitheater. A slit would always open in the madding crowds, an opening wide enough so that she could see her children in the distance, and then the princess would tear herself away from her adorers and come running to Leitzel or Alfred or both of them. Always the dreams ended the same way. They would find La Belle Nellie, or she, them, and then the three would be together forever. Neither Leitzel nor Alfred knew if that day would ever come, but if it did, they were sure, it would be the happiest of their lives.

✦ ✦ ✦

And the day did come.

Late in 1901, Nellie and Edward Leamy called upon the Pelikan family to leave Breslau and come to London to live with them. During all the years she was traveling, first with Dosta and then with Leamy, Nellie yearned to be reconnected with her family, especially with Leitzel and Alfred. It was the main reason why she arranged to have them come to London to live with her. But there was another reason, too.

Nellie and Leamy had decided to reconstitute the Leamy troupe. Nellie wanted the act to be entirely a family affair. She wanted her sisters, Tina and Toni, to be a part of the troupe. Most of all, she wanted Leitzel to be in the act. That way, wherever she traveled, they would always be together.

It was a day in February or March when Leitzel and Alfred, along with Julia and Eduard, aunts Toni and Tina, and uncles Adolph and Horace, steamed into the Southampton port in England. The family was still on the ship's deck, waiting for the gangplank to be lowered, when Julia, looking over the rail, saw Nellie and Edward Leamy in the crowd below waiting to receive the passengers. Nellie and Leamy were waving. Julia drew the attention of Leitzel and Alfred to their mother.

Nellie was easy to pick out in any crowd. This day her head was topped with a hat as big as a bird cage, and her waist, as always, was corseted to the circumference of a wasp's. She was always the most fashionable lady in any setting.

Alfred studied the woman blowing kisses up to him, and then started whimpering. He turned his back to her, and then his knees crumpled, and he dropped to the ship's steel floor. He was sure he had been tricked.

"It's not her," he bawled. "It's not her. It's not my mother. I won't go to her."

Julia tried to calm him; Leitzel did, too.

Alfred was four or five the last time he had seen Nellie, and now he was nine. Any memory he had of her from then had become bleached out to blankness, like a photograph exposed too long to sunlight. The only mother he recognized now was the one who regularly visited him in his dreams.

Julia stayed behind on the deck with Alfred after the ship's footway was lowered to the pier, but the other members of the Pelikan clan, including Leitzel, rushed down the ramp. Some several minutes went by before Julia was able to convince Alfred to leave the ship. They were the last passengers to do so.

Nellie tried to engage Alfred in talk, but his head was down, and he hid behind Julia. Finally, he emerged. At first, all he saw was an outrageously large hat that was swathed in ribbons and had feathers sticking up from it. He lowered his eyes to the face of the woman. She was smiling, and her eyes were both imploring and filled with tears.

Alfred recognized her now. She was the princess he had seen in hundreds of dreams. He took the hand that she had extended to him.

The reunion in the harbor was an occasion for joy and tears. After kissing Alfred and Leitzel and embracing her mother and brothers and sisters, Nellie even hugged her father. It was the first time in more than a dozen years that they embraced.

Leitzel wanted to lock her arms around La Belle Nellie and never let go, but, she apparently knew, you do not do that with princesses. Nellie covered her with kisses this day and told her how pretty she was, but Leitzel seemed shy about showing her feelings.

Leitzel's round face was only partially visible through a surrounding wreath of ringlets. Her hair was no longer the pumpkin orange of her toddler years but something closer in color to butterscotch. Her eyes, big and lustrous, were those of a fawn. They took in everything around her, but mostly she stared at the beautiful woman under the great hat.

Nellie studied her daughter with wonder, too. She was instantly smitten with this stranger who had come to live with her. She may have seen in her something of herself half her lifetime ago. Leitzel was tiny, just inches over four feet, but she had the manner of a child who had spent her formative years in the company of classics professors, piano pedagogues, ballet masters, and the children of aristocrats and the elite. Without her having a hand in her daughter's development— without even having a chance to witness her changes—her girl had bloomed into a lady-child of poise and refinement. It was a good thing.

Leitzel would no longer have the time now for additional schooling or the cultivation of new friendships with other children.

✦ ✦ ✦

If it meant it would give her a chance to get closer to La Belle Nellie, Leitzel would climb partway to the moon. She would, if she had to, fly in thin air, swim in it, put her neck at risk, do almost anything.

And she would have to.

Nellie and Leamy lived in a gracious home on Old Kent Road in the Kensington district of southeast London. It was understood by their neighbors that Nellie, twenty-four, and he, fifty-seven, were wife and husband, but the couple had never wed.

Leitzel was overjoyed on learning of Professor Leamy's plan for a new aerial troupe, one made up entirely of family members, including her. Daughter and mother had always been almost strangers to each other, separated not just by being in different places most of the time but also by a lack of any real emotional connection. Now, maybe, Leitzel could find La Belle Nellie in the element she seemed most comfortable inhabiting—the air.

Leamy had already rented a large barn near the family home, in which he had installed the trapezone rotaire, and before another week or two went by, he and Nellie began their training of Leitzel, Tina, and Toni. Tina, about twenty-three at the time, may have been resentful that she had to take part in the classes. For several years before leaving Breslau, she had been making regular appearances in the city's Zirkus Renz, performing on both the trapeze and Roman rings.

Before a month or two of strength training and practice on a low trapeze had gone by, Leamy decided that the day had come when his pupils were ready to join Nellie on the trapezone rotaire.

Toni was wide of girth and bosom and had thick thighs. It had already been determined that she would pedal the bicycle that propelled the trapezone rotaire. Because of her beefiness, it took exceptional will for her to move her body up the ladder, but from the instant she settled on the bicycle's seat, she was able to keep Leamy's marvel revolving at the even speed of a merry-go-round.

As installed in the practice barn, the trapezone rotaire was some forty feet in the air, a more rarefied elevation than that at which Tina had usually performed. The new condition had little effect on her artistry. She went through the same routines she had essayed hundreds of times at the circus in Breslau and elsewhere. While adroit, her trapeze and rings work lacked much bravura, though. That was fine with Leamy. Nellie, of course, would be maintaining her position as the troupe's true star.

So anxious was Leitzel to put on a show for La Belle Nellie and Professor Leamy that she did not so much climb as scamper up the rope ladder to the contrivance.

From the time she was three or four, Leitzel had practiced every day on a miniature trapeze and a pair of Roman rings that had been gifts from Nellie. Now, when she ascended to her place near to the barn's rafters, she seemed as much at ease as if she were back in the Pelikans' Breslau apartment, flying on her Roman rings. With Nellie and Leamy crying out "Brava, Brava," she reprised all the feats she had seen her auntie Tina perform minutes earlier.

Then she tried something new. She stood on the bar of her trapeze and, with her legs pumping, began driving her swing farther and farther into space. Soon her trapeze ropes were exactly parallel with the floor four or five stories below. She drove the trapeze still higher. Leamy was on the ground, watching through a telescope as she continued on her joyride. He was becoming increasingly uneasy. He worried that if her pendulum lifted even a foot or so higher, she would crash into the trapezone rotaire's undercarriage.

"Stop! Stop!" he shouted up to her. "Stop this instant!"

Leitzel may have been enjoying her ride so much that she did not hear him. Her legs continued pumping the trapeze bar.

Then, at the point when her trapeze had swung out to the farthermost distance in space, her slippered feet lost their grounding beneath her. In another instant, unaccountably, she surrendered her grip on the trapeze ropes at her sides. Her body started falling backward.

Nellie, Tina, and Toni shrieked. Leitzel was going to plummet to the floor.

Then she did something surprising. While tumbling backward, she neatly caught the trapeze bar, as it swung back toward her, by the back of one knee. She hung in this position for what seemed a half minute until the trapeze came to a stop. Next, still hanging upside down, she reached for the bar, drew herself up, and resumed her seat on the perch.

She pushed her hair away from her face and was beaming. She had just taken the ride of her life.

Her expression was still bright when, at Leamy's insistence, she returned to the ground. Nellie, who followed her down the rope ladder, was quick to peel it away.

"Show off!" she scoffed. "Peacock! And just eleven years old. You could have broken yourself into a thousand pieces. You're not expected to do anything up there but sit pretty. I'll be the star a while longer if you don't mind."

Leitzel's lower lip started to quiver. She clamped her hands between her knees and bowed her head. She had so hoped to make a great impression on La Belle Nellie in her first appearance on the trapezone rotaire.

In the days that followed in the barn, Leitzel toned down some of her skylarking, but over time, as Leamy gained more confidence in her, her performances became ever more daring.

"She was just having too much fun whenever she was up there," Alfred said. "And from the start, she had made up her mind that, like our mother, she was going to be a star. No one was going to stop her. From her first time that she performed on the rotating trapeze, she had already outshone Tina."

Alfred was present for the rehearsals every day. He had feelings of envy as he sat alone on the ground and watched his sister treading in air like some Icarian figure. He, too, wanted to follow in the family tradition and become a performer.

"I was circus crazy," he said. "I had become pretty good at juggling and had learned some fancy bicycle riding from my uncles. But there was no place in the Leamy act for a boy. Over my protests, my mother insisted I was to continue in school. She wanted me to be a doctor."

CHAPTER 6

Leitzel and Alfred moved through the terminal as part of a torrent of bodies that included the other passengers who had ridden the crowded train with them on the two-hundred-mile trip from London to Blackpool in northwest England. The human rapids rushing to the exit door appeared to be about equally divided between single men and women in their middle teens to early twenties. Many of the day-trippers were running through the station as though they could not wait another minute to get outside.

As children who had grown up in a bleak ghetto, Leitzel and Alfred could not believe their eyes at the sight of the place that was revealed to them when they pushed through the door. They emerged into a sparkling town that seemed dream-borne, a wonderland where every desire of the heart was available. They were wonderstruck.

It was May of 1902, and Leitzel and Alfred had traveled to this magical place with Nellie and Professor Leamy, along with their aunts Tina and Toni. The hearts of Tina and Toni were likely pounding as furiously as those of Leitzel and Alfred. They had never been to the holiday town before either, although Nellie had visited at least two or three times before for appearances at the Blackpool Circus. The old Leamy Sisters troupe had always been received as a sensation here.

Up and down the streets, everywhere they walked outside the terminal, they saw public houses, shooting galleries, wax museums, and theaters offering both movies and live entertainment. There were organ grinders with dancing monkeys that pushed tin cups out at passersby, and kohl-eyed fortune readers with rings on all their fingers. Vendors were selling pastries, devils on horseback, crumpets, whitebait, and saltwater taffy, and electric tram cars, the first in any city in the world and flashily painted in gold and green, clattered over the streets, ringing their bells.

By far the grandest sight of all, though, one easily visible even fifteen or twenty miles away on clear days from both the sea and countryside, was the soaring tower of open latticed steel that rose above the stone Blackpool circus and entertainment center.

❖ ❖ ❖

Blackpool was the most popular resort in all of England by the turn of the twentieth century. The city itself had a population of fifty thousand, but the resort drew ten or twelve million guests each summer, most of them arriving by trains at one of the city's three stations. Most of the vacationers were factory workers, miners, shop clerks, and knitting mill employees from north England and Scotland, and the majority of them were young, single, and on the make.

Blackpool's beach stretched for seven miles before the blue Irish Sea. Small yellow-and-red-striped tents rose here and there, offering such attractions as Punch and Judy shows, mind readers, and a five-legged cow. Almost everywhere else on the beach, the golden sands were carpeted with sunbathers, and day and night, the promenades and stilted piers swarmed with tourists. The fun seekers shopped for romance, fed coins into the peep shows, and haggled with stall operators over the prices for seashell necklaces, saltwater taffy, and steamed clams.

With their mother or one or the other of their aunts, Leitzel and Alfred spent much of their days exploring Blackpool. As clotted with people as the seafront was, Alfred said, he and Leitzel were less impressed by the hordes of sunbathers than by the buskers from exotic lands.

"There were Indians with their heads wrapped in turbans lying on beds of nails or charming snakes," he said. "There were Chinese acrobats who stood atop one another four or five high. There were Congolese fire dancers. Neither of us had seen Hindus, Asians, or black people before arriving in Blackpool."

* * *

The Blackpool Tower and Circus had lined up the usual array of clowns, equestriennes, jugglers, and acrobats for its summer season of 1902, but the reconstituted Leamy troupe, its name now changed from the Leamy Sisters to the Leamy Ladies, was given billing as the premier attraction.

Nellie, Tina, Toni, and Leitzel spent long hours in rehearsals in the days leading up to the opening. Leamy expected all their routines to have the precision of an expensive watch. He repeatedly tried impressing on the four that with their appearances in Blackpool, they would be performing before some of the most critical circus audiences anywhere.

None in the quartet took the practice sessions more seriously than Leitzel. Like her mother and aunts, she felt honored to be a member of an attraction headlining the Blackpool summer circus. But there was even more at stake for her. She would be making her professional debut as a circus performer. She continued practicing her routines on the trapeze and rings even when her mother and aunts took breaks for naps and tea.

The summer edition of the 1902 Blackpool Tower Circus opened on a night in mid-May. Backstage, in the minutes before the Leamy Ladies were to appear, Nellie instructed Leitzel not to attempt anything rash on the trapezone rotaire. Leitzel nodded her assent.

Nellie, Tina, and Toni were identically costumed in violet leotards when they emerged through the curtained performers' entryway onto the hippodrome floor. Many of the men seated on the ground floor and in the hall's two balconies put opera glasses up to their eyes. The leotards looked like they might have been watercolored onto their flesh, and their bosoms partially gushed from their scooped necklines.

The sisters were well on their way up their rope ladder and the orchestra had already started playing when Leitzel, similarly attired in a violet leotard, appeared. The crowd oohed at her smallness. She was twelve but looked no older than seven or eight. She waved gleefully to every section of the house. Next, as though trying to catch a train just pulling out from a station, she bounded over the floor to the trapezone rotaire's rope ladder, throwing cartwheels and feet-over-head flip-flops on the way.

As choreographed by Leamy, La Belle Nellie was to be the act's nova, its brightest star. Toni had the job of serving as the revolving trapeze's human engine, and Leamy had intended for Leitzel and Tina to function more or less as mere supernumeraries, swaying gently back and forth on their trapezes while gesturing with outstretched hands to Nellie as she executed two- and one-armed handstands on the trapeze bar or sailed on it upside down.

At first Leitzel kept her promise not to try anything on her trapeze that might deflect the audience's attention from La Belle Nellie. After her mother had concluded her turn, though, and was drinking in ringing applause and cheers, Leitzel stood up on her bar and, with legs pumping, drove her trapeze ever farther out into space. When she had her conveyance moving backward and forward in the air, 180 degrees, she crouched down on her bar and, like a bat, hung upside down from it, holding on by nothing more than the upper sides of her slippered feet. She was just at the start of another of her joyrides. She did a headstand on the oscillating bar. She turned herself into a propeller, revolving around and around, heels over head, while gripping the bar. Everyone peering up from the seats seemed to have stopped breathing.

Finally, as her trapeze slowed in its momentum and then became motionless, Leitzel resumed a sitting position on the bar. Everyone rose from their seats. The house rattled with applause, cheering, whistling, and stomping feet. The crowd's outburst might have been less a commendation for the amazing display than a collective hallelujah to the divine who spared the child from death.

Still seated comfortably on her bar, Leitzel wore an expression that seemed to tell the audience, "I appreciate your concern. I really do. But, honestly, there was no need to worry. I was just having fun."

She reached into a slipper and fished out a wad of chewing gum that was about the size of a golf ball. She popped it into her mouth and started chewing. The crowd roared even louder. From her swing perch twenty feet away, La Belle Nellie fixed her daughter with an icy stare. She was likely the single censurer in the house. Minutes passed before the applause and cheering subsided.

Nellie was still in high dudgeon when, after taking her bows, she stormed from the hippodrome to the Leamy Ladies' dressing room. She was immediately intent on giving Leitzel a dressing-down. She had not progressed far backstage when she found her daughter surrounded by a knot of Blackpool Circus officials, all of them praising her to the heavens and telling La Belle Nellie that she may have given the circus world its greatest child star ever.

Edward Leamy was beaming at the attention his protégée was receiving. He determined there and then that the turn Leitzel had presented in her public debut, right down to the end, when she stuffed her mouth with a choking wad of chewing gum, would be a fixture in all future performances of the Leamy Ladies.

CHAPTER 7

The truth about her mother did not come to Leitzel all at once. It fell on her like rain, a day after day, cold and stinging rain. It soaked into her being every day of the first weeks, and then months, that they lived and performed together.

La Belle Nellie was not more devoted to her children than anything else, as Grandmother Julia had always said. She was not selfless. Her mother, as Leitzel came to know her, was insecure and often petty, a woman-child who had been piteously manipulated by others all her life. Maybe because the only real love she had known was from the audiences that cheered her night after night, she resented anyone, even her own flesh and blood, challenging her primacy in the great halls and tents.

The Leamy Ladies played for weeks at the Blackpool Circus, and late at night, when Leitzel and Alfred were in their beds in the hotel room they shared, they sometimes heard Nellie sobbing to Professor Leamy in an adjoining room.

"Did you see her again tonight?" she cried. "Always the show-off. The big star. Always trying to take over the audience as though it were there for her alone."

Her protests to Leamy were always desultory, regularly broken apart by blubbering.

"She makes me feel so bad. She wants to take away everything that is mine. My own daughter, and I put her in the act. She would like it just as well if I wasn't even there. Maybe you would, too. You always seem to side with her. You have to talk to her. You have to put her in her place. You have to stop her from trying to take over the whole show."

Leamy had dealt with prima donnas many times before. He had been managing women trapeze acts for more than a quarter century. He tried assuring Nellie that the audiences still saw her as the star of the Leamy Ladies and would always do so.

"You're La Belle Nellie," he would answer. "The people come to the show to see you."

Leamy was always calm. He tried to show Nellie that he understood her concern, but he gave her no assurances that he would tell Leitzel to tone down her skylarking on the trapezone rotaire.

In her first weeks on the road as a member of the Leamy Ladies, Leitzel held out hope that there would eventually be a lifting of the fog of estrangement that prevented her and La Belle Nellie from seeing eye to eye. Nellie, after all, had been but twelve when she gave birth to her, and then, almost immediately, she was out of her life for most of the next dozen years. How could she be expected to feel, just like that, the same closeness to Leitzel that most mothers who raise their children from birth know?

As more time passed, though, Leitzel seemed to know she and Nellie would never fully bond as daughter and mother.

And Nellie likely knew it, too.

Just as Nellie no longer came close to matching Leitzel's long-held, but now vanished, belief that she was a princess-mother who always had to be separated from her children because she belonged to everybody, Leitzel no longer conformed to Nellie's old idea that her daughter was a child who had been irreparably broken by her abandonment of her. Leitzel had grown into a young woman with a strong will who was independent and self-sufficient. It hurt Nellie that Leitzel did not need her more. She seemed to have done well without her. She had learned to survive without her.

In the stratosphere of the Blackpool Tower, inhabiting the same air, Nellie and Leitzel may have felt that they were birds of the same feather, albeit creatures that competed for the crowds' greatest servings of adulation. But on the ground, down from the trapezone rotaire, each felt completely severed from the other, as distanced from each other as always. Daughter and mother would forever be strangers.

Courtney Ryley Cooper, a circus press agent and noted author, made this observation about the impossibility of Leitzel and La Belle Nellie ever fully bridging the gulf between them: "The yearning that ever existed in the pair . . . lingered. There was mother love and there was child love . . . beating against a barrier of years of separation and a feeling of strangeness which their separation naturally engendered. Surmounting even this was discipline. [Nellie] was an acrobat in a 'sister' act, [Leitzel] herself a child apprentice. . . . In the ring, mother and daughter must be . . . subservient to the commands of the act."

◆ ◆ ◆

Following the engagement with the Blackpool Circus, the Leamy Ladies started on a tour of European cities that was to continue almost without interruption for years.

Leitzel never tired of traveling to one strange capital and then, after a few weeks or months, moving on to another. Each of her days was rich with adventure, and now, for the first time, she had a sense of belonging. Tina and Toni and La Belle Nellie seemed less like blood relatives to her than the dramatis personae of a fable, sorceresses from a missing chapter of *A Thousand and One Nights*. The four captivated entire cities with their magic and beauty.

Wherever the Leamy Ladies appeared in public—in train stations, in cafés, in marketplaces—thickets of curiosity seekers wound around them. Few of the oglers could have known who the three women and the child were, but clearly they recognized the four as somebodies.

Edward Leamy, in fact, always made sure his Leamy Ladies stirred hubbubs when they were out in public. He always inspected the four before allowing them to step outside their hotel room. They were to be dressed in haute couture. They were to have their lips painted, their cheeks rouged, their eyelashes mascaraed, and their eyes rimmed in kohl.

"He had a strict rule," said Alfred. "Whether my mother, sister, and aunts were appearing before circus audiences or strolling through a park in Paris or Berlin, they were to maintain the appearance of royals. He insisted on it."

Leamy himself accompanied the quartet everywhere, always appearing a few steps ahead of them, like a baton major at the head of a parade. With his silvery white hair, tailor-cut three-piece suits, and the large, ever-present, flashing diamond-studded cross just below his neck, he himself was always a figure of wide notice.

Even though Leitzel daubed her cheeks with red and blackened the flesh around her eyes in imitation of the other troupe members, she always appeared to be the odd femme out in the company of the Leamy Ladies. She was tiny, still barely over four feet, and although she was twelve when she became a member of the troupe, she still appeared to be in prepubescence. She could hardly pass for a lady. There was something else that set her conspicuously apart from the others in the quartet. In contrast to her mother and aunts, all of whom were well-coiffed brunettes, her hair was wildly curly and was the color of peach marmalade.

Leitzel was adored everywhere, and just as La Belle Nellie had started to fear, her star began losing some of its gleam once her daughter became a member of the troupe. One indication of this came while the Leamy Ladies were performing in Paris.

The manager of the theater where the company was appearing had arranged for a top newspaper correspondent to interview Edward Leamy and his aerialists. The news that an important journalist would be calling stirred great excitement, especially with Nellie, Tina, and Toni. Not daring to leave anything to chance, the three doused themselves in toilet water. Next, after fastening themselves into iron maiden corsets, which heaved their breasts upward and outward and shrank their waists, they wriggled and stuffed themselves into their most revealing leotards, mauve in color with sprinkles of silvery spangles at the crotch and over their breasts. Leamy sent out for expensive champagne.

The time for the correspondent's afternoon appointment arrived and then passed, and there had been no rapping at the Leamy Ladies' dressing room door. Then another hour ticked by, and then another.

The ice melted and the uncorked champagne lost its fizz. After three hours in their stuffy backstage room, Nellie, Tina, and Toni started to look molted.

Leamy, in a rare pique, finally phoned the newspaper's offices, where he sought out the editor. He demanded to know why the paper's star scribbler had stood up his aerialistes.

"Oh, he was there," the editor replied. "He got a formidable interview from an *enfant* standing outside your dressing room. *Quelle* personality."

✦ ✦ ✦

Because the new Leamy Ladies could boast of not only La Belle Nellie, a circus star everywhere on the Continent, but now also a wunderkind whom the press was calling Madame's protégée, the troupe was a greater sensation than ever. Whether in France, Germany, Denmark, Spain, Portugal, England, or Italy, the theaters and circus halls that could advertise the attraction were virtually assured of turn-away crowds.

Hundreds of thousands would marvel at the quartet in the years ahead. Among their admirers, especially on first-night performances, were kings, queens, marquises, princes, princesses, chancellors, and mayors. Of all the European nobles that took in the act, though, none would be as important to the Leamy Ladies as an American commoner, the son of a harness maker from the dozing farm center of Baraboo, Wisconsin.

A towering figure with an upper body the circumference of a rain barrel, and a head as round as the moon, he showed up in Berlin's Wintergarten Theater on a night late in December 1907.

Alfred Pelikan was on hand the night the American appeared in the Wintergarten. Fourteen at the time, he was on a Christmas season break from Lawn Park High School in London, where he was enrolled in a course of Oxford preliminaries.

"The Wintergarten's show was late in getting started that night," Alfred said. "An announcer kept coming out on the floor, apologizing for the delay. He said the show was being held up because management was awaiting the arrival of some very important guest. One would have thought the Pope was due to arrive, or at least the chancellor of Germany."

The crowd was restless by the time the American finally made his appearance in the hall. He was flanked by a couple aides-de-camp, and following just a few steps behind him was a small retinue of Wintergarten officials. He wore a derby and walked with his right hand wrapped around a gold-balled cane.

Everyone in the house with opera glasses kept them trained on the late-arriving dignitary as he was shepherded to a red plush box normally reserved for Germany's highest officials. The American, likely a stranger to all but a few of the three thousand spectators filling the Wintergarten, comported himself with the hauteur of a man who was aware that whether he was at a circus or throwing back drinks and devouring a couple chickens at a time at Shanley's in New York, he was almost certainly the richest and most powerful figure in the house.

Alfred remembered the circus's tardy dignitary only as being "one of the Ringling boys." In fact, it was John Ringling, or "Mister John," as he was commonly addressed by anyone of lower rank than a viscount. There probably was not a wire walker, clown, or proprietor of a trained flea act anywhere who did not revere Mister John. A big top performer of almost any sort could be pretty well assured of being listed in the final, unabridged annals of circus greats if he or she received notice from Mister John. He was regarded around the world as the absolute potentate of the circus universe.

John Ringling, fifty-one at the time, was well on his way to becoming one of the wealthiest men in the United States. By turns, he was amassing a fortune that included not only stakes in the two largest circuses in America but also eighty thousand acres of land in Montana and another thirty thousand in Florida. He also owned several short-line railroads, oil wells, and a palatial home on the Sarasota Bay in Florida that was modeled after the Doge's Palace in Venice. The possessions he prized among all others, though, were canvases he owned by such masters as Titian, Tiepolo, Rubens, Hals, and Gainsborough. His art collection would ultimately become so sprawling that he would have to build a vast museum on the grounds of his Florida estate to house it.

This was all surprising, since at their start as circus showmen only a little more than two decades earlier, John and his brothers traveled in a tiny, ragtag enterprise with a small secondhand, patched-up tent and a few horse-drawn farm wagons that rolled over rutty roads in Wisconsin, Michigan, and Minnesota. In its first years, most of the Ringlings' ring entertainment was provided by the five brothers themselves, along with the wives of those who were married. Probably the rolling show's biggest attraction its first year was a caged, flea-bitten hyena that the young showmen advertised as "The Midnight Marauding Monster That Robs Graves Under the Cover of Darkness."

After each summer tour, John and his brothers Al, Otto, Alf T., and Charles reinvested their profits in additional attractions and amenities. Within five years, their World's Greatest Shows had grown to such proportions that they were able to retire their farm wagon and buy their own train. This enabled them to start presenting their circus in bigger towns, bypassing the lumbering and farming centers of a hundred or three hundred inhabitants that they visited in their earliest tours.

Traveling circuses and carnivals did not enjoy the highest levels of respectability in the nineteenth century. Most ministers used their pulpits to fulminate against them, telling their parishioners that these here-today, gone-tomorrow shows were vulgar entertainments whose ranks carried bunco men, pickpockets, and chicken thieves. Their condemnation of traveling circuses was hardly surprising. Most of the churchmen noticed precipitous dips in their collection plate offerings at about the same time the first garishly colored posters started blooming on nearby barns and store sides, announcing the coming of the shows.

From the start, though, the Ringling brothers insisted on presenting clean entertainment and policing their circus of grifters. Competing showmen disparaged the boys from Baraboo as goody-two-shoes showmen, the operators of the "Ding-a-Ling Brothers Circus," but the public and press quickly came to regard the new circus as a Sunday school show, fit for families.

Among the boosters of the Ringling Bros. World's Greatest Shows was George Ade, an enormously popular Hoosier humorist, playwright, and nationally syndicated newspaper columnist of the day.

"They found the business in the hands of vagabonds and put it in the hands of gentlemen," Ade wrote in one of his columns. "[They] became the circus kings of the world by following the simple rule that it is better to be straight than crooked."

Each of the Ringlings developed strengths in different areas, including booking, advertising, and personnel management. John, the youngest, was likely the most driven. Early on, he showed a gift for discovering ring performers and attractions that, with proper packaging, would come to be viewed as world-class. After the turn of the twentieth century, he started to make annual trips to Europe, scouring both the great circus amphitheaters and the small tents for attractions to bring to America.

◆ ◆ ◆

When Mister John made his appearance at the Wintergarten that night in 1907, he was shopping for acts not just for the Ringling Bros. World's Greatest Shows, but also for an even more renowned circus, Barnum & Bailey's Greatest Show on Earth. The brothers had acquired the circus lock, stock, and elephant tubs after the death the previous year of James A. Bailey, who had outlived his partner, Phineas Taylor Barnum, by fifteen years.

Mister John's fleshy eyelids always appeared to be at half-mast, but his gaze missed nothing. The Wintergarten was by far the largest and most distinguished of the dozens of performance halls in Berlin. In the moments before the circus finally started, after he and his aides were seated, he threw back his head and stared at the ceiling, taking in a constellation of thousands of softly twinkling electric stars. Next he turned his attention to the Wintergarten's thickly plastered, custardlike walls. They were hung with large portraits of some of the performers who had made appearances in the opulent hall over the years, among them Harry Houdini, the American escapologist; Saharet, the high-kicking, Australian-born burlesque dancer; Grock, the most beloved clown in the world; and Yvette Guilbert, the café singer, a sensation at Montmartre's Moulin Rouge and the subject of paintings by such famous French artists as Henri de Toulouse-Lautrec, Jules Chéret, and Théophile-Alexandre Steinlen.

Mister John may have felt his European scouting trip had been successful even before he turned up at the Wintergarten. Earlier, in France, he had bagged the Sisters La Rague for importation to the United States. The two women, who may or may not have been related, were daredevil stunt drivers whose spectacular act might have been an inspiration to Evel Knievel decades later. One sister piloted a blue car that hurtled down a steeply inclined, ninety-foot ramp and then collided with an obstruction at the ramp's bottom that sent the driver and her roadster somersaulting high into space. Only a split second passed before the second car followed down the ramp and then shot straight out into the air just feet below the somersaulting roadster. In just a second more, one after another, both cars alighted on an elevated bridge fifty or sixty feet away.

Mister John chewed and puffed away on a great panatela as the Wintergarten's circus spilled out before him, said Alfred.

"He appeared to be analytically gauging the nuances of each of the performers that appeared—the equestriennes, the acrobats, the aerialists, even the clowns."

As the Wintergarten's headliners, the Leamy Ladies were the last attraction of the evening. Except for the stars on the ceiling, which continued their glimmering, all the lights in the great hall were switched off. Toni took her place on the trapezone rotaire's bicycle, and Nellie, Tina, and Leitzel assumed places on their trapezes below the great wheel. Then the trapezone rotaire began its slow turning, and at the same time, all its lights started brushing the dark air with color.

If the Leamy Ladies took any notice of the fat man in the royal box seventy feet below, they likely were as uncertain about his identity as were all the spectators in the house. Their display that night, as every night, proceeded with the millisecond-by-millisecond precision of the circling planets. It was spectacular. Near the absolute end of the Leamy

Ladies' presentation, Leitzel, Tina, and Toni descended the rope ladder. La Belle Nellie was left alone in the air, seated on her trapeze, hanging below the trapezone rotaire. In a moment, she rose from her bar, and then pressed her hands to her breast, as though her heart had just been pierced by an arrow. In the next second, she fell forward into space and dove the sixty or seventy feet into the net. Some of those large paintings of Houdini, Grock, Guilbert, and others might have shifted into cockeyed positions on the Wintergarten's walls because of the bombardments of thundering applause and cheering.

Mister John and his aides-de-camp instantly made their way to the office of the Wintergarten's manager. In minutes, someone from the office was sent out to summon Edward Leamy.

"My mother, sister, aunts, and I remained in the dressing room after Mr. Leamy disappeared," Alfred said. "My mother was jittery. It started to seem to all of us that he had been gone for an hour or more, but probably only fifteen or twenty minutes passed. Finally, he reappeared in the dressing room. He appeared more euphoric than any of us had seen him before. He had a rolled-up contract in his hand. 'The Leamy Ladies are going to New York next spring,' he said. 'Madison Square Garden. The Barnum & Bailey Circus. The Greatest Show on Earth.'"

There was much rejoicing. La Belle Nellie, Tina, and Toni were embracing one another, embracing Professor Leamy, and all of them were crying. They were trying to explain to Leitzel what this would all mean, how wonderful it would be.

Alfred Pelikan sat in a corner of the room, a witness to the jubilation but not a part of it.

He so wanted to be able to cross the ocean with his mother, sister, and aunts, so wanted to be inside Madison Square Garden on the night the Leamy Ladies presented their premiere performance there. But even more, much more, he wanted what he always wanted. He wanted to be a part of a family.

In her joy at the news she was going to America, La Belle Nellie kissed and hugged Alfred. She told him that she and Leitzel would miss him terribly, but that they would write often. She told him how proud he had made her, how, through his books and professors, he already had come to know things about God, science, literature, and the world that she could not even begin to understand. He was growing up to be such a fine man, she said.

Alfred managed not to shed any tears during the dressing room celebration. They may have come later, on the train, and then the boat, as he returned to London to resume his studies in Aristotelian value ethics, Latin, medieval history, and the metaphysical nature of being. Parted from his mother once again, he no longer had to hide anything, no longer had to pretend he was a man. He was a boy again, fourteen, and as had been true almost every day and night of his growing years, he ached with loneliness.

CHAPTER 8

So far the show had been going smoothly, close to perfectly, Mister John might have assayed.

He was seated in a box inside Madison Square Garden. As always, his great stomach was straining against a corseting vest, and, just now, the pickle-thick fingers on one of his hands were curled around the gold ball of the cane he held between his legs.

There were eight thousand people in the seats, a full house. It was March 19, 1908, the night of the season-opening performance of a brand-new edition of Barnum & Bailey's Greatest Show on Earth.

The big new show, with about 350 performing artists and 74 separate attractions scheduled, was nearing at its halfway point. Up to now, the audience had reserved its most raucous cheering for Wotan, a riderless stallion that floated upward in a gas-filled balloon to the Garden's eighty-foot-high ceiling, and then glided gently back to the floor. All the acts that had already been rolled out inside the hippodrome and in the air—the wire walkers, bareback riders, jungle cat trainers—had also been generously rewarded with great oohing and ahhing and applause, or, in the case of the clown division of thirty-five funnymen, good-natured jeering.

Still the crowd had not yet seen what Mister John regarded as the show's greatest attractions, its stunt-driving Sisters La Rague, who, the program advertised, carried on an automobile race in which they "passed each other in separate cars while flying and somersaulting in the air," and the aerial femmes who had performed in every major city in Europe, the Leamy Ladies.

Sharing a ringside box with Mister John were a couple dozen of his guests for the night—senators, judges, police commissioners, and other New York potentates, along with their wives and children.

At his side, too, was Mable, his wife of three years. He had waited until his thirty-ninth year to marry. From all accounts, John and Mable could not have been more devoted to each other, but when they were seen together as a pair, they appeared almost comically mismatched. She was pretty, vivacious, small, and delicate. John, ten years older than she, was homely and lumpy, and towered over Mable by at least a foot and a half, even more when he was wearing a derby, which he was most of the time.

This was an evening of special importance not just for Mister John but also for his brothers. While the Barnum & Bailey show had operated under the management of its new Ringling owners the previous year, the 1908 spectacle was the first that was actually produced by the brothers. For weeks there had been speculation in the press about whether the farm boys from Baraboo, Wisconsin, really had the goods to produce a spectacle that could live up to the Barnum circus's long-held honorific as The Greatest Show on Earth.

Mister John had arrived at the Garden that night with every confidence that the critics and public alike would receive the Ringling-produced Barnum & Bailey Circus with at least as much enthusiasm as they greeted any of the previous nineteen incarnations of the most famous big top show in the world. He himself had handpicked several of the heavily advertised features of the new show, among them "The Balloonist Horse," the Sisters La Rague, and the Leamy Ladies, who were slated to be the last attraction before the intermission.

◆ ◆ ◆

The Garden suddenly became dark, and then the lights on the trapezone rotaire started shimmering like distant stars. Like everyone else in the Garden, Mister John was peering up at the ceiling, his head thrown back.

Professor Leamy's massive invention was churning slowly but steadily in the air, animated by Toni, who was on the seat of the bicycle. Suspended from trapezes beneath the slightly creaking creation were La Belle Nellie, Tina, and Leitzel. As the four carried out their assignments, their shadows, three or four times their sizes, moved in unison with them on the ceiling and the walls.

Nothing like the rotating trapeze had ever been presented in an American circus before. There was much purring from the crowd in the earliest moments of the troupe's appearance, but then, very soon, in just two or three minutes, the novelty of the attraction already seemed to be wearing thin with the crowd. Now there were only occasional patters of applause as the aerialists went through their routines—cloud swings, handstands on their bars, and two- and one-legged, upsidedown suspensions on their swings.

Mister John had a reputation for having unerring judgment in discovering acts that proved to be great sensations with the public. How could he have so badly misgauged the appeal of the Leamy Ladies, the costliest single attraction in the circus?

Customarily, Mister John's pie-round face never betrayed anything of his emotional state. But it must have been apparent now to Mable and everyone around Mister John that he was suffering perturbation. His face took on the colors of a still-ripening tomato, green, yellow, and red, and it was also dewy with sweat. He was becoming more and more pained by the crowd's tepid reception to the feature he had been sure was going to be received as the circus's pièce de résistance.

There were people in the seats, some of them his guests in the box, who were already looking at their programs to see what act was to follow, and because the program's intermission was next, some of the spectators were leaving the arena to line up at the concession stands in the hallways.

Mister John, a prideful man, likely started to wonder what the critics would say about the Leamy Ladies in the morning papers. How could he have been so badly wrong in bringing the attraction to America? He may also have started thinking about scrubbing the act from The Greatest Show on Earth and sending the ladies back across the Atlantic on the next steamer out.

Then something surprising happened.

Like dancers in a corps de ballet moving to the sides of the stage to give Anna Pavlova the center position, La Belle Nellie and Tina assumed sitting positions on their trapeze bars. The spotlights in which they had been bathing went dark.

In the next instant, Leitzel transferred from her trapeze to a single white rope. The only things preventing her from plunging six stories were the small fingers of her right hand, which she had passed through a silver ring to grasp the rope.

A cry of alarm rose from the crowd. It sounded like a collective plea for her to immediately return to the relative safety of her trapeze bar. Leitzel was seventeen now, but because her face was so delicate and she was so tiny, she still had the appearance of a moppet to those in the crowd.

Like a mischievous child being scolded by a mother for climbing too high on monkey bars, Leitzel put a free hand to her mouth and chuckled. Her eyes bore a trace of deviltry.

"Just you watch," she seemed to say to those in the seats.

And it may have been just about impossible for anyone in the house not to.

Her effect on the thousands below was like that of the moon on the oceans. Her pull was gravitational. Everyone with a seat must have felt its force drawing her or his heart up to her.

Still grasping the rope, hanging from it by one arm in the carefree manner of a gibbon on a jungle vine, she began rocking her body upward, higher and higher. Her swaying, at least at first, was so gentle that her rope hardly moved. Soon, though, her entire body had risen so it was extending out in a position of nine o'clock. She pushed some more. Her body moved higher with each of her forward swings. Now her toes and extended body had risen so high that they were pointing to eleven o'clock. Then, for the briefest of moments, Leitzel was exactly vertical, with her feet where her head would otherwise be. Twelve o'clock.

She started tumbling downward: one o'clock, three o'clock, five o'clock. Upon reaching six o'clock, she started rising again. Now her return upward was eased because of the momentum she had gained from her rush downward. Within seconds she was spinning heels over head, heels over head, her extended right arm serving as the axis for the vertical, propellerlike revolutions of her entire body.

In an instant she was turning so fast that she was a blur of white. She was a human pinwheel in a brisk wind. Everyone present seemed to have sucked in her or his breath. The Garden was as noiseless as a sepulcher.

Leitzel appeared to be on the verge of self-destructing. Her right arm looked like it might tear from its upper socket from the strain. With each of her turnovers, it dislocated from her shoulder for an instant before snapping back into place. With her free hand, Leitzel inconspicuously pulled the bobby pins from the pile of hair crowning her head. Her butterscotch tresses fell and whipped about her face.

Those in the crowd with opera glasses could see the expression on her face. She was beaming.

How many one-armed swings did she turn in her premiere performance in Madison Square Garden? Fifty? One hundred? More? How could anyone even count them? Her spinning body was just a white haze.

The building rattled from cheering, whistling, and applause when Leitzel finally descended the trapezone rotaire's rope ladder and returned to the floor. Everybody in the crowd was standing as she took her bows. This included most of the circus's other performers, many of whom, like the Leamy Ladies, had been imported from faraway countries. The bareback riders, elephant trainers, acrobats, and clowns cried out their praises to her in German, Russian, French, Spanish, and Japanese. Surely no one in an American circus audience had ever before seen another performance quite like Leitzel's. Everyone in the Garden had been instantly stricken with love for her.

One by one, Mister John's special guests started approaching him, shaking his hand and patting him on the back. It may be that his face bore at least a trace of a smile.

Later that night, after the circus was over and Leitzel, her mother, and her aunts tried to exit the Garden, they encountered a long, double-file line of "eager youths and dapper middle-aged men" that had formed near the performers' rear door.

It would be the same the next evening, and the next and the next. Many of the adorers had flowers and boxes of candies in their hands.

Edward Leamy, leading his four charges through the gauntlet, menacingly waved his folded umbrella at the dandies who looked like they might be preparing to move out of the lines.

"He watched those girls like a hawk," said Dexter Fellows, press agent for the Barnum & Bailey Circus. "Not one of those stage-door Johnnies ever got closer to them than the vigilant figure of Leamy as he shepherded his charges . . . to the Preston House just across the street, where they lived."

◆ ◆ ◆

The Barnum & Bailey Circus played exactly a month of its 1908 season in the Garden, finishing its last show there on April 18. The crowds had been great at all the performances, according to newspaper accounts, and despite the earlier concerns in the press and among circus initiates about whether the Ringling brothers were up to the task of continuing the Barnum circus's reputation as The Greatest Show on Earth, *Variety*, the most powerful of the show business trade publications, pronounced the first of the Ringling brothers–produced Barnum & Bailey circuses to be its old and "big and bewildering self."

No small credit for this could be attributed to a four-foot-nine girl with hair the color of a ripe peach.

◆ ◆ ◆

As spectacularly as Leitzel had shown herself in her premiere performances in America, though, neither she nor any of the other Leamy Ladies were aboard the circus's train when, after the final performance of the Garden monthlong 1908 stand, the show started on a six-and-a-half-month, 150-town, coast-to-coast tour. The four, along with Edward Leamy, were making arrangements to return to Europe to fill engagements.

Because of a purely practical reason, the Leamy Ladies could not perform in the Barnum circus when it was traveling the hinterlands. The trapezone rotaire could be safely rigged in permanent amphitheaters like the Garden, but at the time there were few other cities that had such arenas, and thus, when the circus was on the road, its shows were presented inside its acres-large big top. Edward Leamy's massive, multiton, airborne steel trapeze was just too great of a monstrosity to be safely installed in a tent.

Surely La Belle Nellie, Leitzel, Tina, and Toni, along with their manager, must have been disappointed that they could not accompany the other thirteen hundred troupers to such places as Streator, Illinois, Yazoo City, Mississippi, and San Francisco. At the same time, though, the quintet must have been jubilant.

The Leamy Ladies had appeared with The Greatest Show on Earth. Their act had been seen by a quarter million people during their stay in New York City. And, to top off everything, the troupe already had a contract to reappear with the Barnum & Bailey Circus at its opening stand the following spring.

CHAPTER 9

Edward and Hortense Codona had been gazing at their future for a dozen and a half years, ever since they began their Gran Circo Codona. Always it was shimmering in the beyond, but they had a sense they were gaining on it year by year, drawing closer. They saw it every day as they meandered up and down and sideways through Mexico with their tiny tent, tight wire, trapeze, wooden Spiral Mountain, and a single horse.

Then, in an instant, like a star that fell out of the heavens, it was gone. It all happened around 1904 near a small village ten or twenty miles outside Monterrey.

"Papa couldn't stop crying," Victoria Codona said. "There were times every day for weeks when he just broke down."

She was twelve or thirteen, the eldest of the Codona children, when the family's future just seemed to disappear.

"Papa was a broken man. Everything he had been dreaming of for years for the family was gone. None of us thought he could ever go on with the circus."

Edward and Hortense's anticipated ahead-time had always in-cluded a place of their own, a home. It would be planted on green grass and would be in America. Maybe their house would have looked some-thing like the grand white home that Victoria, over and over, from the time she was four, kept drawing in tablets.

Above Victoria's imagined house, in a blue sky with mashed potato clouds, there was always a great orange sun with rays shooting out of it like spikes. The earliest of her drawings showed Papa Edward, Mama Hortense, Alfredo, and she posed in front of the house, all of them smiling, appearing so proud of their grand residence. Then, later, her drawings made room for a fifth Codona, Abelardo, or Lalo as everyone in the family called him. He was born in 1895.

In Lalo's first appearances in Victoria's drawings, he was present as a babe in Edward's or Hortense's arms. After a while, he started turning up in the artworks as a boy. He was always standing in the middle, between Papa and Mama on one side and Victoria and Alfredo on the other. Lalo, blond, was always grinning even more widely than the rest of them.

◆ ◆ ◆

The two desperadoes entered the tent in the inkiest hour of morning when Edward and Hortense and the children were asleep. They were drunk, loud, and boisterous. They started firing pistols, putting flashes of red light in the complete darkness. They were hooting.

"Oh, did we awaken you? Oh, we're sorry. So sorry. We should be more respectful, shouldn't we?"

There was more barking and flaring from their pistols and the men cackled again. The smell of sulfur thickened in the air.

Edward's heart was racing. He lighted a lantern.

The lamp's glow revealed the faces of the intruders. Edward had seen the same men eight or ten hours earlier, as had Hortense and the children. The pair had turned up on horseback for the circus's twilight show. They reeked of alcohol and strode into the tent without buying tickets. Edward did not challenge them. Both were dressed in the uniforms of the Mexican Guardia Rural. They wore wide-brimmed sombreros and gray shirts and britches trimmed with braided silver. They were part of a countrywide constabulary maintained by Mexico's perennial president, dictator Porfirio Díaz, to seize land and property from the indigenous poor. When the men took their seats in the audience before the circus ring, the mothers and fathers sitting around them drew their children nearer.

When the pair entered the tent a second time, well beyond midnight, they demanded money. The Gran Circo Codona seldom drew audiences of more than two or three dozen at any of its presentations. The only cash Edward had in the tent were the receipts the show had earned in the last day or two. He offered the paramilitaries all the cash he had in the tent, but the men started cursing him. The paltry receipts were hardly enough to satisfy them.

They started rummaging through the family's trunks, throwing costumes and cooking utensils to the ground, looking without success for more money. Next they moved to where Hortense and the children were huddled on the blankets. They cast the light of the lantern onto the faces of Hortense and Victoria.

"*Bonita, bonita,*" they appraised. "Ah, *muy bonita.*"

The fear deepened in Edward. He felt suddenly sick, as though he had just swallowed some fast-acting poison.

What would he have been able to do if the armed *rurales* assaulted his wife and daughter? He tried talking calmly to the men, pleading with them not to harm his wife and daughter.

To get them away from his family, Edward led the men from the tent and walked a half mile through the desert with them until they came upon a small village. Parked there, on a railroad siding, was the baggage car that moved the Gran Circo Codona from one stand to another. Edward unlocked the padlock at the door of the car, and, with the *rurales* following, entered the wheeled wooden box. By the light of his lantern, he lifted a floorboard, exposing a chamber containing two or three canvas sacks. The bags were filled with every centavo of the savings Edward had been able to accumulate with the circus over the years after meeting the family's barest living expenses and paying the train operators who towed his show from one place to another. The bandits fit the sacks under their arms and disappeared into the night.

When the sun rose, Edward arranged to have the baggage car moved to some new place up or down the rails. There was no trace of any kind of future visible to Edward when the Gran Circo Codona started rolling again. It had been scrubbed from the far skies, every detail of it, including his long-held vision of Victoria's white house, with the family standing before it.

"All those years, all those sacrifices for the circus, even the deaths of those babies who came before me, my brothers, and sister, who lived for only days or weeks—all this had been for nothing," Victoria said. "Our family lost everything. Papa wept and wept."

In time, though, Edward's spirits gradually started to brighten. He again began to see a future for his family, although just yet it lacked the shimmer of the old one and appeared further away than ever.

"The circus was the only life he knew," Victoria said. "It was the thing he could pass on to his children. He kept the show going for my brothers and me."

◆ ◆ ◆

Dozens of small circuses, most of them horse-drawn wagon affairs, but also a few railroad enterprises of one or two cars, crosshatched the same countryside that the Gran Circo Codona roved in the 1880s, 1890s, and in the early part of the twentieth century. The tented shows were a favorite entertainment of Mexico's poor families. The circuses, most of them presented entirely by members of the same family, were called *carpas*. Most of them combined features of the American and European circuses with elements of clownery and acrobatics that could be traced to the Aztec mountebanks who traipsed the land centuries earlier.

Of all the *carpas* that crisscrossed the countryside early in the twentieth century, though, probably few presented entertainment that was as distinctive, varied, and finished as that of the Gran Circo Codona. Though nearing fifty, Edward continued to ascend and descend the Spiral Mountain at the conclusion of every performance. Hortense walked a tightrope, rode the Codona horse, did some clowning, and also wove through the circus's benches, peddling homemade candies and pastries. More and more, though, it was their children who were becoming the circus's most luminous attractions. This was always what Edward and Hortense had wanted. It had been their plan.

While Alfredo's earliest appearances on the trapeze were as a baby passenger in a leather pouch that Edward kept belted around his waist when he was flying, the boy started begging for a chance to perform in the family tent alone when he was about four. Edward and Hortense were apprehensive, but in time they relented. Still, they always positioned themselves below the trapeze when their son was swinging, holding a stretched blanket between them, ready to catch Alfredo if he should ever fall. He never did.

"We all believed that Alfredo must have gotten his love and gifts from the hummingbirds in Hermosillo," said Victoria. "Papa, Mama, and I always thought back to the days we spent there when Mama was still carrying him and waiting for his arrival. We thought those hummingbirds there must have transferred their magic right through her belly to her womb."

By the time Alfredo was ten or eleven, he was appearing in the circus on both the single trapeze and in a flying, double trapeze act with Edward, who did the catching. Alfredo had yet to turn any midair somersaults in his flying act with Papa, but he started presenting a stunt that was every bit as dazzling. While standing on the trapeze platform, he slipped a black hood over his head. Now unable to see anything, he stepped onto his bar and started swinging farther and farther out into the air. Finally he let go of the ropes and catapulted into space.

He was an eagle, but one that was now blind as a bat. With his arms extended before him, he shot through the air for twenty feet or so. Then with the trueness of an arrow fired from William Tell's crossbow, he hit his bull's-eye: the strong and harboring hands of his father hanging upside down from a bar at the opposite end of the rigging.

The feat never failed to bring everyone in the tent to their feet, cheering. The adoration that Alfredo received did not stop there. He had a shy manner and wavy brown hair, and by the time he was twelve or thirteen, his physique had already started to take on the concinnities of Michelangelo's *David*. He was shirtless and wore tight, white leggings whenever he performed on the trapeze. There were always senoritas, and senoras, too, who were anxious to have a closer look at the boy flyer after the show.

Of all the daredevils who appeared in Mexican circuses, none were more widely esteemed than trapeze flyers. The people saw them as successors to the *voladores*, Aztec neck-riskers from five centuries earlier who scaled one-hundred-foot poles, attached themselves to ropes, and then, in imitation of condors, leaped into space and soared and circled around and around their tower.

As virtuosic as young Alfredo's trapeze performances were, Victoria may have been an even bigger favorite with the families inside the tent of the Gran Circo Codona—*Primero en Su Clase*. She had so many talents that she seemed to be something close to a full-blown circus by herself.

Almost always, the circus began with Victoria appearing in the ring as an equestrienne. While the family horse cantered in a circle of sawdust, she pirouetted and did handstands on its back, and bounded into the air, throwing backward somersaults, always alighting on its hindquarter, inches from its tail. Two or three acts would pass, and then she would reappear, this time to perform on the single trapeze. Her presentations there, while lacking the dazzle of Alfredo's, were always more than merely creditable. Next Victoria might reappear before spectators to join with her mother and brother Lalo in a clowning routine. Finally, usually as the last feature in the tent before Edward led the audiences outside where he ascended the Spiral Mountain, Victoria would return before the audiences yet another time.

The mere sight of her was breathtaking. She was a vision costumed in a skirt of multilayered red and black cloth with multiple ruffles and an off-the-shoulders white peasant blouse. Her expression was demure as she stood before the audience, and because the benches were so close to the ring, it was possible for everyone to gaze into her eyes. Was there another young woman in the whole of Mexico whose eyes were that color? They were purplish blue, almost the color of lilacs. Her hair was wavy and black, and glinted as though there were specks of gold in it.

She ascended a ladder of eight or ten steps to a taut, braided wire that was hardly thicker than a telephone cable and stretched eighteen or twenty feet between securing frames at both ends. At first she merely pranced back and forth over the cable. Next, with the lightness of a sparrow, she moved over it in little hops.

And then she transformed herself from a child of innocence to a young gypsy lady of bewitchery. She gathered her ruffles in one hand and lifted her skirt a few inches above her feet. With her other hand, she started clicking a castanet. Her gold slippers jabbed at the wire over and over in a rapid staccato. She might have been in a smoke-smeared cabaret, moving among the tables, as she danced a flamenco.

She was not quite finished.

Edward, in a black tuxedo and always nearby when she was in the ring, made adjustments to her cable, changing her half-inch-wide performing stage from a tight wire to a slack wire. He loosened the strand so greatly that it drooped to within a foot of the ground at its midpoint. Victoria repositioned herself at the lowest point of the wire, bobbling a bit because of her shaky underfooting. Slowly at first, she started rocking the wire laterally from side to side with her feet. The slack wire moved a little higher right and left of her with each of her pushes. Eventually it was oscillating to her sides a full 180 degrees. Her head and feet were now exactly horizontal, and, impossibly it seemed, she was able to maintain her balance on the whipping strand. The wire moved even higher. Finally she allowed it to fling her into the air. She sailed a dozen feet and then landed safely in her father's arms.

✦ ✦ ✦

Victoria was surpassing as a circus artist, and so arrestingly pretty, that her reputation soon began to extend well beyond those arid places of sand and steer bones where the Gran Circo Codona mostly raised its tent. Agents from the circuses that only played the big cities started turning up at the Codona *carpa*, trying to arrange with Edward to have Victoria make special appearances with their shows.

One of these circuses was the Orrin Bros. Great Metropolitan Circus. It was the largest circus in all of Mesoamerica, and also the oldest. Victoria was still short of her thirteenth year, but Edward could not turn away the offer. It had always been his and Hortense's dream that their children achieve wide renown. When Victoria appeared in the

Great Metropolitan Circus's tent, it was before an audience of thousands, not one of a dozen or two that typically entered the tent of the Gran Circo Codona.

Three or four years later, on a December 12, Victoria's wire was stretched from one stone wall to another in Mexico City's El Toreo, not a circus, but the most famous of Mexico's bull rings. Her appearance there was a part of a celebration commemorating the Feast of the Virgin of Guadalupe, a high holiday in Mexico. There were mariachi bands, *voladores*, a chariot race, even bullfighters, but none of the attractions was quite as sensational as "The Venus of the Wire," as Victoria was beginning to become known.

The coliseum was absolutely hushed as she moved forward, inches at a time, over her wire highway in the sky. Sixty or eighty feet below her was the same soil where the blood of dozens of bulls and at least a few matadors had been spilled over the years. When she finally reached the end of her journey, El Toreo erupted in a storm of roars. So great was the tumult that day, in fact, that one newspaper observed five years later that Victoria's "ovation [was] still remembered . . . in the gay capital."

Among those on their feet, cheering and blowing kisses to Victoria, was a man occupying a special box in the stadium decorated in red, white, and green bunting, the national colors of Mexico. He was surrounded by dignitaries and wore a helmet and a military coat whose front was covered with two or three dozen medals and ribbons. It was a man whom Edward frankly despised, Porfirio Díaz, then nearing eighty, and in his eighth term as Mexico's president. Through his henchmen, the dictator had once stolen a future from Edward and his family. Probably that was not so much on Edward's mind this moment, though.

The cries of "*Brava! . . . Brava! . . . Brava!*" just kept ringing out for Victoria, the Venus of the Wire, from the crowd of fifty thousand on their feet in the stone arena, and Papa Codona was enjoying what likely was the proudest moment of his life. Alfredo was, too. He revered his sister. He might also have been hoping that a day would come when his father would be just as proud of him.

CHAPTER 10

Alfredo had never seen a fairy before.

She was impossibly small and delicate, as fragile-looking as a but-terfly, and so beautiful. She was all in white—tutu, stockings, slippers. Her hair was the color of gathered sunlight.

A luminous nimbus glowed all around her. She looked like a saint on a holy card. She might have been seventy or eighty feet up in the air of the Coliseum in Chicago, seemingly somehow kept aloft by nothing more than the beams of phosphorescent white light aimed at her.

How Alfredo wished he could be up there, too, joined with her in an aerial pas de deux, floating and fluttering in nothingness. Her beauty moved in and through him, flooding him everywhere with feel-ings he had never known as deeply before. He was sixteen.

In the parlance of the circus, Alfredo was a flyer, or as he was identified by other big top performers, a "leaper." Leitzel was an aerial-ist. Immediately, though, he saw the two of them as birds of a feather. Both were more at ease in the air than on earth.

There were times when Alfredo had a sense that she had made eye contact with him as she performed. Just him. That was foolish, of course. Even he must have known that. He was inside the cavernous arena, watching her from a dusky aisle between the seats. Thousands of others were peering up at her, too. It was the first night of a new season for the Barnum & Bailey Circus.

As young as he was, Alfredo even by then was regarded as the most beautiful male with the circus. In stolen moments in dark and empty tents, he had been with other young women before, showgirls, and sometimes young town girls who might have come to the circus with their parents one night, and then, after seeing him, returned a second night, unaccompanied and free.

After Leitzel descended from the Coliseum's stratosphere to take her bows and harvest the cheers and applause, Alfredo ran to a performers' dressing area in the building where Victoria, as a headliner of the circus, had a small, private, curtained-off cubicle with a mirror and makeup table, a cot, a costume rack, and a Taylor trunk. Papa Edward was with her.

"After seeing Leitzel that first time, Alfredo was changed, all right," Victoria said. "He was giddy. He was gushing. He was breathless. He said he had just seen the loveliest creature he had ever seen in his life. He would marry her someday, he said. He sounded loco, just plumb crazy."

Alfredo always seemed to be on wires, jittery, his attention ping-ponging from one subject to another, but she had never before seen him quite as discombobulated as he was this night. She suppressed an urge to laugh at him. How many times had she herself turned boys into mooncalves simply by appearing in the circus ring?

"Alfredo was in love, crazy in love, and for the first time ever," Victoria said. "He was all mixed up, happier than a lark and also aching because he had just seen the girl of his dreams."

It was the night of April 1, 1909, and the first time in the Barnum & Bailey Circus's three decades' history that the show had opened a new season in a city anywhere outside New York. In the past, it had always rankled on the Ringling brothers that the Barnum show had a lock on Madison Square Garden, the most prestigious of the circus halls in America. Because they were now in possession of not just the Ringling Bros. World's Greatest Shows but also the Barnum colossus, they decided to premiere their eponymously named circus in New York, and the Barnum show in the Windy City.

✦ ✦ ✦

By 1909, the Codona family finally had their own house, a home in El Paso, Texas, with a small barn in the backyard that Papa Edward hoped to turn into a school for aspiring circus athletes. Alfredo and Victoria, along with their father, traveled by train to Chicago's Coliseum, arriving just a few days before the circus's opening. Hortense remained in El Paso, caring for Lalo, then thirteen, and another child who had been born into the family, Edward, five.

Leitzel, too, had only recently arrived in Chicago. She, along with the women in her family, had been playing engagements in Europe for most of the past year, and they had returned to America for a second appearance with the Barnum show.

Leitzel was already well on her way to becoming world renowned. She was eighteen and already a darling with circus audiences everywhere abroad, as well as with the quarter million people who had seen her the year before in the Barnum circus's opening stand in New York's Madison Square Garden. Alfredo, on the other hand, was unknown to all but the audiences before which he had appeared with the Gran Circo Codona in the tank towns and deserts of Mexico. The position he had been given in the Barnum & Bailey Circus was that of an extra, one of those nameless performers whom the audiences saw only peripherally, if at all, while focusing on the genuine stars in and above the center ring. Alfredo, in fact, would not have had a place in the Barnum circus at all had it not been for his sister.

An agent for the big show, Ernie Thompson, saw Victoria performing with the family circus in Veracruz, Mexico. He was besotted not just with her dazzling feats on the slack wire but also by her surpassing beauty. He immediately wired his Ringling bosses at their circus winter quarters, in Baraboo, Wisconsin, assuring them that she would be a major sensation in the show.

"Give her the moon if you have to," Thompson urged. "No expense should be spared."

Otto Ringling followed the agent's advice but maybe not to a tee. He flashed a wire to Papa Edward, declaring that the Barnum circus was prepared to give Victoria a place in the show:

FEB 13, 1909

CAN OFFER YOU $125 PER WEEK AND BOARD AND TRANSPORTATION.
THIS IS THE BEST WE CAN DO. CAN PLACE ACT IN CENTER RING.
TELEGRAPH ANSWER, BARABOO, WIS.

OTTO RINGLING

Even as long ago as 1909, $125 a week might have been considered laughably low for a center ring attraction of Victoria's caliber. But Papa Codona not only accepted Otto's proposition, he also offered to throw in his services, along with those of Alfredo. He regarded $125 a week as a king's ransom next to the receipts he typically took in with his circus, some of which were in denominations of chicken eggs and grilled goat meat.

When Edward, Victoria, and Alfredo reported to the show just days before its Chicago opening, the circus, looking for a place where Alfredo might fit in, added him to the Siegrist-Silbon Flyers, a trapeze troupe that already had fourteen or fifteen artists. Trapeze flyers were always ranked with the most elite of circus artists. But on the Barnum show of 1909, they seemed to be only slightly less common than the flies in the horse stables. In addition to the big Siegrist-Silbon troupe, the spectacle also featured two other flying acts.

If Alfredo was little noticed by the people occupying the seats, it was a different matter for the single young women who traveled with the show, working as seamstresses in the wardrobe tent, washing pans in the cookhouse, or appearing as window dressing in the lavish biblical and historical productions of a hundred or more anonymous, camel- and burro-leading players that the circus spilled out on the hippodrome floor. He had lustrous and dreamy eyes that were about the color of beer bottle glass and softly waving brown hair. Like most trapeze flyers, he was smallish, just five foot eight, but every square centimeter of his arms and chest seemed to have been carved and polished by a Renaissance master. Even his muscles appeared to have muscles. Probably the most apt physical description for the boy leaper came from a stage actress who apparently had some knowledge of herpetology.

"When he moved"—she sighed—"the muscles on his back moved like copulating snakes."

A good number of the showgirls drifted to sleep at night with publicity photographs of Alfredo in their hands. The pictures, taken when he was still traveling with the family's Gran Circo Codona, showed him shirtless and wearing leggings that appeared to have been whitewashed on his lower body.

He likely would have discovered many of these fellow travelers to be easy conquests. Even at sixteen, though, it was not in Alfredo's nature to pursue much in life that was his for the mere taking. He was up for a greater challenge. He wanted only Leitzel.

Many of the circus's single women, and likely some married ones, too, were desolate when it became widely known that Alfredo was love drunk on Leitzel.

"You would have thought the show had suddenly been hit by some epidemic—one that only struck the girls on the show," said Charlotte Shives, one of the showgirls. "When it became known that Alfredo was putting out his cat for Leitzel, almost every girl on the show seemed to stop believing life was worth living. There was a lot of moping, a lot of crying, a lot of talk by the girls of leaving the circus to enter the convent."

Shives appeared in the hippodrome spectacles riding atop a float as Betsy Ross and sewing stars on an American flag. She was also a member of the Living Statues, a small group of exceptionally attractive young women and men who covered their near-nude bodies in white greasepaint and appeared in the center ring where they assumed the poses of the figures in such famous artworks as Leutze's *Washington Crossing the Delaware.*

While she shared the view of the other showgirls that Alfredo was the most beautiful male specimen in the circus, she herself was never smitten with him, Shives insisted.

"For one thing," she said, "I don't think Alfredo knew more than a hundred words of English at the time, and the only word of Spanish I knew was *sí,* which could have resulted in a dangerous relationship. For another thing, I thought my chances of ever being singled out by Al-

fredo were about the same as my chances of winning the Irish Sweep-
stakes. Whether they were sixteen or forty, almost every other single
girl on the show wanted him."

✦ ✦ ✦

Now and again romances did blossom on the Barnum & Bailey Circus, but hyphenations of performers or workers who met each other on
the show were extremely rare, maybe falling into that broad category
identified as eternal mysteries of nature. This was because the circus's
front office was always quick to run in with icy water if it saw signs that
sparks were beginning to arc between a male and female on its payroll.

Charley Ringling, who was in charge of the show's personnel, even
hired a detective, an Officer Black, to regularly peer into the circus
baggage wagons and the shadowy areas of the animal tents to look for
coupling employees. A camel groom or clown who was caught trying
to woo a showgirl would discover on payday that he had been docked
$10. This was not an insignificant amount when the average workman
earned $25 a month, a minor performer $37.50.

The Ringling brothers' reason for discouraging the development
of intracircus romances may not have been motivated entirely out of
overdeveloped senses of rectitude. Love could lead couples to the altar
or justices of the peace. This complicated matters—for the circus and
for the newlyweds. For one thing, the show's sleeping accommodations
fell short of those at the Waldorf Astoria. The five Ringlings, a few
of the show's other executives, and one or two center ring stars had
staterooms on the train. But most of the performers and all the animal
men, canvas men, and showgirls, whether married or not, were housed
in "sixty-four cars," so-called because each was shared by sixty-four
men and women. Fred Bradna, ringmaster for the circus, compared the
arrangements to those of the Yagua, an Amazon River tribe that lived
in grass communal huts, with each couple sharing a hammock against
a wall.

"Nothing is quite so frustrating to the newlyweds as the married
people's car," Bradna lamented. "The company is excellent, even sym-
pathetic. But space is crammed and privacy is limited. . . . Privacy is

obtained by turning one's face to the wall. A man . . . in such a position is, by common consent, not present. No one looks in the direction."

Whatever the sanctions management imposed to keep the men and women segregated, though, none worked perfectly. It was one thing for the circus to expect an animal trainer to stick his head into the oral cavities of his lions for two performances a day. It was quite another for Charley and his brothers to insist that males in their teens and twenties ignore the showgirls of ripened figures that abounded on the show.

Necessity being the mother of invention, though, the circus's attachés found ways to foil Officer Black, according to Francis "Butch" Brann, one of Alfredo's coflyers in the Siegrist-Silbon troupe.

"Every town had a post office," he noted. "If you picked up a signal that one of the ballet girls might be interested in you, you'd get word to her to meet you on the post office steps after the last show. If you had a night off and knew what movie houses were in a town, you could ask the girl to wait for you in the theater's balcony." Brann may have sounded knowledgeable about ways to skirt the circus's measures for keeping the sexes apart, but his own skills in such maneuverings might be called into question. By his own admission, his pay was docked so many times for his attempts at amorous connections that at the close of most circus seasons, he often had to borrow money to get back to his home in Canton, Ohio.

◆ ◆ ◆

The circus's patrons have always tended to view its spectacles as dream-splashed, rainbow-colored phantasmagoria that are populated by demi-gods who, in their strength, fearlessness, and ability to relax the usual rules of gravity, have taken on the traits of beasts and birds. The men and women responsible for putting on the spectacles, though—the ringmaster, the performers, even the faceless men with shovels who clean up after the elephants and camels—tended to have a different view. Most of them became blasé about their workplace after relatively short stays on the job. They rarely regarded the sideshow's bearded lady or the human cannonballs and high-wire daredevils with any more fascination than people who were in the workaday world viewed their mailman or corner butcher.

Even so, when Leitzel was performing, great numbers of her fellow circus travelers stopped what they were doing to take in her act. Many of the interlopers were young males who were single, recently detached, or detaching. Leitzel was easily the most widely desired of all the pretty young women traveling with the circus. She also may have been just about as unreachable and unobtainable to her love-stricken as Selene, goddess of the moon.

Of all the bareback riders, daredevils, tumblers, clowns, cookhouse dishwashers, and stablemen who interrupted their routines to take in her performances, Alfredo likely was the only one with a perfect attendance record. He was present for each of her afternoon and evening appearances.

In addition to the hindrances that the circus threw up to frustrate the flowering of amour between its single employees, there was an even more formidable obstacle that Alfredo would have to surmount to carry on any attempts at wooing Leitzel. Edward Leamy remained as vigilant as ever in keeping Leitzel as well as the other Leamy Ladies stonewalled from any would-be suitors, whether they were part of the circus or paying customers.

Brann made this observation: "If the old man had any suspicion that some young buck was lusting after his Leitzel, or, for that matter, any of the Leamy Ladies, he probably would have put out his eyes with his umbrella."

Victoria said that certainly Alfredo knew he was engaging in risky behavior by pursuing Leitzel, but he could not stop himself.

"Over and over, Papa warned him about getting on the wrong side of Mr. Leamy," she remembered. "Papa said that if the Leamy Ladies' manager found out that Alfredo was trying to romance Leitzel, he would have marched right up to Mister John and seen to it that he was thrown off the show. Maybe I'd have lost my job, too. Alfredo was so crazy in love, though, that he would have walked through fire for her. He wouldn't listen to Papa."

✦ ✦ ✦

Within a few days after the circus's new season began, though, Leitzel secretly started providing Alfredo with intimations that maybe she was a little bit interested in him, according to Charlotte Shives, who had become close to the star.

"I think this was all a game for her, at least at first," she said. "Even then, she was a big star, and Alfredo was a nobody. It wasn't until Leitzel found out that the show's other girls were gaga over Alfredo that she paid any attention to him. I loved Leitzel, but she was fiercely competitive, whether playing Chinese checkers or trying to show up the other performers. As a star, she seemed to believe she was entitled to anything that made her heart flutter. When she heard that the other girls were turned into mush by Alfredo, she decided to put her name on him. If that meant taking him out of circulation from the other girls, well, so be it."

Leitzel and Alfredo eventually found a way to start snatching private, if brief, moments together. Their liaisons required help not just from Alfredo's friends but also from La Belle Nellie, Tina, and Toni.

Each night after the show, Leamy shepherded his foursome to a rooming house some blocks from the Coliseum. He always kept a few steps ahead of them, ready to wrap his umbrella around the heads of any mashers. Always on these late-night strolls, Leamy stopped at a pool hall along the way to pick up cigars for the next day. The hall was a popular late-night hangout with circus performers, among them Butch Brann, Toto Siegrist, also a trapeze flyer, and Orrin Davenport, a trick horse rider. Because women were prohibited from entering pool halls, the Leamy Ladies waited outside while their manager took care of his business inside.

"What Leamy didn't know," said Brann, "was that Alfredo was always hiding in the shadows at the side of the pool hall. The instant the old man entered the hall, Leitzel separated from her mother and her aunts, and got together with Alfredo. Me and Toto and Orrin were always at a billiards table. When we saw Leamy, we'd tie him up in conversation, talking about the weather, the circus, this and that. This gave Alfredo and Leitzel some time for smooching. When Leitzel's mother and aunts saw through the window that their boss was at the cash register, settling up for his cigars, they signaled the lovebirds to break from their clinch. Leitzel quickly rejoined her mother and aunts. Leamy never found out about these little trysts."

◆ ◆ ◆

Alfredo could be moody much of the time, even melancholic, Brann said, but after he and Leitzel started seeing each other, he brightened.

"He even talked to me and Toto and some of the other guys in the Siegrist-Silbon Flyers about borrowing money to help him buy an engagement ring," said Brann. "He thought that if Leitzel agreed to marry him, old man Leamy would have to let them carry out their romance in the open. I never saw anybody fall harder for a gal than he did. He seemed to be getting crazier every day."

To Papa Edward, the most alarming change that came over his son at this time involved a new obsession, a madness. Alfredo had become preoccupied with the thought of accomplishing the most dazzling of feats ever to be presented under a big top. He wanted to execute The Triple, three somersaults in midair while streaking at speeds up to seventy miles per hour from one flying trapeze to another.

The flying trapeze act—the spectacle of a performer being catapulted from a flybar and then shooting through space to another athlete, a catcher—started becoming a feature of the bigger circuses by the 1870s. Very soon some of the more daring flyers added a somersault to their flights to make their displays appear even more eye-popping to their audiences. As spectacular as these exhibitions were, though, they still did not have enough razzle-dazzle for the most brazen of flyers. By the 1890s, some of them had started turning two somersaults while shooting the air.

But three somersaults from a flying trapeze to the hands of a catcher, a Triple?

Such a feat was thought to be absolutely impossible, as inconceivable at the time as the idea of any man ever being able to run a mile in fewer than four minutes, as preposterous as the notion that a day would ever come when a man could walk on the moon. Maybe there were gods somewhere who could execute a Triple, but a mortal? The idea was absurd, not even imaginable.

And then, not many years into the twentieth century, a Triple was executed. It was accomplished by Ernie Clarke, a British-born circus daredevil.

There were accounts, some of them published, that Clarke, at least now and then, may have begun throwing his first Triples as early as 1902 or 1903 when he and his brother, Charles, his catcher, were performing in Australia and New Zealand. Not all experts on the early twentieth-century circus believe these claims, but there appears to be little doubt that by the time Ernie was appearing with the Publiones Circus in Cuba in 1909, he was regularly presenting The Triple.

Word of Clarke's feat spread quickly through the big top world. Alfredo was immediately determined to follow his lead.

"If he could perform The Triple, it would make him famous the world over," Victoria said. "He also believed that if he could ever perform the feat, it would make him more worthy of Leitzel."

Papa Edward had started training his son on the flying trapeze when Alfredo was as young as four or five. When a dozen years later Alfredo approached his father and begged help from him to add The Triple to his repertoire, the senior Codona's response was immediate and adamant.

"No," he said. "Not on your life and not on mine."

Edward was fifty in 1909. He must have thought he had already sacrificed enough for the circus, all those babies who were stillborn or died soon after they were born while he and Hortense were traveling with their Gran Circo Codona in Mexico. He did not want now to also lose his sixteen-year-old son.

◆ ◆ ◆

Triple midair somersaults had started taking the lives of circus daredevils years before the first flying trapeze acts started appearing in the big circuses late in the nineteenth century. Emerging in the circuses in the 1830s and 1840s was a species of intermittently insane supermen who ran down long, steeply inclined wooden ramps to gain speed, and then, at the bottom of the ramps, jumped onto springboards that shot them sixty or seventy feet through the air before they alighted on straw-filled mats. These athletes were called "leapers," a name that would later be passed on to somersaulting trapeze flyers. Almost all of the first leapers could throw at least one somersault while moving in their parabolic arcs in the air, and a few could turn doubles. Almost all of the madmen who tried to execute triples, though, killed themselves, if not in their first tries at the stunt, then in their second or tenth.

One of the best accounts of the perils of The Triple may have been provided by George Brinton Beal, an author, Boston theater critic, and one of the most alert observers of the circus's arts.

"Nothing in the entire list of acts . . . is more heavily laden with possibilities of disaster than the triple somersault," he wrote. "The great risk involved . . . is . . . after the second turn is accomplished, and the third turn is attempted. The performer 'loses his catch,' or, translated from show language, loses control of his body and is governed by gravity. Because his head is heavier than his feet, he is most likely to land on his head and break his neck."

When Alfredo told Papa Edward that he was going to try to find The Triple, even if he could not count on his help in his search, Edward wept. He pleaded with his son to give up the idea. It was only after he became fully convinced that his son's mind could not be changed that he agreed to work with him.

The Barnum & Bailey Circus had settled into the Coliseum in Chicago for a month at the start of its 1909 season. Hours before the show's matinee each day, while the great arena was empty of spectators, Alfredo ascended the rope ladder to his trapeze pedestal, and with Edward opposite, hanging upside down from another trapeze, son and father started their search for The Triple.

"*Estoy listo!*" Alfredo would cry out, and then, ready to go, would grab his flybar. Next, he would swing as high as possible, and then let go of the bar, starting the first of his heels-over-head backward somersaults while at the same time shooting forward en route to the hands of his father, hanging upside down on another trapeze at the opposite end of the rigging.

One . . .

Two . . .

Thr-r-r-r . . .

Butch Brann, along with other members of the Siegrist-Silbon Flyers with whom Alfredo performed in the circus, was often present to watch the sessions.

"Alfredo could always throw a double somersault, sometimes even something close to a two and a half," Brann said. "But The Triple? No. Never. He'd spin wildly out of control just as he was entering the third turn, and then end up crashing into the net. He'd cuss in Spanish, totally frustrated. But then he'd climb back to his pedestal. *'Estoy listo!'* he would again cry out to his father."

There were times when Alfredo believed he was getting closer to executing The Triple. Other times, he felt he was no closer to success than the first day he and Papa began the pursuit. He was cross with himself at the end of each practice session and feeling aches everywhere on his body from his spills into the net.

✦ ✦ ✦

As angry at the fates as Alfredo would become because they did not permit him to execute The Triple, there was another matter that troubled him even more. He and Leitzel continued to steal a few moments together outside the pool hall each night, but she made it increasingly clear to him that she was not interested in seeing the relationship advance beyond a puppy love stage.

"I think she saw her clutches with him as mere rehearsals for a day when there would be someone else in her life," said Charlotte Shives. "Each day, men from outside the circus, young men with elegant manners, were sending her flowers, candies, and letters, and begging for a chance to see her. Because of Mr. Leamy, of course, none ever got anywhere with her."

Brann said Alfredo became worn down by Leitzel's refusal to commit to him.

"He would get teary and say, 'Who am I to think that she would ever promise herself to me?' Leitzel, of course, was already a major star, someone management counted on to draw people to the ticket booths. Alfredo was just another 'kinker,' a no-name performer like me whose job was to provide filler between the premier acts like the Leamy Ladies and Victoria Codona, who were getting all the promotion."

Brann probably was at least partly correct in suggesting that Leitzel was reluctant to become serious about Alfredo because the two were so distanced from each other on the circus's social scale. But there was another reason why the time was not right for Leitzel to make a commitment to Alfredo, or to anyone.

Their romance, she told Alfredo over and over, necessarily had to be a "summer love," or, more accurately, a "spring love"—one that could only have the duration of the four or six weeks that the Barnum & Bailey Circus was playing in its season-openers in the Garden in New York or the Coliseum in Chicago.

After that, Alfredo, along with most of the circus's other performers and workers, would board the show's train and, for the next seven months, start crosshatching the country. Neither Leitzel nor any of the other Leamy Ladies would ever be on the train, though. Leamy still had not been able to find a way to safely hang his ponderous trapezone rotaire in the circus's big top, and once the show left the permanent halls in New York and Chicago to go on the road, the Leamy Ladies were scrubbed from the program. They, along with their manager, would then return to Europe to resume their peregrinations there.

＊ ＊ ＊

Leitzel and Alfredo were again in the shadows outside the Chicago pool hall late in the night of April 26, 1909, but this would be the last of their minutes-long embraces there. The circus would be presenting its final show in the Coliseum the next day.

As circus artists, they were committed to the life of vagabonds, stateless souls who, like migratory birds, move here one day, and there the next. Maybe sometime, somewhere, their paths would cross again, Leitzel told Alfredo. Maybe things could be different then, she said. But maybe, too, that might never be.

Professor Leamy exited the pool hall moments later with a new supply of cigars to get through the next day and, joined by Leitzel, Nellie, Tina, and Toni, then resumed the walk to the group's hotel. Alfredo remained in the shadows for a while, watching the five disappear down the street, and then rejoined his fellow Siegrist-Silbon Flyers at the billiard tables, but, according to Brann, he was unable to stop crying.

CHAPTER 11

ℑt all happened so fast. Leitzel was left stunned, uncertain now about everything.

Days earlier, she was a darling of Barnum & Bailey's Greatest Show on Earth, America's biggest circus, adored by hundreds of thousands. Now she was out of work, and without prospects for immediate employment. Even more wrenching, just like that, she had lost her attachment to her mother, her aunts, Edward Leamy, everyone with whom she had been closest.

She was even without a country.

What upended everything, finally, was a final blowup between La Belle Nellie and Professor Leamy.

From the time Leitzel had begun touring with the Leamy Ladies, she had often heard her mother and Professor Leamy arguing in low voices. Most of the time, their quarrels took place late at night as she lay in hotel beds while her mother and Leamy were in an outer room.

Their whispers went back and forth, moving like sweeping brooms at opposite ends of a room.

Shiss . . . shiss. . . . Shiss . . . shiss. . . . Shiss . . . shiss. . . .

Occasionally Leamy's murmurings rose to the sound of wind: *SHISS . . . SHISS . . . SHISS . . . SHISS . . . SHISS. . . .*

Leitzel strained to listen to the fusses. Their words were too indistinct to make out. Often, though, after the bickering quieted, she heard

La Belle Nellie sobbing. When she saw her in the morning, her eyes were puffy and red.

While Leitzel never knew exactly what Leamy and her mother quarreled over, she was sure their difference had to do with his control. He chose the clothes she wore, as well as those of Leitzel and Nellie's sisters. He subjected the four to dress inspections before he allowed them to go out in public. He paid for the clothes, train tickets, hotels, and meals for all the Leamy Ladies and also provided them with allowances. But there was a feeling among Nellie and her sisters that maybe they were not getting honest shares of the money the act earned.

Maybe what was most upsetting to La Belle Nellie was that he refused to allow her to accept dinner and theater invitations from admiring men. And although he himself seemed never to have a romantic interest in her, or in any woman, he refused to ever let her out of his sight.

◆ ◆ ◆

The Leamy Ladies' separation from their manager took place soon after April 22, 1911, when the Barnum & Bailey Circus ended a six-week appearance in New York. It had been the fourth consecutive year that the circus had brought the troupe to America for its season opener.

"My mother always felt indebted to Professor Leamy," said Alfred Pelikan. "She respected him. He rescued her from Willy Dosta. He turned her into a world-class circus star. But was he controlling? Oh, yes, I'd say he could be despotic. He insisted on running every detail of her life, as well as mine and my aunts'. I was a young boy at the time. I didn't know all that went on when the Leamy Ladies were touring. Leitzel, though, told me about the tension that always existed between my mother and Professor Leamy. Finally, after being together for years, the two of them decided they just couldn't go on together anymore. They went their separate ways, and that was that."

Nellie sailed to Berlin, and Tina and Toni returned to London to be reunited with other members of the Pelikan family, including patriarch Eduard, who had found work producing finely crafted display cabinets for the British Museum.

Leitzel was desolated by Leamy's departure from the Leamy Ladies. She had never felt any bitterness toward him. He was kind and good, and she had always loved him like a father. Now she was unsure if she would ever see him again.

Leitzel, now twenty, decided to remain in New York to search for opportunities as a solo performer.

♦ ♦ ♦

⁋If La Belle Nellie felt new freedom after the falling-out with Professor Leamy, she must have also felt some fear. She was thirty-two, and from the time she was fourteen, there had never been a day or night when he was not there to chart all of her moves.

It was not long after Nellie settled in Berlin, though, that the entertainment world started taking greater notice of her than ever. She received offers to make appearances in theaters throughout the Continent, and caused tongues to wag wherever she traveled.

She had reinvented herself as "Zoe, the Aerial Venus." The handbills printed for her act carried a tagline in big type that described her act this way: "A Beautiful Woman Completely Disrobes While Clinging by Her Teeth to the Handle of a Lace Parasol."

It was the Belle Epoque, a rash and brash era ushered into Europe with the tango. Even so, it seems improbable that there were halls where Nellie was permitted to "completely" disrobe before audiences. She did not put on her shows in dives but in opulent performing halls and circus theaters whose gilt-filigreed boxes were occupied nightly not just by dukes, archdukes, counts, and viscounts but also by mayors and police magistrates. As liberated as the "Beautiful Age" was, especially in contrast to the Victorian era, any public exhibitions of nudity likely would have brought out police raids.

Jack Leontini may have seen her "disrobing" as often as anybody—and for free. In 1911 he was working as a bareback rider and errand boy for the Adolfi Circus in Göteborg, Sweden, where Nellie had an extended engagement.

Leontini was interviewed in his seventy-fifth year and said the impression Nellie's stratospheric striptease left on him was still "indelible."

Probably this was not surprising. He was a schoolboy, just ten or eleven, when he saw her performances. Leontini, who years later would become manager of the Great Wallendas, the famous high-wire daredevils, had this memory:

> She was elegantly attired when she appeared in the ring, twirling a parasol and flirting with the men. After a while, she hooked the top of her parasol to a cable that was rigged to a pulley. A couple of strong men pulled at the cable and, while she was hanging by her teeth on the parasol's handle, she was hoisted almost to the ceiling. The spotlights changed from white to red. Then, while swaying back and forth in the air, she started stripping. Her buttoned shoes dropped to the ring first, then her garters, then her stockings and petticoats. She was covered in a lot of frills which she took off one by one, very slowly, and let them flutter to the floor. I was sure at the time that Madame Zoe was stripping completely. I became a hero among all my friends because I told them I had seen a naked woman. Because I was so young then, though, I really didn't even know what nude ladies looked like. Maybe I only thought I was looking at a completely nude lady night after night because this is what I wanted to believe. I was told years later that Madame Zoe only stripped down to flesh-colored tights. Maybe so, maybe not.

Then, as today, European circuses shaped their productions for adults. The circuses of America, on the other hand, were crafted for families. Enterprises like Barnum & Bailey and the Ringling Bros. would have considered Madame Zoe's skyborne disrobings far too risqué for their audiences. Nellie would, though, return to the United States the following year, where she found bookings in New York and Washington, D.C., theaters, as well as an extended engagement at Luna Park on Coney Island, where, for several months, she shed her raiment not as "Zoe, the Aerial Venus," but "Zoe, the Famous Parisian Novelty."

"In Europe, at least, there was no bigger sensation at the time than

Madame Zoe," Leontini said. "She appeared with just about every major circus. In the equivalent of American money at the time, she was probably earning $400 or $500 a week, a staggering amount, likely more than any other single circus performer of the time was commanding."

◆ ◆ ◆

All of Leitzel's days started the same way in the first weeks she was alone in New York. Each morning, she entered one or another of the office buildings on Forty-Sixth Street near Broadway that were dovecotes of talent promoters and booking agents. She would ride an elevator or sometimes climb the stairs to the sixth or eighth floor. Next, she would start entering the offices, one after another, some hardly bigger than phone booths, and almost all of them with air thickly smeared in cigar smoke.

She spread her newspaper clippings on the desks of the agents, showing them how she had always been singled out for her performances with the Leamy Ladies. She could easily recraft her act into a solo feature that would play well in the vaudeville houses, she assured them. Inevitably, her importuning brought a response along these lines: "You know how many 'dumb acts' I already have on file, sister? Got hundreds of 'em. Maybe a thousand. What theater managers are looking for today are real entertainers—Eva Tanguay, the Marx Brothers, Fanny Brice. Big stars. Dumb acts? You can hardly give 'em away anymore."

The expression "dumb act" was not a pejorative, but rather defined vaudeville acts like juggling, trick roller-skating, and acrobatics where the performers did not communicate vocally with their audience. Dumb acts were usually slated as the first and last features of the vaudeville lineups, when the patrons were either noisily entering the theaters or leaving them.

Although she had endeared herself to uncountable numbers of New Yorkers who had seen her in her appearances in the Garden with the Barnum & Bailey Circus, the bookers for the vaudeville houses apparently had doubts about whether her trapeze act would translate well inside theaters. After being turned away at a talent agency, Leitzel would move on to the next, and then the next. Hours later, by the time she finally descended to the ground floor, her spirits would be beaten down. She would walk out into the sunlight, wondering how much longer she could survive without employment.

◆ ◆ ◆

After weeks of searching, Leitzel finally did find work—on vaudeville's so-called silo circuit. She had been given marching orders to make appearances at a series of what the bookers referred to as "slabs," vaudeville houses in small, sleepy towns and farming centers well outside New York. Because of the remoteness of the cow towns to which she was dispatched, she often found herself traveling not in passenger trains but on milk trains.

The dives at which she appeared, often with fewer than a dozen people in the audience, were open from late morning until late at night. Because the theater managers were usually too stinting to hire more than three or four features, she put on her grueling act on her aerial rings eight or ten times day, and when she was not onstage, she often assumed assignments like operating the popcorn stand. She knew better than to complain. The silo circuit was a purgatory in which nearly all new vaudevillians served terms. Troupers who groused about their assignments were often left marooned a few hundred feet from nowhere, with their future booking erased, and without funds from their agents to return to New York.

While gazing out the windows of the trains as they delivered her to one Podunk one week and then another the next, she often saw barns blazing with luridly colored posters advertising the Barnum & Bailey and Ringling Bros. and other circuses, and then became wistful. She loved the circus life more than any other. She wondered if she would ever return to it.

There are no reliable accounts of all the travails Leitzel might have endured while traveling the boonies, but the time she spent playing the slabs of vaudeville was relatively short. By December 1911, just eight months after she started her peregrinations through the wilds, she made her Broadway debut. By then she had been taken under the wing of Gene Hughes, longtime president of the Showmen's League and one of the best connected agents in New York. A roly-poly man with a tomato-colored face, he had a talent for sifting through the armies of aspiring entertainers and identifying the few who had genuine star potential.

Hughes teamed Leitzel with another aerialist, a Jeanette Diaz, who, coincidentally, had been a former member of the Siegrist-Silbon trapeze troupe and, thus, like Leitzel, was a Barnum & Bailey alumna. In contrast to the small, fair-skinned, and comely Leitzel, Diaz was thickset, dusky in color, and had the protruding brow and long, over-large nose of an Easter Island monolith. In their appearances, the two women could hardly have been more mismatched. Hughes, though, retailed the new duo as the Leitzel Sisters. His pairing may have been carefully calculated. Leitzel's Dresden doll smallness and delicateness was only accentuated by Diaz's coarser appearance.

The Leitzel Sisters' New York vaudeville debut took place on the night of December 11, 1911, at the Columbia Theater, Forty-Seventh Street at Broadway. The Columbia, a theater that advertised itself as "The House That Brought Distinction to Burlesque," was not a regular stop for New York's smarter set. Now and then, the Columbia featured some of vaudeville's bigger stars, but to hold its costs down, the theater padded its entertainment with "startling, beautiful, living pictures."

Most nights, the Columbia's eighteen hundred seats were predominantly occupied by newly arrived immigrants and foreign students who were enrolled at Columbia University. These ticket holders viewed the Columbia as a place where they could improve their English by reading the movie subtitles and matching them with the action on the screen.

In great part because of Hughes's efforts, the Leitzel Sisters' debut was well attended by a good number of vaudeville house managers, as well as the important critics. When the act was announced, the shy Jeanette stayed in the background, but Leitzel strode to the center of the stage.

"O-o-o-h-h." She shivered as she looked up and down at the crowd in the balconies and the ground-floor seats. She seemed genuinely surprised that so many people turned out.

"O-o-o-h-h . . . o-o-o-h-h . . . o-o-o-h-h. . . ."

Leitzel showed so much style just in making her stage entrance that the aerial rigging behind her almost seemed extraneous. But then the kettledrums in the pit began rumbling. Then the house lights went out and a single spotlight alighted on a white, velvet-wrapped rope, or web, that had been dropped from the stage's ceiling.

Leitzel untied her cape and, in a gesture that was almost imperious, tossed the shoulder wrap to Jeanette. Next, she slipped her feet from her size one and a half mules.

She did not appear so much to climb her web as to float upward on it. She appeared incorporeal, lighter than air. Her ascent was punctuated by momentary stops during which she appeared to be reclining on air, with her body extended perpendicular to the rope. During these pauses, she dallied with the spectators, causing them to applaud, cheer, and whistle their adoration.

She continued her journey. Up. Up. Finally, when she was thirty feet above the stage floor, she reached out for a pair of Roman rings suspended a few feet from the web. She slipped her feet through the rings and drew herself up into a sitting position. She seemed as tickled as a child who had just been presented with a new swing set for her birthday.

Leitzel began swinging at the same time the pit orchestra started playing a waltz. Next, she began dishing out the little fillips of her act: handstands, forward and backward rollovers, upside-down hangs during which she dangled from the rings by her hocks. All aerialists performed the same stunts, but probably none with quite her style.

She again drew herself up into a sitting position on the rings and, now swinging gently, looked out at the crowd and, with a buoyant expression, seemed to put a simple question to everyone: "How do you like me so far?"

The crowd tittered, and then roared. There was piping from spectators blowing on empty Black Crows and Cracker Jack boxes. Leitzel blushed.

Now she drew a tiny envelope from beneath a flounce at the neckline of her bodice. She tore open the packet and dusted her palms with the powder she found inside.

It was time.

She reached out with her right hand for another rope a few feet away. Then, in an instant, she veered off her place on the rings and hung by a single hand from the looped end of the second rope. She writhed forward and then backward, forward and backward, and then, with a mighty effort, threw her body feet over head.

One!

Then she rocked her body up and over again.

Two!

Now another time.

Three!

The kettledrums began tolling off each of her revolutions and then the crowd started picking up the count: "Nine, ten . . . twenty-five . . . forty . . ."

Her body was now moving in a wild, jerky motion, like a loose airplane propeller about to fly off its shaft. At the same time that she was spinning, her near waist-length yellow hair came loose from the top of her head and swished in the air. The sight was almost unsettling, but no one could turn their eyes from her.

"Seventy . . . seventy-five . . . eighty-five . . ."

"Ninety-eight . . . ninety-nine . . . ONE HUNDRED!"

She descended to the stage via her web. With the audience now on its feet, applauding, cheering, she bowed and bowed and, still a little dizzy from her rigors, exited the stage on wobbly legs.

Variety summed up the performance this way:

> The Leitzel Sisters closed the show at the Columbia . . . with a flying trapeze and ring act that attracted some little attention. . . . The smaller sister is the act. The girl has many things in her favor. The most important is a fetching style of working that means more than all the complicated tricks that could be devised. Also, she turns off several tricks on the rings that few male exponents

in the line have shown. As a finish, she does a one-hand circle on the loose rope, turning over and over. It is a . . . capital finish for the act. The heavier girl fills in the time between the smaller girl's tricks with familiar work on the trapeze. The Leitzel Sisters can easily hold down the opening position on big bills. . . . They are of the original Leamy Sisters turn.

Behind Leitzel now were the slabs where the entertainers were expected to put in twelve- and fourteen-hour days. From now on, she would be contracted to appear in theaters where two performances a day were the rule. Gone, too, were the hick town boardinghouses with the scent of cow manure wafting through the windows. She would now be staying in modern hotels with maid service and clean sheets. In what may have been close to record time for a new vaudevillian, she had slogged her way from flyspeck towns to the Great White Way. Moreover, she proved that she belonged there.

Gene Hughes had gotten the Leitzel Sisters a tour of theaters on the Keith-Albee vaudeville chain. The theaters were mostly in larger cities like New York, Boston, and Chicago, and were among the most lavishly appointed anywhere. Benjamin Franklin Keith and Edward Franklin Albee, ex–circus men, paid their entertainers more than other theater owners. As a result they were able to attract vaudeville's biggest stars, among them Charlie Chaplin, Ed Wynn, W. C. Fields, and Fanny Brice. Leitzel was featured in the same variety shows as these luminaries, as well as with others who were just as esteemed by vaudeville audiences. She was starstruck in the presence of all of them. But she felt a different set of emotions for an entertainer of less eminence, one who had started appearing on the bills with her after she had been on tour for about a year.

◆ ◆ ◆

His name was Alexis Sousloff, and he was a tango dancer. He had slicked-back blond hair, prominent cheekbones, and piercing eyes the color of blue ice. When he appeared onstage, the women in the front rows commonly started fanning themselves with their programs. Some of them opened the upper buttons on their blouses.

While most other members of the vaudeville enjoyed one another's company, playing checkers and lunching together, Sousloff was never a part of the fellowship. An outsider, he spent much of his nonperforming time auditioning new partners and replaced his dancing halves about as regularly as the vaudeville company moved to different stops on the Keith-Albee circuit. His stage comrades, of course, had suspicions about his frequent changes of partners, since all his dancers moved well and all of them were beautiful.

Sousloff, though, apparently was as smooth with words as he was on his feet. To the surprise of others, he and Leitzel were soon going out for late-night, postshow dinners. Next, hand in hand, they started spending free afternoons at movies and ballet performances.

Other than the brief and barely grazing romance she had carried on with Alfredo three years earlier, Leitzel had never before been in a relationship with a man.

Before a month passed, Sousloff proposed marriage.

Oh, yes, she sighed. Oh, yes, yes.

For a day or two after the proposal, Leitzel was giddy, happier than she had ever been.

There was another matter that filled her with sweet anticipation. Edward Leamy had wired her from Syracuse, New York, where he had been living in an apartment building, the Florence. He told her of the pride he had at learning of the success she had been having in vaudeville. He also informed her that he would be taking a train to New York in a few days and would love to see her. Leitzel was overjoyed.

On a Sunday morning in August of 1914, a week or so after receiving the wire, Leitzel stepped outside her hotel and strolled past a newsstand. Her heart stopped. All the newspapers had the story, most of them on the front page.

Edward Leamy lay near death in Bellevue Hospital, badly beaten and unconscious.

The "Silver King" or "Prominent Showman," as he was identified in most of the headlines, had been found midway down the stairs of the subway station at Broadway and Times Square at two o'clock in the morning three days earlier. Police had determined that he had been at Shanley's Restaurant, dining with several theater friends, including the superintendent of Hammerstein's Theater. He excused himself from his friends sometime after midnight, saying he was going to the Astor Hotel, where he was staying.

Leamy died of massive head injuries four days after he had been conveyed by ambulance to Bellevue. Ironically, his demise was likely brought about by the object he treasured above all his other material possessions, the diamond-studded cross that he always wore around his neck when he was in public. The cross, valued between $2,000 and $5,000 by the newspapers, had been stripped from him when he was found on the subway stairs.

The meeting she and Leamy had planned was to have been their first time together since he had disbanded the Leamy Ladies two and a half years earlier. Leitzel was desolate.

◆ ◆ ◆

Less than two weeks later, on August 20, Leitzel and Sousloff were married in New York. The union took place hardly more than a month after he had proposed to her, but as short as the betrothal period was, the marriage, it would turn out, would be similarly fleeting.

From the start of their engagement, Sousloff had promised Leitzel they would spend their honeymoon in the coziest of love nests. This started Leitzel speculating about which of the finer New York hotels they would be registered at. She was crushed when, following the pair's marriage proceeding, carried out before a justice of peace, Sousloff took her to a boardinghouse where he kept a small, gray, airless room.

George DeFeo, a theatrical producer who owned the boarding-house, had doubts about whether the marriage was ever consummated. The two started fighting from the instant Sousloff led her into his room, he said, and the battle raged on night and day for weeks.

DeFeo said he thought that after they married, Sousloff, still in his twenties, revealed to his bride that he was entering retirement. He viewed Leitzel as a meal ticket whose earnings would allow him to loaf during the day and carry on assignations with other women at night while Leitzel was working in the theaters.

"She wanted him to go to work and he refused," DeFeo said. "One word brought on another, and he told her to get out of the house, and, if she didn't, he would put her out."

Within two or three weeks, the new bride did move out, taking a room at a New York hotel.

"My wife and I visited her a number of times in hopes we could bring them back together, but he was obstinate and would not live with her," DeFeo said.

In a retreat that was uncharacteristic for her, Leitzel surrendered New York to Sousloff and decamped for Chicago, where she set up housekeeping in an apartment building in the heart of the entertainment district at 4700 Broadway. Within days, she was traveling the vaudeville circuit again and was garnering critical praise wherever she appeared.

A line from *Billboard*'s review of the engagement at San Francisco's Orpheum Theatre: "Miss Leitzel, on the vertical rope and Roman rings, was a sensation. The audience interrupted the act with continuous applause during the entire act."

A *Columbus* (Ohio) *Dispatch* critique of her performance at the city's Keith Theatre: "[Miss Leitzel] possesses chic and alertness. A charmingly impertinent thing, she is with square shoulders and slender legs, a witching face and, heaven knows, she does whirl herself about on rings and ropes and things. This is a marvel because she does . . . a variety of things in such an insouciant manner. . . . Truly she is a headliner because what she does requires years of hard work [and] can't be easily taught."

Reviewing her act at Chicago's Majestic Theatre, the city's most opulent house, *Billboard* weighed in a second time on the vaudevillian whose star just kept rising: "Miss Leitzel['s] . . . act and personality should bring her the title of 'Eva Tanguay of the Air.'"

Leitzel was an aerialist, Tanguay was a singer, but the comparison *Billboard* drew between the two had a certain aptness. What was extraordinary about Leitzel was that she seemed to take sport in battling with the Grim Reaper each time she performed. When she was doing her one-arm planges, especially, she gave everyone an impression that she was on the verge of coming apart. Roland Butler, a press agent, may have put it best: "People got the idea she was flying apart at the seams, like an airplane under stress." Danger of a different sort was also present in all of Tanguay's performances. She seemed to be running a risk of being arrested and thrown in jail every time she stepped onstage. While other chanteuses of the day seemed to favor such sappy hits as "The Bells of St. Mary" and "M-O-T-H-E-R," Tanguay's repertoire was made up of selections like "Go As Far As You Like" and "I Want Somebody to Go Wild with Me." Her vocals seemed less like songs than solicitations, and when she was moving across the boards, she presented an impression that she was plugged into a light socket. Her hips were shimmying and her breasts were waggling.

One thing is clear: Leitzel's manager, Gene Hughes, liked the *Billboard* observation that she had a lot in common with the "I Don't Care Girl." It was not long before Leitzel was being merchandised on the Keith-Albee vaudeville posters and in newspaper ads as "The Eva Tanguay of the Rings."

◆ ◆ ◆

Standing before Leitzel, just outside the door of her dressing room at the Orpheum Theatre in South Bend, Indiana, were two men, one of them the manager of the theater, the other a stranger who started praising her for the stage performance she had just presented. He introduced himself as a representative for the Barnum & Bailey and Ringling Bros. circuses. Could he, the caller wanted to know, talk to her?

It was a November night in 1914. Leitzel extended her hand to him and invited the pair into her room. There may have been a twinkling in her eyes, but if so, her tone was probably frosted with a hint of sarcasm

"You're late," she told the circus man.

She had been expecting and hoping to hear from an emissary of the Ringling organization for a long time, probably, in fact, since she had started attracting glowing reviews in the trade papers for her appearances in vaudeville.

The agent was Fred Warrell, who, it turned out, had a home in South Bend.

He opened a leather briefcase, drew out some printed forms, and got right to the point. He was acting on behalf of the Ringling brothers. More than anything, he said, they wanted her back in their organization.

Warrell started reading from notes he apparently had made while taking directions from one or another of the Ringlings.

The circus could offer her $250 a week to start. She would be given star billing. He assured her that when she was presenting her act, she alone would be the single artist appearing in the great tent.

"You're late," Leitzel said again to Warrell. She was taking sport in playing hard to get.

Warrell may have been worried that his continued employment depended on his success with Leitzel. He threw out more blandishments.

Few of even the biggest vaudeville theaters had more than fifteen hundred seats, he noted. She could appear before ten times that number of people in just two performances a day in the Ringling brothers' big top.

There would hardly be a place anywhere in America where she was not recognized as the Ringlings' premier artist, Warrell went on. The circus would honor her with her own posters, giant bills three, four times larger than life that would be pasted on billboards and the sides of stores, factory buildings, and barns. In the entire history of American circuses, there had not been more than a dozen individual stars that had been accorded such a distinction. Finally, Warrell told Leitzel that if she wanted, she could return to vaudeville during the circus's off-season.

Leitzel's mother had been born into the circus, and before her, Leitzel's grandparents. Her father, Willy Dosta, wherever he was now, had also been a *saltimbanque*. As much as Leitzel had come to love the popular stage and its players, she had never stopped feeling a powerful urge to return to the circus. The call always came in spring, and it was perhaps inbred, like the urge, atavistic, irresistible, and eternal, that sends the swallows winging from Argentina to Capistrano each March.

Leitzel did not gibe the Ringling representative again for the tardiness of his call on her. She asked for his pen and the contract.

PART TWO

A caravan similar to the one that Willy Dosta would have driven, taking twelve-year-old Nellie Pelikan away from her family. *(Author's collection)*

Leitzel, age two, in Breslau. *(Author's collection)*

Lalo, Victoria, and Alfredo Codona when they were appearing in their first circus, a small one-ring family show organized by their father, Edward, that toured Mexico. Lalo is dressed as a clown. Victoria and Alfredo are dressed as aerialist or acrobatic performers. *(Courtesy of Circus World Museum, Baraboo, WI)*

Leitzel and her brother, Alfred Pelikan, in Breslau circa 1898. *(Author's collection)*

Edward Leamy, manager of the
Leamy Ladies and the Leamy Sisters.
(Author's collection)

Members of the Pelikan clan circa 1897. Seated at the far left in the dark dress is Julia, matriarch of the family. In the foreground is Alfred Pelikan, and to his right, Leitzel and Nellie. Others in the photo likely include Leitzel's aunts and uncles, Tina, Toni, Adolph, and Horace. Nellie was the star of the world-famous Leamy Ladies at this time, and the family portrait was created during a visit home to the family in Breslau. *(Author's collection)*

Leitzel and Nellie, both members of the Leamy Ladies aerial troupe, around 1904. Mother and daughter were separated by just twelve years. *(Courtesy of Circus World Museum, Baraboo, WI)*

The Leamy Ladies around 1905, when they were a major circus attraction throughout Europe. From left to right: Leitzel, fourteen; her aunts, Tina and Toni Pelikan; and her mother, Nellie Pelikan, along with Lily Simpson, not a part of the family, who toured with the troupe for a brief period. *(Author's collection)*

The Leamy Ladies made their first appearance with an American circus in 1908, when they were headliners with the Barnum & Bailey Greatest Show on Earth, along with the Sisters La Rague, daredevil automobile stunt drivers, and Wotan, a "balloonist" horse. An inset that is part of this poster, from that same year, shows the Leamy Ladies performing on their "trapezone rotaire," a massive revolving contrivance that was invented by their manager, Edward Leamy. *(Courtesy of Circus World Museum, Baraboo, WI)*

Barnum & Bailey Circus, 1909—La Belle Victoria's first year in America and her first season with The Greatest Show on Earth. Victoria's father, Edward, and Alfredo look up at her on the slack wire. *(Courtesy of Greg Parkinson, Baraboo, WI)*

Studio portrait photograph of Lillian Leitzel and her brother, Alfred Pelikan. *(Courtesy of Circus World Museum, Baraboo, WI)*

Nellie as "Zoe, the Aerial Venus" circa 1918. *(Author's collection)*

Leitzel circa 1918, likely taken during the time she was performing in Ziegfeld's *Midnight Frolic. (Author's collection)*

CHAPTER 12

Leitzel gazed through the window of the taxi as it traveled the streets from Baltimore's train station. She rarely rolled more than a block or two without seeing the woman looking back at her. She felt excitement every time she saw her.

She was way larger than life, ten feet at least, maybe twelve. She was also so sultry in appearance that she may have caused Leitzel's cheeks to redden. Her pale skin was bare from her shoulders to the point where her breasts began their swell. She was posed on an ornately carved love seat with a white angora coverlet, and was wearing a spaghetti-strapped, gold camisole that was patterned with twining black flora, along with a tutu of apple-blossom pink and white ballet slippers. Her eyes were greenish blue.

Leitzel would have recognized the woman anywhere. She saw her every time she looked in the mirror, although never in such Amazon-like proportions. The woman was her. Her outsize likeness seemed to be everywhere in the city, appearing on gigantic, richly colored posters blazing from billboards, fence hoardings, and the exterior walls of department stores, car dealerships, and butcher shops. Each of the posters bore the same legend in orange block lettering:

Ringling Bros.
World's Greatest Shows

WORLD'S
MOST MARVELOUS
LADY GYMNAST

Dainty Miss Leitzel

BALTIMORE MAY 12–13

Never before had Leitzel received such extravagant billing. She also must have wondered whether she really looked quite that sexy when she was costumed for the circus ring.

Ten or twelve hours earlier, before it was light, she had boarded a train in Chicago and had traveled all day. She was exhausted but in high spirits as the taxi carried her the last miles of her trip in Baltimore to the tents of the Ringling circus. She had been with the show when it opened its 1915 season in Chicago a few weeks earlier, but then had to stay behind in the city for a short time to appear for the divorce proceedings in the Cook County courthouse in Chicago that she had started against Alexis Sousloff. As it turned out, Sousloff failed to show up in court to contest any of the claims Leitzel made against him. Her petition for the marriage's dissolution was granted.

Leitzel was excited at having a chance to appear before the Ringling crowds again, but there was another reason why she was eager to rejoin the circus. She was twenty-three now and believed that the time was right for her to execute a plan, one she had been plotting for a long time.

◆ ◆ ◆

She could scarcely believe her eyes when the cab came to a stop at the circus grounds. Although she had appeared with the World's Greatest Shows only a few weeks earlier when it was playing in the Coliseum in Chicago, she had never before seen the Ringling circus set up on a show lot. She was astonished at its immensity.

It looked like a municipality, a community made almost entirely out of canvas. The circus's fifteen-thousand-seat big top dominated the setting, but there were twenty-two other tents, among them a hotel-size cookhouse large enough to seat several hundred workers and performers at one time, stables for the more than seven hundred horses, and a zoo for the show's thirteen hundred wild animals, including jungle cats, zebras, gorillas, emus, and hippopotami.

Charley Ringling greeted Leitzel as she stepped from the taxi and immediately started leading her through the high grass on a tour of the lot. The two strolled past tents that had the form of the pyramids of Giza, and seemed almost as large. Next, they passed before the side-show annex on the midway. Hanging from cables outside the annex and flapping in the breezes like laundry on a clothesline were garishly painted, ten-foot-high banners advertising such human wonders as an Indian rubber man who could tie his arms and legs into Boy Scout knots; a fat lady about a quarter the size of a boxcar; and Princess Wee Wee, a midget claimed to be "Just Twenty-One Inches High—The Smallest Woman in the World."

Women sat outside the wardrobe tent, making needle-and-thread repairs to richly ornamented camel and elephant robes and polishing navel stones for the showgirls who would appear with a cast of hundreds in the circus's opening spectacle, "Solomon and the Queen of Sheba."

It all seemed like Camelot to Leitzel. She was almost too excited to speak.

Finally Charley led her into the big top. Its seats were empty, but equestrians and equestriennes, clowns, wire walkers, trapeze flyers, and acrobats were everywhere, rehearsing their routines. She followed her guide into the center ring, where the Three Jahns were practicing their perch pole act on a twenty-five-foot-long wooden shaft that Carl balanced on his shoulders while his brother, Hans, and Hans's wife, Gretchen, performed at its top. May Wirth, the circus's premier equestrienne, was also rehearsing in one of the rings.

Charley directed Leitzel's attention to the big top's ceiling. There, fifty or sixty feet in the air, were her trapeze and Roman rings. She could not wait to return to them, but not this day. What she needed most at the moment was a good night's sleep.

She was stifling yawns as Charley kept talking, and then she put a question to him that she had been wondering about all day.

"Do you know the living arrangements that have been made for me on the show?"

Charley looked at her with solicitude.

"Oh, forgive me, my dear," he said. "Of course you must be bone tired. You've been on a train all day. We'll see to it that a porter fixes a bed for you. You'll be in a sixty-four car, one for the single girls."

Leitzel's expression of wonderment dissolved in an instant. She was incredulous. She could not believe what she had just heard from Charley Ringling. A bunk, maybe a shared bunk, in a sleeper with sixty-three other performers? This for a star advertised on the posters as the "World's Most Marvelous Lady Gymnast"?

She folded her arms in front of her, stewed for a bit, and then launched into a tirade.

"With all due respect, Mr. Ringling, you can go straight to hell if you think you're going to put me up in a car with sixty other girls like so many piglets going to market," she hissed. "I know I'm a star and you know I'm a star. I expect to be treated accordingly. Consider me to be on strike until you can provide me with my own private quarters."

Invectives continued to spew from her like fiery magma exploding out of Vesuvius.

Charley unbuttoned his suit jacket from his paunchy middle, and then rebuttoned it. Then he unbuttoned it again and, once more, rebuttoned it. His normally pinkish face turned ashen. He looked as if he might have lunched on some tainted pork stew in the cookhouse and was now suffering severe stomach cramps.

By now, the Three Jahns had interrupted their practice but remained in the center ring. "Our jaws had dropped," May Wirth said. "Here was this little bitty thing dressing down our big boss."

Charley's attempts at placating Leitzel went nowhere. The pair exited the big top and rapped at the door of Mister John's office wagon.

"The three met there for at least an hour," Wirth said. "Leitzel was all sweetness when she stepped outside again. Mister John appeared to be in good spirits, too, although Charley was still looking a bit wan."

The solution that had been worked out in the first of what would be numerous summit meetings between the three was designed to take care of the immediate crisis, as well as ensure that Leitzel would be comfortably and peacefully cosseted in the long term.

She was to spend the first of her nights with the circus in the rail car that Charley shared with his wife, Edie. After that, she would be moved into quarters on the train that were entirely her own. This second step would necessitate the shifting of one of the show's top executives from the private and quiet lodging he had been enjoying to a bunk in one of the sixty-four cars.

✦ ✦ ✦

From its beginnings a century and a half ago as a multiple-ring, railroad-traveling enterprise with Notre Dame Cathedral–size big tops, the modern American circus has had its kings. Before the Ringling brothers, there were Phineas Taylor Barnum and James A. Bailey, and before them, a few other monarchs whose reigns did not last long enough for their names to get permanently written on the public imagination. Never in its history, though, did the circus empire have a genuine queen.

Although born illegitimately and without a pedigree of royal lineage, Leitzel decided at an early stage that she alone was destined to fill the vacancy. She had carried that plan with her the day she traveled to Baltimore. Without filling out an employment application or submitting to a job interview, and certainly without the pomp and circumstance of a coronation, she simply assumed the position. She was sure the circus public wanted it this way. Where was there another star in pink tights who was washed over with the kind of love and adulation that she received when she appeared before audiences?

Leitzel, of course, never openly declared to the Ringling brothers that she was the circus's first, only, and last queen. But they knew very quickly that something momentous had changed in the royal court, and that somebody new was calling a lot of the shots.

Leitzel made another change about the same time she assumed occupancy of a throne that had remained empty since the very beginning of the circus. She changed her first name from Leopoldina to Lillian, apparently believing that her christened name was just too Old World–sounding and that the time was now right to assume an identity that was more American. In presenting her to crowds, the ringmasters starting intoning her name as "Le-e-E-E-tol-l-l Lillian Leitzel" and, in not much time at all, her name began appearing as "Lillian Leitzel" on her posters and in the circus's press materials.

◆ ◆ ◆

Within a week after setting up housekeeping in her new apartment on the train, Leitzel had a creature comfort delivered into the space, a shiny, new spinet piano. Late at night and sometimes at one or two o'clock in the morning, to the pleasure of some but not all her neighbors on the train, she played Mozart, Chopin, and the rags of Scott Joplin as the circus flyer rolled through the coal towns of Virginia and the cornfields of Kansas.

Then, soon after gaining her own private train quarters, Leitzel knocked at the door of Mister John's office wagon again. She was swarmed by worshippers wherever she appeared on the lot, she explained. She loved the attention, but now and then she needed moments to herself, yet more privacy. She needed her own tent where she could take sanctuary.

No other circus performer had ever had such a perquisite. John balked but acceded when Leitzel showed him a collection of telegrams she had received from theater agents pleading with her to return to vaudeville.

Her tent was always staked near the rear of the big top, close to the performers' entranceway. Fit for a sultana, it was appointed with satin drapes, Oriental rugs, and rattan furniture.

As resistant to Leitzel's cottage as Mister John was at first, he came to view it as an important capital improvement, a place where visitors of rank could feel they were being received with special hospitality.

Leitzel held tea parties in her tent for President and Mrs. Calvin Coolidge whenever the circus was playing in Washington, D.C. The Coolidges returned her hospitality. On at least one occasion, they invited her for a sleepover at the White House. Leitzel accepted the invitation, but not wanting to appear overly anxious, she turned up at 1600 Pennsylvania Avenue NW late enough to look fashionable.

Henry Ford was another regular caller at Leitzel's blue-and-white-striped tent and train apartment. The industrialist was among the most ardent of her admirers, and on all his visits, he presented her with bouquets of flowers. Dropping in day and night at Leitzel's canvas residence, too, were senators, governors, mayors, newspaper publishers, and bank presidents, as well as such major stars of the stage and screen as Will Rogers, Fanny Brice, the Marx Brothers, and Charlie Chaplin.

Most of the guests receiving entrée into Leitzel's private sanctum were there only because they were eager to spend a social hour or two with the circus's most glamorous artist. But Leitzel apparently was also welcoming to at least a few visitors, some of them midnight callers, who came to her door with other intentions.

Mister John was not at all amused when he received a report from the show's detective that Leitzel was regularly entertaining gentlemen in her stateroom late at night. Management promptly delivered a carefully worded letter to her, spelling out the circus's policy on such matters. The missive, in part, read: "We have always had a rule that persons not connected with the show are not to be admitted to sleeping cars or dressing rooms. This has never been considered a privation by anyone, and should not be so considered by you as there is nothing personal to you in its application." Leitzel ignored the directive. As queen of the big top, she was above taking orders from Parliament.

✦ ✦ ✦

Of all the potentates who streamed to Leitzel's train quarters and tent, none was more warmly welcomed by Leitzel than Colonel H. Maxwell Howard of Dayton, Ohio.

Colonel Howard was the founder and president of one of the country's largest paper manufacturing operations, the Howard Allied Paper Mills, which had four plants in Ohio. He lived in perhaps the showiest residence in the Dayton area, a three-story Norman castle perched on a high hill on the city's outskirts, and also maintained a stable of racing horses. Several of his ponies were to gain immortality in racing's annals, including Stagehand, who pounded past Seabiscuit at the finish line in a Santa Ana Handicap that many horse racing historians still regard as the most thrilling Thoroughbred run ever.

Colonel Howard and Mister John, perhaps because both were fabulously wealthy, appeared to be the closest of friends. The two often strolled the circus lot together, or sat with each other in a box inside the big top. It seemed likely to many on the show that Mister John introduced the colonel to Leitzel.

✦ ✦ ✦

Because the colonel raced ponies, lived in a castle, and considered circuses to be his favorite form of entertainment, it seemed surprising to others that there was nothing at all flashy about his outward appearance. He could have passed as a mortician. He wore rimless glasses, was bald except for a fringe of white hair that half circled his head, and wore expensively tailored three-piece suits that were either mouse gray or brown.

Howard was twenty-five years older than Leitzel. He also had a wife back home. Some of Leitzel's fellow travelers on the show wondered why she was attracted to him. The colonel was not just a millionaire but a *multi*millionaire, and this was in an era when there were fewer than two hundred people in America whose net worth reached a million dollars. It seems unlikely, though, that Leitzel was unduly impressed with the Daytonian's riches. She was well short of qualifying for millionaire status herself, but she was by far the most richly compensated artist with any circus.

Soon after the two became chummy, Howard set Leitzel up in an apartment overlooking Central Park in New York, a place he visited often to carry out business for his papermaking operations. On each of his reunions with his inamorata, whether on the circus lot or at her apartment, he also presented her with furs and jewelry, although she tended to respond more warmly to such lagniappe as chocolates and flowers. On one occasion, he simply placed an envelope in her hand. Her face crinkled in an expression of distain when she opened the envelope and removed its papers.

Leitzel might have hoped that the envelope contained a letter in which Howard poured out his love for her, or perhaps described a future in which the two lived together as husband and wife.

"Now I just took the liberty of bringing along these shares of General Motors preferred," the colonel said by way of explaining his offering.

"Money, money," she snapped upon seeing the stock certificates. "What do I care for money? Get them out of my sight."

Always unaccompanied, Howard turned up on the circus lot in different towns a half dozen times or so each touring season, and when he did, he typically stayed three or four days before disappearing, according to Fanny McCloskey, a perch pole artist, elephant rider, ballet girl, and close friend of Leitzel's. Neither she nor any of her fellow performers fully understood the nature of Leitzel's relationship with him, but all of them had suspicions.

"Leitzel never answered any of our questions about the colonel," McCloskey said, "and he was always private around others on the show. Everyone suspected they were lovers, of course, but because they were so secretive, none of us knew for sure."

"Mostly," McCloskey went on, "he and Leitzel spent all their time together behind the closed door of her train quarters or the flap at the front of her private tent. On those Sundays when the circus wasn't able to play because of local blue laws, they'd often borrow one of the cars that Mister John and Charley carried on the train, and travel into town for dinner or a night at the movies."

✦ ✦ ✦

Leitzel's demands on management continued without abatement. As pleased as she was about having her own private tent and a stateroom on the train, she quickly discovered that such pieds-à-terre required constant spiffing up, especially because of the distinguished and discerning guests who were often stopping by. She called on Mister John and Charley again.

What could she possibly want now? they wondered.

She had to have her own full-time maid, she insisted. By this time, Leitzel had proved herself to be by far the circus's biggest draw. The queen was also responsible for generating more favorable press coverage for the show than it had ever received. Charm oozed from her like juice from a ripe peach whenever she was interviewed by a journalist.

As outrageous as some of Leitzel's requests seemed to them, Mister John and Charley rarely objected to her petitions anymore.

Leitzel got her maid, Mabel Clemings. She was the wife of Harry Clemings, one of the forty clowns touring with the circus. Mabel was as faithful to Leitzel as a Saint Bernard. Perhaps somewhat curiously for a woman who was married to a Pierrot, though, she always looked dour and seems never to have had even the slightest curl of a smile on her lips. She had fewer curves than a yardstick and favored ankle-length dresses, all of which were in shades of shadows.

✦ ✦ ✦

Some of Leitzel's fellow travelers may have been resentful of the favored status that she alone enjoyed with the circus, but probably not many of them. Most of them took the position that what was good for the queen was also good for the show. She appeared to have been revered by all but a small few of the more than one thousand zebra grooms, tent stake drivers, living skeletons, bearded ladies, human cannonballs, and high-wire-dancing lunatics crisscrossing a nation with her. The open love her confreres had for her might be explained by the generosity she extended to everyone on the show.

Not only did she allow her private tent to serve as a hospitality center for visiting dignitaries and celebrities, but she also turned it into a gathering place for her fellow troupers, among them the dozen or two children traveling with the circus. Five mornings each week, Monday through Friday, the tent served as what came to be known as Auntie Leitzel's Free Elementary School, with Leitzel herself serving as its marm. There she read stories to the kids and gave them their first lessons in penmanship and arithmetic.

Eventually a time would come when Leitzel's tent would also bulge with young people in the early evenings. In an age when radios cost about the same as a Model T Ford, she bought one of the receivers, an Atwater Kent. Her new acquisition had the immediate effect of turning the circus's children into evenly blithesome boys and girls who seemed unable to ever stop singing.

At the time, *The Man in the Moon*, the first of radio's children's programs, was starting to be broadcast coast to coast. Bill McNeary, the show's host and "The Man in the Moon," read such stories as "The Adventures of the Gingerbread Man" over the airways and urged each of his young listeners to look up into the night sky and pick out a star as their very own. The Man in the Moon assured his earth children that their stars would always remain glowing as long as they cared for them properly.

"It's easy," he promised. "The way to keep your star shining is to sing as much as you can and never pout."

Because Leitzel had the only radio on the circus, there were also times when her tent served as a prime social center for the circus's performers and working men and women. On occasions of such historic broadcast events as presidential addresses or Gene Tunney and Jack Dempsey fights, so many troupers streamed to her cottage that Leitzel had to limit the stays of each listener to three or four minutes.

◆ ◆ ◆

Charley Ringling was in his early fifties by the time Leitzel joined the circus, and though he was more than twice her age, he clearly was smitten with her.

His wife, Edie, was regarded by everyone on the show as an

extraordinarily indulgent woman, but there had been times in the past when she had learned of trysts her husband had arranged with ballet girls. She had threatened to leave him on those occasions, and made it clear to him that if they ever did enter a divorce courtroom, she would peel away as great a stake of his wealth as the judge would allow.

Charley devised a stratagem for spending time with Leitzel without arousing the suspicions of either Edie or the newspaper gossip columnists. He founded what he called the "Once in a While Club" and installed himself as its president, treasurer, and entertainment director. The club had a membership that usually hovered around a dozen showgirls, and in an effort to convince his Edie that his conduct was always unimpeachable, he sometimes even brought her along as a guest for the picnics, swimming parties, and tables in fine restaurants.

The club, he told Edie, was created with the sole purpose of providing wholesome and chaperoned activities for the show's unattached and lonely female employees who were distantly separated from their families.

"In reality, the Once in a While Club was started only because Charley believed it could give him some quality time with Leitzel," said Fanny McCloskey, herself a member.

Leitzel enjoyed Charley's company in a way that a child might adore a generous and fun-loving uncle, but she was not willing to let their relationship move beyond that stage. After being rebuffed repeatedly by Leitzel in his efforts to get away with her in some private love nest, Charley eventually quit the pursuit. He did not disband the Once in a While Club, though.

He found the mechanism useful in developing a romance with a second choice, Anna Stais. She was a member of "The Living Statues," that group of Aphrodite-like women and Adonis-like men who appeared in the center ring covered in white greasepaint and mimicked the poses of the human subjects of famous art masterpieces that were familiar to the public through pictures in the Sunday rotogravures.

Unlike Leitzel, Stais apparently was willing to let the relationship with her boss move further than just the toasting of hot dogs and marshmallows around a campfire encircled by a dozen or more other young women.

The trapeze flyer Butch Brann had just started dating a pretty, black-eyed showgirl who would eventually become his wife.

"Because of the show's rules for keeping the sexes apart, Delores and I had to go through all kinds of sneaky stuff to be alone with each other," he said. "Once, we arranged to meet at a movie house in town. I got there first, bought a ticket, and waited inside. In a while, Delores came in, and then entered the darkened theater. I watched as she walked down the aisle and then slipped into a row with a couple empty seats. I waited five minutes to make sure no show detectives were around and then slipped into the seat beside her. Then I saw who was in the row just ahead of us. It was Charley and Anna Stais. He had his arm around her and his head was resting on her shoulder. Delores and I hightailed it out of that row. We found new seats in the balcony."

CHAPTER 13

The voice coming through the closed door was deep and resonant, songful.

"Come in, please. Come in. Come in."

Surely Leitzel had heard the voice before, if not in a music hall or on a vaudeville stage, then on the Victor and Columbia records. The voice may have been more widely recognizable to Americans at the time than that of President Woodrow Wilson.

Leitzel was making the rounds of the dressing rooms inside Florenz Ziegfeld Jr.'s Aerial Gardens on the rooftop of the New Amsterdam Theatre building on Forty-Second Street near the corner of Seventh Avenue in Manhattan. Leading her on the tour was a young woman in a floor-length evening gown with carrot-colored hair and a light sprinkling of freckles on her nose. She was so pretty that maybe she should have had a tiara on her head and a magic wand in her hand. She put a gloved hand on the brass knob and turned it. Leitzel's excitement rose.

The occupant on the other side of the door materialized before the two women through a white-blue cloud. He looked like a divine, like the mythic being everybody up and down Broadway regarded him to be. There was, as always, a smoking cigarette in the V of his fingers. Two or three others were burning in ashtrays. The air in the room seemed almost sliceable.

Leitzel would recall her reaction this way: "My arms turned to gooseflesh at the sight of him. My heart was drumming."

The man, thick around the middle, grinning widely, and wearing a black tuxedo with swallowtails, took Leitzel's companion into his arms and held her in a long embrace.

"Like a god and a goddess hugging," Leitzel would remember.

The man was Bert Williams, song-and-dance man and comedian. He was the highest-paid entertainer on Broadway and, along with Al Jolson and Nora Bayes, one of the three biggest-selling recording artists in the world. He was likely also the most widely beloved black performer in America. Booker T. Washington said of him: "He has done more for our race than I have. He smiled his way into people's hearts. I have been obliged to fight my way in."

In Williams's arms was Billie Burke, an esteemed stage and film actress, but even better known the last four years as Mrs. Ziegfeld, wife of the impresario widely regarded as "The Man Who Invented Broadway."

In time Billie, in fact, would acquire both a magic wand and a crown, and then be forever identified with them. She would also become known eternally to almost every child born, and to be born, in the Western world. But the royal accoutrements and her everlasting fame would not begin until years later, when she portrayed Glinda, the Good Witch of the North, in *The Wizard of Oz*.

That was not to be until 1939.

This night was December 9, 1918, and it was late.

When Billie introduced Williams to Leitzel, he took her hands in his, a cigarette still popping up through his fingers. He told her of seeing her perform in the Ringling circus a year or two earlier. "I'll never forget it," he said. "When you finished and returned to the floor, I whispered a thank-you to the Lord for making my life such an easy one."

Leitzel could not believe it. She could not believe any of it. She was high above the sidewalks of Times Square, as close to heaven as any Otis elevator could lift her. She was inside the most sumptuous entertainment temple in all of New York. And she was in the company of Bert Williams and Billie Burke, *the* Bert Williams and *the* Billie Burke.

She was also frightened, more terrified than at any time in her life.

The clock was nearing midnight. Opening in a little more than an hour would be the fourth annual production of the show New York's smart set anticipated with greater excitement than any other—Flo Ziegfeld's *Midnight Frolic*.

And Leitzel was to be a part of it—she and Bert Williams, and such other luminaries as Fanny Brice, Will Rogers, W. C. Fields, Eddie Cantor, and Lillian Lorraine, advertised as "The Most Beautiful Woman in the World."

A month earlier, Leitzel had concluded another tour with the Ringling Bros. Circus, her fourth. She was now free to accept whatever stage engagements were offered to her, and the invitation to appear in a Ziegfeld *Frolic* was by far the most prestigious theater assignment ever to come her way.

Billie Burke continued in her role as tour guide for Leitzel. After introducing her to Williams, she led her to the dressing rooms of the 1918 *Frolic*'s other entertainers.

"I had to keep pinching myself to make sure I wasn't dreaming all this," Leitzel told her brother, Alfred. "I don't know when there were a greater number of so many truly distinguished entertainers in one place at one time. What was I doing in such company? I was a circus performer.

"They were all so gracious, though. Everybody told me I was now one of them. I thanked them for trying to make me feel welcome, but I wasn't so sure I really belonged in this place with them. Here I was, among the great aristocracy of the entertainment world, and surely I had big doubts about whether I really belonged."

As jubilant as she was at meeting most of her costars, she may have become standoffish when Billie presented her to Bird Millman, a slack-wire performer who had been a sensation with the Barnum & Bailey Circus the last few years. Audiences recognized in the first minute of Bird's performances that they were seeing someone unlike any other circus artist. A petite figure of radiant beauty, Bird discharged pirouettes and entrechats with about as much grace as Isadora Duncan performed the feats, but with a difference. Instead of performing her twirls and liftoffs on a wide and deep wooden stage, Bird presented them on a cable, three-quarters of an inch thick and thirty-six feet long. To make things even more interesting, all the time she pranced on her wire, she sang with the sweetness of a nightingale. Her lilting soprano carried to the most distant seats. Audiences adored her.

Bird had a reputation as the sweetest-tempered woman appearing with any circus. As unassuming as she was, she seemed not to have any other ambition but to always put on a good show for the folks, and have fun doing it. Leitzel, though, viewed her as a bit of a nemesis. Because Bird was so lovely and so broadly cherished, Leitzel believed, she was her greatest challenger to the throne she had assumed as queen of the circus world.

Certainly Leitzel recognized Bird's exceptional artistry. It irritated her, though, that the circus gift wrapped the wire dancer's appearances in such pomp and ceremony. No other star, Leitzel stewed, not even her, had enjoyed such favoritism. More than once, she had complained to one or another of the Ringling brothers that the circus was going way over the top by providing Bird with an eight-member choir to accompany her as she warbled songs like "Would You Like to Spoon with Me?" and "Tiptoe through the Tulips" while mincing over her wire. As upsetting as the choir was to Leitzel, what galled her even more was the ostentatious manner in which Bird's consorts were costumed. According to one magazine writer, the accompanists were gowned in "vestments not dissimilar to those of the Vatican choir."

Variety observed that Ziegfeld's *Midnight Frolic* "drew the classiest after-theater patronage ever known." In an age when the pay for skilled workers averaged four dollars a day, there was a five-dollar cover charge for admission to the *Frolic* shows, by far the highest anywhere in Manhattan. Ziegfeld did not intend for the rooftop productions to attract just anybody. The plebs, he said, could take in his long-running, dollar-a-head *Ziegfeld Follies*, which were presented in a sixteen-hundred-seat theater on the ground floor of the New Amsterdam building. The *Frolic*, though, had been confected expressly for New York's most beautiful people.

Begun in 1915, the *Frolics* had many of the same ingredients as the enormously successful *Follies*, including A-list comics, singers, and, of course, dozens of chorines, each handpicked by Flo with a critical eye for exceptional beauty, long legs, and pleasing topographies of flesh. There was a difference, though. Because the *Frolic* was presented in a far smaller playhouse and limited to about five hundred guests, the clubbers had such intimate contact with the performers that they could sniff the Sen-Sens on their breaths.

The *Frolics* also tended to be more risqué than the *Follies*. Many of the *Frolic* comedians salted their monologues with stories that were too racy to present to the wider public, and among the two or three dozen showgirls who were featured in the productions, there were always a few who had little compunction about removing just about all of their coverings but their nail polish. The *Frolics'* management not only tolerated a certain restrained revelry by the guests but also encouraged it. In all of the productions, there was always a number when Ziegfeld's Broadway belles circled the floor in costumes made mostly of inflated balloons. The rowdier of the male patrons took sport in approaching the dancers and, with lighted cigars, popping the balloons.

No circus performers were featured in any *Midnight Frolic* of the first two years. It was Billie who persuaded her husband to open the programs to the day's big top novas. As much as she adored the great entertainers of the stage, Billie considered the circus's wanderers to be the noblest of all performing artists. She had spent much of her girlhood in the presence of equestriennes, lion tamers, and fire. eaters, as well as such storied professional human oddities as Jo-Jo, the Dog-Faced Man, and George, the Turtle Boy. Her father, Billy Burke, briefly operated a small circus in the 1870s, and later became a popular singing clown who made center ring appearances with such major enterprises as the Barnum & Great London Circus.

✦ ✦ ✦

By the time Leitzel headed to her room to change into her costume, the first of the clubbers had already started appearing in Ziegfeld's aerie. They turned over their fox and raccoon coats to the coat check girls and made their way to the floor, where small, round, glass tables were set with wooden hammers and interhouse phones that allowed the patrons to ring up not only the waiters but also other diners across the room.

No other club in New York had the opulence of the Aerial Gardens. Ziegfeld commissioned the great Joseph Urban, a Vienna-schooled architect and a top stage designer, to create the jewel box. The playhouse's walls were decorated with woodland scenes, painted à la Georges Seurat's softly shimmering, pointillist *A Sunday Afternoon on the Island of La Grande Jatte.* All around the space there were inner-lighted crystal columns with bouquets of gold foil flowers at their tops. The theater's movable stage was made of glass, as were the staircases on either side of the floor that led to box seating.

At the stroke of midnight an orchestra dramatically started playing and two or three dozen showgirls surged onto the floor and took their places on the stage and the staircases. A few of the bolder men in the audience left their wives and girlfriends at the tables and took positions beneath the transparent staircases for worm's eye perspectives on Ziegfeld's Broadway belles.

◆ ◆ ◆

Leitzel was seated in her dressing room, waiting for her turn onstage, when she was disturbed by the noise the first time. It was a loud, rushing clattering that rattled not only her room but also her nerves. After a few moments, the annoying commotion filled her room again, though now filtered by the sounds of the orchestra or the laughter Fields or Brice were drawing from the crowd.

Then, in a little time, the clattering returned, went on for thirty seconds or a minute, and then again quieted, but never for long.

Leitzel was becoming more and more disturbed by each of the noisy disruptions. As it was, she had already been experiencing opening-night jitters. As she would comment later, "In all my years in the circus and vaudeville, never had I been as nervous about appearing before the public as I was in Mr. Ziegfeld's club."

There was a knock at Leitzel's door, and then it opened a crack. The stage manager called in that her act would begin in minutes.

She left her room, moved through a hall, and stopped at a curtained entranceway that opened onto the floor. Then her name was announced by the emcee, and the frightful clattering started again, only this time, because she was outside her dressing room, the disturbance was louder than ever. Now she understood its source. The clubbers were pounding at their glass tables with wooden mallets. Ziegfeld had provided the hammers for what he said was the protection of the guests. He knew he had the most spectacular show in town. By showing their approbation for the entertainers by pounding the mallets, the guests could spare their hands from turning into bloody pulps.

Bobby Cronkleton, Leitzel's rigger and property boy, was already on the stage when she took her first steps onto the floor. At first sight of her, he may have thought she was nude. She was wearing a flesh-colored, loose-fitting, barely-there tutu. Under the arms of her bodice were two large openings through which Cronkleton likely got his first look at his employer's bare bosom. Cronkleton, nineteen or twenty, had been with Leitzel two or three years, carrying out the rigging for all her circus and vaudeville performances. He had never before seen her in such a revealing costume.

If Leitzel initially had any qualms about appearing before the public in such revealing dress, she likely disburdened herself of them after seeing the examples of the *Frolic* showgirls. She had observed that Ziegfeld's girls, though half naked, commingled with the crowds with hardly any more self-consciousness than the veil-faced matrons filing into St. Patrick's Cathedral Sunday mornings.

But it may have been a man, rather than any of Ziegfeld's enchantresses, who gave Leitzel her greatest lessons in merchandising her sexuality to the audience. Alfred Cheney Johnston listed his occupation as a portrait photographer, but such a characterization was hardly any more descriptive than calling Van Gogh a "colorer." Johnston, who maintained a studio in the Hotel des Artistes with neighbors such as Noël Coward, Isadora Duncan, and the painter Howard Chandler Christy, served as a kind of Professor Henry Higgins to all of Ziegfeld's new hires. He was a brilliant photographer, but his greater importance was in mentoring waitresses and shop clerks who aspired to places in the impresario's chorus line. He directed them on how to color their faces with rouge and lipstick and kohl. He coached them on how to move, how to pose, how to bat their eyelashes. He showed them how, with one-dollar swatches of satin, silk, and tulle not much bigger than handkerchiefs, they could create costumes whose effect on the male animal could be as incendiary as any getup Cleopatra ever wore inside her boudoir.

Leitzel had spent part of two or three weeks in Johnston's studio before turning up for her first performance in the *Midnight Frolic*. Johnston must have found her to be a malleable subject. He produced at least a dozen eleven-by-fourteen-inch, hand-colored photographs of her, depicting her variously as an innocent with her virginity still available, as a gypsy peasant, and as a seductress.

✦ ✦ ✦

The clattering of the wooden mallets was rushing at Leitzel as she curtsied before the audience.

Her preshow jitters vanished. There was no place in the world where she was more at ease than on her trapeze bar and Roman rings.

In an instant, she was again frolicking in air, soaring on her trapeze, cartwheeling while gripping a hand ring. Her perpetual motion was reflected in flashing blurs on the glass stage and staircases.

The audience applauded appreciatively, and a few patrons pushed themselves up from their chairs to give her a standing ovation, but the reaction from the clubbers was nothing like the din that resounded whenever she finished her act in the big top or on the vaudeville stages. Maybe the subdued response she received was simply because the *Frolic* audience was far smaller than those before which she usually performed, she concluded. Or maybe it was that the people of the high life had unusual reserve. Or maybe it was because the patrons believed that as a circus performer, she was completely miscast in the company of the belles and beaux of Broadway, and that was the thought that was most in her head as she left the floor.

✦ ✦ ✦

℘t was three or four o'clock in the morning. Leitzel had changed into her street clothes, but she was almost too tired to leave for home. The crowd had thinned, but some revelers were still in the Aerial Gardens, drinking, dining, and dancing to an orchestra.

Bird Millman was the first to drop by her dressing room. She embraced Leitzel, congratulated her, and told her she was the greatest circus performer she had ever seen.

In time, Bert Williams, Eddie Cantor, Fanny Brice, and all of her other coheadliners dropped in. She had been a sensation in her *Frolic* debut, each said, and told her they felt honored to be able to appear on the same stage with her. Each then wished her a good night, or what little was left of it, and disappeared.

Finally appearing were Billie and Flo. Billie covered Leitzel's cheeks with kisses. She told her how proud she and her husband were to have her in the revue. Ziegfeld was more reserved, but he shook her hand. He was carrying a first edition of the morning *New York World* and opened it to the theater page. He drew her attention to a column headlined "New Ziegfeld Frolic Loveliest of All," and then pointed to an observation a critic had made about her performance.

"Lillian Leitzel, 'Aerial Frolic,' deserves—and will get—a paragraph by itself. She is the most amazing performer on the flying rings and the dangling ropes that this metropolis has ever seen."

Billie and Flo were in their coats. Their car was parked on Forty-Second Street right outside the New Amsterdam, with their chauffeur at the wheel, the motor running. It would be no trouble at all to drop her at her apartment on their way home, Billie assured Leitzel.

"What a grand, grand night it had been," Leitzel would later report to her brother, Alfred.

As she rolled through the dark and now quiet and nearly empty streets with her deliverers, Leitzel was still thinking about her newly acquired friends, all of them nobles. She revered them all—even Bird Millman. Maybe especially Bird Millman, for a long time her nemesis and now, after this night, a dear and lovely friend.

CHAPTER 14

It was a question debated by the stable hands shoveling manure in the horse tents, the chalk-faced clowns, and, most animatedly, by the midgets, bearded lady, living skeleton, and Frank Lentini, the three-legged man, in the sideshow annex.

How could it have happened?

Leitzel changed suitors with about the same frequency that she changed earrings. In every town where the circus appeared, trails were beaten in the grass to her train quarters and private tent. Many of her callers were young men with high posts in finance, manufacturing, or show business. With such a wide field of admirers, how could it happen she would tumble for, of all people, Clyde William Ingalls, manager of the sideshow?

"The pairing of Clyde and Leitzel seemed no less astonishing than the creation of the first centaur," observed Merle Evans, the circus's bandmaster. "Who would have predicted that there would be an attraction between two beings that were so distinct from one another? The romance that flowered between them may be the best example since time began that love is blind."

Ingalls had a prognathic jaw that some thought gave him the profile of a Neanderthal man. He towered over Leitzel by almost a foot and a half, weighed about two and a half times her ninety-five pounds, and, at forty-six, he was nearly twenty years older than she.

The contrasts of the pair did not end with their eye-jarring physical distinctions. Leitzel was by far the most fabulously compensated contract employee with the circus; Ingalls, in the words of Merle Evans, "didn't have a pot to pee in." Ingalls also had what a lot of single women might have regarded as another drawback to the budding of a serious romance. He already had a wife, a shy girl from Iowa named Neil. She was at least the second Mrs. Ingalls, maybe the third.

The romance between Leitzel and Ingalls started in 1919.

This was a momentous year in the history of both the Ringling Brothers and Barnum & Bailey circuses. The year before, at the end of the tours of the two circuses, John, Charley, and Alf T. Ringling arrived at a decision that shook the ground of the show world. The two giant circuses would no longer exist as separate entities. The following spring, the two circuses were to be merged into a single megashow, the Ringling Bros. and Barnum & Bailey Combined Shows, or what the press was quick to characterize as "The Colossus of All Amusements."

The consolidation was dictated, in large part, because the brothers saw a need to achieve greater economies in their operational costs. By joining the two formerly competing shows as one, they could make vast cuts in their transportation costs by moving with just one train instead of two. Even more significantly, they could slash their labor costs. Hundreds of workmen had been needed on each of the shows to load and unload the trains, and put up and take down the tents. Not only had the circus been paying these workers each week, but it had also been providing them with meals and bunks. Through the merging of the Ringling and Barnum & Bailey shows, the labor costs could be halved.

But there was yet another reason why the time had come to join the two amusement behemoths. During the thirty-four years the Ringlings had been touring as showmen, there had been times when there were as many as seven brothers to handle the top management posts. By 1918, the brothers' ranks had been significantly thinned by deaths. John, Charley, and Alf T. were the only brothers still active in the circus operations, and Alf, director of press relations, was in failing health.

In their crafting of the new supercircus, the Ringlings drew up a list of their most valuable and loyal employees, including performers. The remainder of their attachés, likely a thousand or more men and women, were let go.

As the most famous circus performer in the world, Leitzel, of course, topped the list of contracted employees whose jobs were secure. Ingalls, formerly manager of the Barnum & Bailey Circus sideshow, was also retained. A condition of his employment was that he bring along his most celebrated freaks. With his switch to what would be a brand-new circus, Ingalls apparently believed the time was also right to make another change in wives. He wasted little time in going after Leitzel.

Different theories evolved among the circus's travelers about how Leitzel could have fallen under Ingalls's spell. Some, including Evans, thought she may have viewed him as a stand-in for the father she never had. But it seemed more widely conjectured that Leitzel was drawn to Clyde because of his undeniable gifts of persuasion.

Like the anteater-nosed Cyrano de Bergerac, Ingalls may have had some physical features that a lot of young women might have found off-putting in their first meetings with him. But, also in common with the rapier-wielding Cyrano, Clyde was a master wordsmith. He could string them together in sentences that gleamed like strands of pearls against black velvet. Ingalls cultivated his skills at declamation through years of lecturing midway crowds on the virtues of the tattooed lady, the ossified man, and the two-and-a-half-foot-tall midget mother with a six-foot-two son.

"They're all real, they're all alive, and they're all anxious to meet you, ladies and gentlemen, girls and boys," he would tempt the towners from an elevated platform outside his one-hundred-by-three-hundred-foot-long tent. "You can talk to them, they will talk to you. The cost for entering our capacious, clean, and comfortable pavilion is a mere twenty-five cents for the gentlemen and gentle ladies, a thin dime for the young ones. A great bargain, if you ask me, for making new friends you'll have for life. You can stay inside for as long as you wish. You'll thank me on the way out for presenting you with the time of your lives."

If all human beings were equipped with lungs like Ingalls's, the loudspeaker would have been an unnecessary invention.

"His voice was so booming you could hear him a quarter mile away," said Freddie Freeman, a clown, bareback rider, and trapeze flyer. "It also had mellifluence. When he was lecturing, his voice reminded you of those scenes in those biblical movies by Cecil B. DeMille where the clouds part, the sky opens, and, in a tone that's like roaring wind, God says something like, 'Hey, Noah, I want you to build an ark.'"

The effect was always the same once Ingalls gathered a crowd, or what circus people called a "tip." He would start his lecture, and instantly, the sideshow tent, as though it had been turned into a powerful vacuum cleaner, would begin sucking the towners off the midway and through its canvas flaps.

Some believed W. C. Fields studied Ingalls's manner before developing his portrayal of J. Eustace McGargle for the movie *Sally of the Sawdust.* Ingalls wore loud checkered suits, boutonnieres, alligator skin shoes, and Panama hats with brims that seemed large enough to provide shade for two.

Because he was still married, he and Leitzel, at least early in their relationship, tried carrying on their romance in secret. Merle Evans recalled an occasion when he unintentionally surprised the pair. It happened in an early morning after Evans woke in his bed inside the parked train and heard a galop playing inside his head. The bandmaster was quite commonly treated to such predawn musical interludes. Evans was the originator of much of the circus's music, whether the marches for the grand entries or the lilting waltzes to which the trapeze artists flew. Most of the compositions that Evans heard playing in his head in the predawn hours were, in his view, just so-so, even derivative. He was able to turn them off and go back to sleep. Now and then, though, he heard melodies that struck him as being quite good, although none was ever perfect in its playing.

"I looked at these tunes as fixer-uppers," Evans said. "With a little tinkering, maybe beefing up the brass section here, putting in some crashing cymbals there, I could often turn them into music that was a little more, oh, Sousa-like."

When Evans awoke to hear a new composition coming on, he would quietly slip out of bed, careful not to disturb Neva, his sleeping wife. He would put on a robe, gather some blank music paper and the instrument on which he did all his composing, his cornet. He then went out into the darkness, trying different things with his muted horn to bring refinement to the tune in his head.

"One early morning while I wandered the circus lot, playing with different passages, I happened on one of the most heavily billed freaks of Clyde's freaks, 'Zip, The What Is It?' Zip, who was advertised as 'The Last Living Link between Ape and Man,' was an ancient, stooped-over man with a head no bigger than a Jonathan apple. He was also an imbecile—didn't even have the intelligence of a four-year-old—but he was harmless.

"Zip was lying in some weeds and bawling like a baby," Evans went on. "He was wearing the same outfit he always wore on Clyde's stage, kind of a caveman's getup made of leopard skin, with one strap over a shoulder. Zip had no idea where he was. Maybe he had gotten into a bottle of hooch. I felt sorry for him. I took his hand and led him back to the sideshow. The tent was pitch-black inside, but I heard rustling near the stage. I lit a match and moved toward the noise. That's when I saw Leitzel and Clyde. Both were straightening their clothes. 'What are you doing here at this hour?' they asked me. And I replied, 'No, the question is, what are you are doing here? It's three in the morning.'"

Evans could not remember paying any future calls at the sideshow during the dead of night. More than once, though, he said, when it was lights-out everywhere on the lot, he spotted Ingalls entering Leitzel's stateroom.

"On the circus, everybody's crowded together like candy in a gumball machine," he noted. "No secret can survive long. I think everybody on the show soon knew of the hanky-panky between Clyde and Leitzel."

Certainly Neil Ingalls learned of her husband's dalliances. The newly combined Ringling Bros. and Barnum & Bailey Circus had been on the road for only a month or two in 1919 when, with her heart broken, Neil left for her hometown of Burlington, Iowa. She promptly began legal proceedings. Within a year, the couple was divorced.

◆ ◆ ◆

Leitzel and Ingalls wed on the afternoon of January 29, 1920, in a Baptist church in West New York, New Jersey. Because it was off-season for the circus, most of their fellow troupers were scattered everywhere in the country and unable to attend. Still there were well-wishers on hand, and it is likely the church pastor, the Reverend John Lehment, had never before seen his house of worship filled with a stranger mix of high and low congregants.

On the bride's side of the aisle were some friends from Broadway like Billie Burke, Fanny Brice, and Ed Wynn. Among the attendees from the circus was May Wirth, the loveliest and most dazzling of the circus's equestriennes, and Bird Millman, with whom Leitzel had become especially close since their working together in Ziegfeld's *Midnight Frolic*. Wirth, as always, made her appearance at the church in exceptional style. She was dressed entirely in white and had been ferried to the church in a white limousine driven by a chauffeur who was also liveried in white.

Several of Ingalls's charges filled the pews on his side of the aisle, among them Eddy Masher, a "living skeleton," advertised as weighing just thirty-three pounds; Jim Tarver, a giant, at eight foot three; and Alistair MacWilkie, a Scot with a twelve-foot-long red beard. It was Lionette, though, who attracted the greatest attention on the groom's side. Not only did the seventeen-year-old "lion girl" have flaxen hair that fell silkily from the sides of her head, but much of her face was covered with it, too.

The newspapers hailed the wedding as a major event in show business history. The *New York Mail*, for one, observed that, like Fifth Avenue, the sawdust ring could make claim to at least a few nobles, and called the joining together of Clyde and Leitzel as "a marriage of circus high life." The *New York Sun*, referring to Ingalls as "the prince of side showmen" and Leitzel as the "queen of the flying rings," pronounced the union to be a "marriage of circus aristocracy."

And Ingalls undoubtedly did feel like a freshly minted aristocrat soon after the ceremony. He started experiencing the cushiest lifestyle he had ever known. Not only did his bride have a well-appointed Manhattan apartment with around-the-clock doormen, but she also had her own car, a big, new, gleaming black phaeton, along with a chauffeur. She also had Mabel Clemings, who was always there to serve not only as her maid but also as secretary, bookkeeper, confidante, and worshipper.

On average, Leitzel fired Mabel four times a day—usually before and after each of her matinee and evening shows. After finishing her turns on the Roman rings and harvesting the audience's applause, Leitzel would head toward the tent's exit and, with Mabel trailing behind her, launch into a critique on how badly she thought her employee had carried out her job in the big top.

"Where were you, Mabel? I turned to you to put the wrap on my shoulders and you were six feet away. Six feet! Think of it! And where were my clogs? Where were they? I ask you. Oh, well, you'll never learn. Don't come near me! Don't touch me! I never want to see you again, Mabel. And you say you love me, that you think of me constantly when I'm up there in the air. Don't try to answer me. I've heard it all before. Why don't you say something? Are you stricken so dumb that you can't even answer me?"

As lashing as they were, Leitzel's tempests rarely lasted longer than it took for her and Mabel to walk to the star's private tent or train quarters. Leitzel would slump into a chair, blame her rage on the strains of her employment, and beg Mabel for forgiveness, promising she would try harder never to fly out of control again.

"There, there, ducky," Mabel would coo. "I understand. Now let me fix you tea."

◆ ◆ ◆

The roustabouts, with all their worldly possessions carried inside bedrolls, along with clowns, daredevils, and bareback riders, started appearing in Madison Square Garden the second and third weeks of March 1920. The Ringling Bros. and Barnum & Bailey Circus was scheduled to launch another new season on the night of March 26, and then, following the New York stay, begin another cross-country tour.

Because only a small number of Leitzel and Ingalls's fellow troupers had been able to attend their church wedding, the newlyweds were swarmed in the Garden by well-wishers. All their fellow travelers were trying to kiss the bride and shake the groom's hand, and some of them were bearing gifts. According to May Wirth, though, it was evident that the marriage, just a month and a half old, was already in trouble.

"Leitzel and Clyde appeared cold toward one another. A few of us girls got together with Leitzel privately and asked if we could organize a little party to celebrate the marriage. 'No,' she said. 'I wouldn't want anything like that.'"

Because Ingalls rarely ever accumulated enough money to buy his next pair of alligator skin shoes, he was as anxious as anyone to get back to work, to again start getting paid. But that was not the only reason why he was anxious for a new circus season to start. Now, maybe, he would be able to see his bride with some regularity. This had not been the case with the newlyweds up to now.

Because she had been engaged for a second season in Ziegfeld's *Midnight Frolic* during the circus's off-season, she had disappeared from the couple's apartment most nights and did not return until a few hours before dawn.

The few nights when she was not performing in the New Amsterdam Theatre were mostly taken up by appearances at soirees, many of them thrown by people who were connected to the worlds of the circus and theater. She permitted Ingalls to tag along on some of these nights out, but some of the invitations she received, she told him, had been extended only to her.

As she was leaving their apartment alone for these nights out, she would often call back explanations to her new husband that might sound something like this, according to Fanny McCloskey.

"Flo and Billie want me to meet one of their dear friends, the owner of a chain of department stores or something like that," she might say. "Oh, it's going to be such a boring night. Probably a lot of talk about luggage and white sales. No need to wait up. I'll be late getting back."

At least some of the merriments in which she participated were organized as just two-person affairs, Leitzel and the host, who more times than not, was a gentleman. Flo Ziegfeld and Charley and John Ringling not only encouraged her participation in such outings but sometimes also helped arranged them. They valued her as a potent emissary for their enterprises and believed her liaisons with manufacturers, bankers, newspaper editors, theater managers, and politicians could be useful to them.

Leitzel seemed not to deny that the expectations she had in a marriage partner could be beyond reason to an extreme, even allowing for her to carry on dalliances with other men. Still, she believed that as a queen, she was entitled to make all the rules in relationship matters and, on at least one occasion, openly discussed her ideal of the perfect man, whether a husband or lover.

"He must be ever there, waiting for my commands," she said, "my wishes must be his law. I am high-strung and nervous as a result of my strenuous work, and he must remember this and make allowances for my fits of temper and unreasonableness."

She went on to say that she would always react sharply to any man who might try to control her in any way, even if he regarded some of her ways as being capricious.

"He must be comforting, but he must not be forever under my feet. He must remember that ego is the curse of the professional woman, and he must cater to it."

✦ ✦ ✦

The Ringling Bros. and Barnum & Bailey Circus opened its 1920 season with a five-week run at the Garden that ended in May, and then, once again, started rolling elsewhere across America. The apartment that Leitzel and Ingalls shared on the train immediately gained a reputation among the other troupers as an arena for some of the great fights of the century.

It is likely that at least some of Ingalls's differences with his bride had to do with Colonel H. Maxwell Howard, her multimillionaire suitor. She was still seeing him at least now and then.

Harry and Gracie Doll, brother and sister midgets from Germany who sang, danced, and rode horses in the big top, shared a train compartment adjoining Leitzel and Ingalls's quarters. A lot of mornings, the Dolls' eyes were rimmed with dark circles when they entered the cookhouse for breakfast.

"Oh, they were at it again last night," Harry would explain. "Like cat and dog they were snarling at one another all night. We got no sleep at all."

During one especially pitched battle, Leitzel lopped off one of Ingalls's fingers with a kitchen knife, according to Henry Ringling North, a nephew of the Ringling brothers who was traveling with the circus at the time. After that, whenever Clyde recognized that the tensions were escalating to a dangerous level, he surrendered. Perhaps fearful that he might be risking the loss of a body part even more dear to him than a finger, he gathered a blanket and in the black and blue of night, skulked to the sideshow tent.

✦ ✦ ✦

Leitzel and Ingalls had been married a little more than a year when they received a cablegram from Captain Bertram W. Mills, the biggest of Britain's circus impresarios. He was lining up acts for his second annual Bertram W. Mills International Circus and Christmas Fair. He wanted to sign Leitzel as his headliner and Clyde as head of the sideshow, as well as the announcer for the arena shows. Leitzel and Ingalls's marriage was already badly deteriorated, but the offer was hardly one they could pass. Mills's Circus and Christmas Fair, held each year in Olympia Hall in West Kensington, London, brought together many of the world's greatest circus all-stars.

Mills chose two other features for his production from the Ringling-Barnum circus, the nine-member Siegrist-Silbon trapeze troupe and bandmaster Merle Evans. The Americans boarded the *Adriatic* for the nine-day voyage on November 30.

"Leitzel and I got so seasick we were sure they'd be burying us at sea," Evans remembered. "As sick as Leitzel was, though, she put up her rigging in the ship's hold and practiced every day. She worried that if she laid off too long, she wouldn't be in shape to perform in Mills's show."

The change in continents had little effect in moderating Leitzel's instinct for constant socialization. She had hardly stepped off the *Adriatic*'s gangplank when she became swept up in a whirlwind of endless lunches, dinners, parties, and nights at the theater. As always, Clyde was excluded from most of her rounds. As hurtful as this must have been to him, there was another matter that left him humiliated. Within days after he and Leitzel arrived in London, many of the city's newspapers began publishing pictures showing Leitzel in the seminude. The photographs, many of them produced by Alfred Cheney Johnston, were too risqué for American newspapers, but such pictorial cheesecake was de rigueur in the British papers, especially the tabloids.

Mills's International Circus opened under the patronage of Queen Alexandra to a full house in the five-thousand-seat Olympia the afternoon of December 16. The queen mother, eighty-eight years old and in fragile health, was not present, but the premiere did not lack for glitter in the royal boxes. Princesses Beatrice and Victoria were there, along with the Lord Mayor, Edward C. Moses, and Queen Maud of Norway. Also present were hundreds of wounded World War I soldiers and children from orphanages and institutions for the blind.

Mills's production was roundly praised in the press as the most spectacular circus seen in London in years. The circus continued for four weeks, and when it was over, Leitzel and Ingalls made a side trip to Berlin, Germany, to visit for a few days with Nellie, who, at forty-two, was still making regular appearances as a striptease aerialist. Leitzel and Ingalls then sailed back to New York.

◆ ◆ ◆

The couple was home for little more than a week when Leitzel began skipping out on Ingalls again, disappearing to fit in some vaudeville engagements before the start of a new circus season.

In its publicity in the early 1920s, the circus made the claim that Leitzel was earning $6,000 a week. Clearly the claim was absurd. It may have overstated her pay by as much as the third zero.

Whatever the amount of Leitzel's pay, it was surely the richest sum awarded to any single big top performer. But few of the troupers begrudged her earnings. She functioned as kind of a one-woman benevolent society whose principal beneficiaries were her fellow travelers. Gretchen Jahn was often a witness to her acts of generosity.

"There'd be times when the two of us would be walking around the lot and Leitzel would spot some old workingman with raggedy clothes, and shoes that were bound together with twine," Jahn said. "She'd hand me a twenty-dollar bill and tell me, 'First chance you have, get this to that man and tell him to shop for a new outfit.' Other times, she'd learn of someone on the show who didn't have train fare to visit a sick mother or father somewhere. She'd get train money and extra cash to the worker or performer, and get word to him or her not to worry about ever paying her back."

Merle Evans, too, had memories of Leitzel's largesse.

"She considered my drummers to be the most important players in the orchestra because they tolled off the count for the crowds as she did her one-arm swing-overs—fifty . . . fifty-one . . . fifty-two, and so on," he said. "She'd come around once a week and slip each of them ten spots. She also gave weekly ten-dollar allowances to the boys who put up and took down her private tent. She handed out ten spots like they were sticks of gum." Of all the people who came to Leitzel with their hands extended, none called more frequently than Ingalls. Because of the support payments he was making to his earlier wives, and the tabs he had running with several haberdashers, he was broke most of the time.

Evans was paid twenty-five dollars a week as conductor of the circus's big orchestra, and he speculated Ingalls was probably drawing similar pay as manager of the sideshow. If that were so, Clyde's salary was probably but a twentieth of his wife's salary. He regularly asked Leitzel for handouts.

"I loathe money," Leitzel would scream at him. "I never touch it. Talk to Mabel."

Ingalls would move on to the maid.

"How much do you need?" Mabel would inquire.

Ingalls seemed ever hopeful that one day he would find that Mabel, like Ebenezer Scrooge, had experienced some dramatic transformation that would fill her with the spirit of Christmas.

"Oh, three or four hundred should see me through," he would reply.

"Here's a tenner," she would reply. "See that you don't fritter it away foolishly."

Leitzel was never sure where her stipends to Clyde were going. Still, she seems never to have directed Mabel to cut off the allowances. Maybe she considered the payouts a form of penance for not just once, but now twice, failing to vet her prospective mates more closely.

The two continued to operate in separate spheres, Leitzel the social butterfly, Clyde the stay-at-home husband.

By the third year of their marriage, if not earlier, Ingalls finally concluded that coexistence with the world's greatest circus star would never be possible. He started shopping for a new mate. Ultimately he found one in a neighboring tent on the lot. She was Kathleen Baines, a Brit, thirty-three and widowed, and the exhibitor of a gorilla, John Daniel II.

Leitzel was awarded a divorce from Ingalls on a finding of "irreconcilable differences" on October 15, 1924, in Shreveport, Louisiana. Six months later to the day, the minimal waiting period for divorcees to remarry, Ingalls and Kathleen Baines became husband and wife in New York City.

The third time—or was it the fourth?—was charmed for Clyde. He and Kathleen had two children, a boy and a girl, and remained together until his death in Sarasota, Florida, on March 17, 1940, at age sixty-four.

PART THREE

Alfredo Codona and Leitzel, following their marriage ceremony on July 20, 1928, on Chicago's lakefront where the Ringling Bros. and Barnum & Bailey Circus was performing. The open top landaulet in which the newlyweds traveled had been modified by clown Myron "Butch" Baker so it could rear up on its back wheels like a rodeo horse. (Author's collection)

CHAPTER 15

For the residents of Wichita Falls, Texas, who left their houses the morning of April 17, 1919, it all must have looked like something that had slipped off a star, something magical and sparkly that dropped from the sky and landed on, of all places, their town. On a dusty scrap of land near the railroad tracks that the day before was a patch of barrenness with only some rusted cans, tumbleweeds, and prairie dogs, tents were rising. Scattered here and there around the canvas stables, sideshow, and big top were a couple dozen gilded and rainbow-splashed parade wagons and floats that took the morning light and flung it back at the sun.

Sometime after midnight, when all of Wichita Falls was sleeping, the Sells-Floto Circus train had stolen into town. It arrived in style, on a forty-car train, all white with blue lettering, "the prettiest thing that ever moved over the rails," *Billboard* declared.

The town's forty thousand citizens should have felt well favored. The Sells-Floto Circus's Wichita Falls matinee and evening performances would be the first of its planned 165-town 1919 tour. Immediately upon their arrival, the roustabouts, working by torchlight, started unloading the train of its caged wild animals, elephants, horses, tents, parade wagons, and other cargo. By the time the first light of the new day appeared, the show's here-today, gone-tomorrow encampment was largely established.

The invading gypsies must have struck the townspeople as

members of some lost and ancient tribe. They were black and white, and red skinned, coffee colored, and faintly yellow. They appeared to have come from everywhere, and quite possibly they did.

Strolling the circus grounds were five or six dozen showgirls, many of them appearing bored at having been deposited in a place of such dusty forlornness. Even in their everyday housedresses, even with curlers in their hair, they were striking, all of them gorgeous enough to be contestants in a beauty contest.

Greatest in number in the circus tribe were the whiskered, gray-faced, and sweat-soaked men who threw slabs of meat to the lions and tigers, pitched hay at the horses and zebras, and rhythmically swung sledgehammers at the tent stakes.

There was another distinctive subculture with the traveling show that was not yet seeable to the Wichita Falls townsfolk making early morning explorations of the new show ground. Its members included Carlos Traveno, "The Two-Headed Mexican"; the "Honduras Siamese Twins"; and Kyko and Sulu, a brother and sister from Zanzibar whose heads looked like they had been shaped by a giant pencil sharpener. These "Marvelous Human Prodigies," along with a dozen and a half others just as remarkable, were hidden behind the canvas flaps of Professor W. F. Palmer's sideshow annex. Their tent would not be open to the public until closer to the time of the big top's matinee. By then, Professor Palmer would stand on his bally platform outside the freaks' showplace, trying to lasso customers from the midway with his rodomontade:

"You'll see them all, ladies and gentlemen. You'll see 'The Living Venus de Milo,' a young woman more beautiful than dawn who was born without arms. You'll see the fattest lady in the world. She weighs more than a piano and is just as wide. There's a man inside our commodious emporium who twists his arms and legs into pretzels.

"You've got plenty of time to see them all before the big top show starts. Tickets for the show inside here are just a quarter of the dollar for the ladies and gentlemen, a dime and a nickel for the little ones."

✦ ✦ ✦

Somewhere in the same setting, probably inside the big top and string-ing up his trapeze with his brother Lalo, was the circus's newest sensa-tion, Alfredo Codona. He was in the highest of spirits. He was back in America. He had been out of the country for most of the last half dozen years, traveling first with the Siegrist-Silbon trapeze troupe in Australia and New Zealand, and then, after 1915, touring Europe and South America with his own unit, The Flying Codonas. Over the last two years, Alfredo, along with Lalo, who was now his catcher, had been in Cuba and South America, as headliners with the Santos y Ar-tigas Circus. Not only was Alfredo happy to be back on United States soil, and appearing with the Sells-Floto Circus, The Show Beauti-ful, but, probably even more cheering to him, he was reunited for the first time in years with his father, Edward, and sister, Victoria. Now twenty-eight, married, the mother of a three-year-old son, and still arrestingly beautiful, Victoria was regarded as the Sells-Floto Circus's first lady. With Hortense in El Paso, Texas, looking after the home she and Edward had bought there, Edward was still touring with Victoria as her manager.

Alfredo was married now, too. Five months earlier, while in Ha-vana, Cuba, he married Clara Curtain, an aerialist who had begun her career in entertainment by appearing in the twenty-five-cent vaudeville houses in Chicago and her hometown of Cincinnati.

✦ ✦ ✦

Even though it was a Thursday afternoon, and most of the town's men were at work in the oil fields, the circus's opening show drew ten thou-sand people, a full house, a quarter of Wichita Falls' population. The show opened with a spectacle titled "The Birth of a Rainbow." As the-ater, the many-act production had no more coherence than a wino's dream, but it did give the circus a chance to roll out just about everything it had brought to town. There were pom-pommed horses; twenty-five clowns; a small herd of elephants, each caparisoned in satin; a caged ape; and about sixty costumed showgirls. A dozen of them hung by their teeth from ropes, and another four dozen twirled awkwardly *en pointe* on the sawdust-covered ground. After twenty minutes or so, a pot of gold was drawn before the audience on a pony-drawn float. The pageant finally ended, and the circus began rolling out its acts.

Three world-class bareback riding acts—The Lloyds, The Hobsons, and The Hodginis—performed simultaneously in the circus's three rings. There were clown acts, acrobatic feats by a troupe called the Bonomoor Arabs, and then twenty or thirty elephants appeared in the arena, each of them carrying a showgirl.

It was not until well into the program that Princess Victoria appeared. Like a swimmer determining the temperature of the water in a pool, she started by tentatively placing a toe on her wobbly slack wire. Alfredo and Papa Edward were on either side of the cable, to try to catch her if she should fall the sixteen feet to the ground. In another moment, Victoria was moving back and forth over the sagging wire, cakewalking at first and then doing her flamenco dance while clicking castanets. Then she began the crowning display of her act, and in seconds, the Wichita Falls crowd, like all the audiences that had ever witnessed it, became stupefied. Her wire started to move laterally higher and higher, faster and faster, until it was whipping back and forth like a telephone cable in a tornado. Somehow, impossibly it seemed, she was able to keep her gold-slippered feet on the wire as it flung her horizontal body right and left in the air almost to twelve o'clock. After finishing, she took her bows, and then left the big top, but the crowd, through its roars and cheers, called her back into the tent two or three times before it would finally let her go for good.

There were more clown acts, more acrobats, and a dog in a woman's dress and hat pushing a puppy-filled baby buggy. Then, after two hours, the time had come for the circus's finale, what was likely the inaugural appearance in the United States of The Flying Codonas.

A gasp rose from the audience at Clara Curtain's first appearance on the trapeze perch. She was dazzling, with porcelain skin, an undulant figure, and curly, fire-colored hair, and the spotlight seemed to strip her of her brief coverings so she appeared nude.

Clara and Alfredo each took turns presenting solo flights on the trapeze. Clara could perform all of the trapeze's basic maneuvers, but as stunning as she was in her physical appearance, she was not a flyer of much expressiveness. When Alfredo was flying, on the other hand, he gave the impression of a bird that had just been freed from a cage. He soared through the air in ecstasy. He pirouetted. Sometimes, while in transit to the hands of Lalo, he left his trapeze and then seemed to move through the air with the loping leaps of Nijinsky. Other times, he seemed to hang in space motionlessly for what seemed like seconds. The audience cheered and cheered.

And then it was time for Alfredo's pièce de résistance, a feat he had presented in Cuba and South America, but never in the United States.

He wormed himself into a gunnysack, and then, with only his arms free through the top of the bag, slipped a blindfold over his eyes. He pawed into the air to locate his flybar, and then, with fingers locked around the baton, shot out into the air. He made three or four forward swings, each higher than the one before it, and then released his grip. What appeared to be a sack of potatoes started ascending into the air and then made two full backward revolutions. Next, the sack was boring forward in space, with only Alfredo's outstretched arms seeable outside its opening. In another blink of the eye, he was caught in a wristlock by Lalo.

No one in the seats could have really believed what they had just witnessed, but Alfredo's feat was still not quite finished. Lalo then flung him back into space, and still blindfolded, still stuffed in the burlap bag, he twirled like a top. Next he reached into the air for the flybar that Clara had just thrown and that was hurtling to him. He caught it and then neatly rode his conveyance back to the perch.

The feat that Alfredo had just presented seemed utterly impossible. It may even have been beyond any rational person's ability to imagine. Yet ten thousand of Wichita Falls' townspeople had just seen it with their own eyes, and another ten thousand would also see it at the evening show.

❖ ❖ ❖

Ten years. Ten damn years.

Still, Alfredo had not gotten it. What did the gods want from him? Had he not worked long and hard enough to gain The Triple?

The Sells-Floto Circus presented the last show of its 1919 season on November 9 in Opelousas, Louisiana. After the single season of touring America with his Flying Codonas, Alfredo was already starting to receive mention from circus experts not just as the greatest trapeze flyer of his time but maybe even of all time.

That was fine with him, all just fine. But still, after a decade of searching for it almost every day, he had yet to find the rarest, most wondrous, and most spellbinding big top feat of all: The Triple. It ate at his insides.

The Flying Codonas had a contract to rejoin the Sells-Floto Circus for its 1920 season. Alfredo made up his mind that he was going to be ready to present The Triple when the show opened at the Coliseum in Chicago the following April, or die trying.

Both Papa Edward and Lalo begged him to abandon his quest for the feat before it killed him or, worse, left him such a pathetic cripple that he would be belted into a wheelchair for the rest of his life. Alfredo could not be persuaded.

By and large, circus people are superstitious. They believe that there are gods above them that rule their destinies. People in the ordinary world may be governed by fates, too, most circus people might concede, but the gods that govern the *saltimbanques* are different. They may be more extortive than any other gods. They may be more demanding in the payments they expect for their special favors.

If Alfredo had a prayer, it was to accomplish The Triple before he became too broken from falls or too old for that to be possible. He was sure that there was no other daredevil who wanted anything half as badly as he wanted the stunt. It was the four-minute mile of the big top world, the most elusive goal for every flyer aspiring to true greatness, to immortality.

Alfredo revered Ernie Clarke, the Brit who, beginning in 1909, if not earlier, began presenting The Triple to circus audiences. At the same time, though, Alfredo may have been resentful of him. Why had the gods favored Clarke over him?

Alfredo was twenty-seven. He had been carrying on his search for

The Triple since 1909, almost from the first moment he saw Leitzel, performing in the Barnum & Bailey Circus in the heavens of Madison Square Garden. His madness had started out of his first love. If ever he was to be worthy of such a divine, he thought back then, he would have to gain the circus's rarest feat.

Did he still, even fleetingly, think of Leitzel with amorous longing anymore? And did he wonder, too, whether she ever thought of him in the same way?

So much had happened in both of their lives since they had been secret lovers on the Barnum & Bailey Circus. For one, she had gone in and out of two marriages, and he had entered into one.

Even if Alfredo had tried to push Leitzel out of his head and heart, that, as a practical matter, would have been impossible. By the mid-teens, she was already established as the first darling of the circus universe. The popular press, as well as the entertainment papers, detailed all her comings and goings.

She had become one of America's earliest poster girls and even a bona fide sex symbol. During the waning days of World War I, a vote was carried out by the thousands of American soldiers fighting in the trenches of France and Belgium to select "The most beautiful and attractive woman in all the world." When the last of the ballots had been tallied, Mademoiselle Leitzel had finished well ahead of any of the other contenders, including Mary Pickford, Mae West, and Theda Bara. An emissary from the American Expeditionary Forces was dispatched to New York to hand deliver the proclamation to her. The document, prepared in Claumont, France, on stationery bearing the official seal of General John J. Pershing's army, informed the circus star that she had been selected as "Queen of the Flock." The proclamation went on to acknowledge to Leitzel that "you now stand No. 1, and in view of our absolute confidence, you need have no fear that your present position will ever be usurped by another, no matter how beautiful." Thereafter, Leitzel posters and photographs started appearing on the inside locker doors of soldiers billeted in barracks throughout the United States and Europe.

✦ ✦ ✦

Alfredo's search to find The Triple had taken on new urgency after he returned to America and, along with Lalo and Clara, joined the Sells-Floto Circus.

Ernie Clarke, the first flyer to at least now and then successfully complete hands-to-hands triple somersaults on the flying trapeze, had by now eliminated the stunt from his performances. Even when the Brit was at the top of his form years earlier, he was never able to complete The Triple more than once or twice in every half dozen tries, and Clarke apparently came to the realization that he was engaging in a form of Russian roulette every time he attempted the feat.

If Clarke had given back The Triple to the fates, Alfredo may have believed, they might now be more inclined to pass it on to him as the second mortal worthy of the most cherished of all big top treasures. But now there was a new matter tormenting Alfredo. He had been receiving reports that another flyer, Ernie Lane, the star leaper with the Flying Wards, was also seeking to gain the feat. Some who had seen Lane in his rehearsals said he appeared to be very close to taking possession of it. The former Iowa farm boy had started showing a devil-may-care daring in all his flying for the last two years. He had lost his wife when an empty troop carrier crashed into the Hagenbeck-Wallace Circus's train just outside of Hammond, Indiana, in the early morning hours of June 18, 1918. The railroad accident, the worst in circus history, took the lives of eighty-seven performers and workers.

✦ ✦ ✦

Alfredo found an ideal place to resume his pursuit of The Triple after the Sells-Floto Circus presented the last of its 1919 shows in Opelousas, Louisiana: the Coliseum on the fairgrounds in Shreveport just 190 miles to the south. The Coliseum, a dirt-floored exhibition hall, was largely vacant over the winter months.

When Alfredo entered the Coliseum each morning along with his brother and father, it was in a spirit of humility, as though he were entering a church for the most solemn of occasions. He seemed willing to turn over his life to the gods to do with it whatever they thought was best.

"I had adopted a fatalistic attitude," he said. "If this was to be the end of my efforts, very well, then, it would be the end."

Each new day in the Coliseum, just as he had done thousands of times before over close to a dozen years, Alfredo ascended the rope ladder to the trapeze. Lalo, hanging upside down at the opposing end of the rigging with his legs entwined with the ropes of his trapeze, started swinging. Then, when he reached exactly the right speed and lift, Lalo sent out his familiar cry.

"Listo."

Alfredo would then lunge into space and, gripping his flybar, swing higher and higher. Then he would let go of the baton and, with his body tucked into a sphere, start turning his backward somersaults while at the same time streaking forward in space like a comet. Always, though, when he started entering into the third of his spins, he would black out, momentarily losing consciousness. Alfredo had a term for these slivers of time during which he believed he ceased to exist.

He experienced, he said, "the little death."

When he came to, another second would pass before he regained awareness of who he was, where he was, what he was trying to do. By then, it was too late. He was too far off course to make any corrections. Sometimes he slammed into Lalo, sometimes their hands brushed, but always the attempts ended with Alfredo tumbling into the net. His body was always bruised and abraded from net burns, and his mood ugly, when he left the Coliseum each day. He cursed himself. He also cursed Lalo and Papa, as though, preposterously, they shared any blame for his inability to find the trick. Mostly he blamed the damned gods. There was no one on earth who wanted The Triple more badly than he did. Probably there never was. Why did they not see that?

◆ ◆ ◆

Two or three two months went by, and then a morning came when Alfredo did not so much seem his customary humble, almost penitential self when he stepped inside the Coliseum. Rather, his spirit was one of excited anticipation.

He clambered up his ladder to his perch and waited for Lalo's call.

"*Listo*."

Once again, Alfredo hurtled into space on his flybar, then released his hands from the baton and scrunched his body into a ball.

He started somersaulting.

One.

Two.

Three.

And this time it happened.

When he came out of the third turn, he leveled out, and this time, like a bullet from a sharpshooter's rifle, traveled the remaining ten feet to Lalo, and this time, hallelujah, their hands interlocked around each other's wrists.

Had it all been a fluke?

The brothers were almost afraid to try again, but after just moments, Alfredo was back on the rope ladder, climbing to his perch.

"*Listo*."

Alfredo was again moving through space, his feet rolling over his head in three blurring revolutions, and then, hardly a second later, he was moored once again in Lalo's powerful grip.

Perfect.

The brothers tried a third time, and once again, everything ended perfectly.

Alfredo had it.

He had The Triple.

Had he made some irrevocable promise to the fates the night before in exchange for it?

After a few seconds of hanging in his brother's wristlock, Alfredo fell into the net, this time deliberately. A moment later, Lalo left his bar and also fell to the net.

The brothers hugged each other on the ground, then collapsed to the earthen floor, and, like a couple of bear cubs, started playfully rolling together in the dirt. Then they pulled Papa Edward to the ground, and all three of them were rolling and squealing with laughter.

"If any other people had entered the Coliseum just then, they would have thought that all three of them were crazy, absolutely loco," said Anita Codona, Lalo's wife, who was a witness to it all.

Ten years. Yes, ten damn years.

CHAPTER 16

Alfredo fell in love with Leitzel all over again.

It happened in the same place it had occurred the first time, nearly a dozen and a half years earlier, on the floor of Madison Square Garden.

This day, though, the Garden hardly seemed a likely setting for love to strike a second time. Several hundred Ringling Bros. and Barnum & Bailey Circus employees, performers, and workmen were in the arena, and more were streaming in by the minute. At the same time, roustabouts were rolling wheeled and iron-barred dens onto the floor with lions and tigers, a gorilla, and even a hippopotamus. Other circus employees were working near the ceiling, guying cables for the wire walkers and stringing up the riggings of the trapeze artists.

Some of the tumblers, clowns, and bareback riders had found corners on the floor where they could begin practicing their acts, but most of the performers were still milling around, talking with one another, and waiting for some directions on where they might fit into the chaos.

Weaving through the jumble, a cigar moving in and out of his lips, was Mister John. He was sixty-one now, and the last of the Ringling brothers. Charley had died four months earlier, at sixty-three. A question John could have had on his mind was how he and his lieutenants were going to be able to shape all the formlessness before him into another show. They would just have to do it. There was no other choice. Completely ready or not, The Greatest Show on Earth was scheduled to open its 1927 season on April 12. That was three or four days away.

When Alfredo turned up in the Garden, accompanied by Clara and Lalo and Lalo's wife, Anita, one performer and show executive after another kept approaching him, shaking his hand, and telling him how excited everyone was to learn that The Flying Codonas would be the headline attraction of the new show.

He was now regarded as a mythic figure by the circus's other nomads. The fates had been good to him. Perhaps because of some Faustian bargain Alfredo had made with them six years earlier in a fair park building in Shreveport, they finally presented him with the most zenithal of the big top's prizes, The Triple. And, furthermore, they had given him exclusive possession of the treasure, although, for a brief time, he had to share it with another leaper.

Ernie Lane, the flyer who had been competing with him to be the second man after Ernie Clarke to perform The Triple, finally gained the feat, too, but the gods apparently intended for their gift to him to be a short and temporary one. On a spring day in 1921 while Lane was rehearsing his trapeze act, he lost all control while trying to revolve in space. With his arms and legs flailing crazily, he fell from the air and tumbled face-first into a net. He was pronounced dead of a fractured skull and neck injuries upon his arrival at Chicago's St. Bernard Hospital.

Alfredo was the foremost male circus artist in the world at the time Mister John signed The Flying Codonas to appear as headliners for the 1927 edition of the Ringling Bros. and Barnum & Bailey Circus. He and his troupe had been abroad for much of the past four years where, night after night, in months-long engagements, they appeared at such major venues as Berlin's Wintergarten and Paris's Cirque d'Hiver and Cirque Medrano. Not only was Alfredo revered as the only artist on the planet performing The Triple, but he was also esteemed because of his role in *Varieté*, a motion picture by the brilliant German director E. A. Dupont. The photoplay, starring Emil Jannings and largely filmed in the Wintergarten, was released in Europe in 1925 and became an international hit. Alfredo had performed all of the movie's stunning trapeze sequences, including The Triple, or the Salto Mortale, as the sometimes lethal feat was known to Europeans.

Alfredo was still inside the Garden, receiving welcomes from his new Ringling colleagues, when it happened.

He saw Leitzel across the floor, and, at the same time, she spotted him.

She started making her way to him. Her eyes were kindled, and she was beaming.

Then she was before him, and extending her hand.

"Well, look at you," she said. "Just look at you."

And that is what she did. She looked him up and down for several moments without saying anything. She may have been trying to unite the figure standing before her with her memory of the sixteen-year-old boy she had kissed good-bye seventeen years before outside a pool hall in Chicago.

At thirty-three Alfredo was still as trim and boyish-looking as ever, but now, differently, he could have passed for a movie idol. He looked as though he might have stepped outside a tailor shop five or ten minutes earlier with a completely new set of expensive clothes. He wore a sport coat whose shoulders were two times the width of its waist. His trousers were so sharply creased they looked like they could cut bread. There was a fedora on his head, and, on his feet, shoes waxed to a high polish.

Alfredo had thought for years about what their reunion might be like if one should ever occur. He had even had dreams about it.

Now his feelings came rushing back, the same ones he had the first time he ever saw her.

Clara was at Alfredo's side when he and Leitzel reunited in the Garden. He may have resented her presence there. She did not belong there, he must have felt. She had never been present in any of the dreams he had of reuniting with Leitzel.

Alfredo was transfixed by the sight of Leitzel. He had not seen her face-to-face in a dozen and a half years. He was tongue-tied at first. Finally it occurred to him that he had subjected Leitzel, as well as his wife, to a social gaffe. It was not until then that he introduced the two women.

Leitzel took Clara's hand and welcomed her to the show. She told her that if there was anything at all that she could do to make her more at ease in her travels with the circus she should feel free to call on her at any time. She told Alfredo she had seen him in *Varieté* so often that she had lost count of how many times she had taken in the movie. She told him how glad she was that The Flying Codonas were now a part of the Ringling circus. She inquired about Victoria and his father, and asked him to remember her to them.

And then the moment that Alfredo had been thinking about for so many years was over. It had been so perfunctory, so businesslike. He looked sad as Leitzel drifted away.

Clara tried talking to him. She told him that she found Leitzel to be "absolutely charming." Alfredo probably did not hear a word of what his wife said. He appeared to be lost in his thoughts and had a look in his eyes that Clara had seen before, a faraway gaze.

◆ ◆ ◆

He was indistinguishable from the anonymous and faceless drones who shuffled behind the elephants, camels, and horses with shovels. He wore the same baggy coveralls as the drudges who mopped up the urine and droppings of the animals.

He strode out onto the oval floor fifteen or twenty minutes before each of Leitzel's performances and climbed her web hand-over-hand until he was near the ceiling. There, in near darkness, he went about his tasks swiftly. He sat on Leitzel's trapeze bar, bouncing on it to make sure its ropes were not frayed and could hold her weight. He swung from her steel rings, testing them to make sure they were securely fastened. Few sitting in the stands took notice of him. The crowd's attention was focused on the forty elephants that trainer George Denman was presenting in five rings on the great oval floor. After two or three minutes, the workman finished his checks on the rigging, and then, expertly and quickly, descended Leitzel's web and disappeared, but only for a short time.

Still in his outsize coveralls, he was back in the hippodrome five or ten minutes later as Leitzel was beginning her routines fifty or sixty feet in the air. He was inside the center ring, exactly below her, with his head thrown back and his gaze fixed on the sprite suffused in silvery light. If, heaven forbid, she should ever fall from her trapeze or Roman rings, he would be there to catch her, or die trying.

Everyone traveling with the circus, performers and workers alike, knew the identity of the figure in the too-big work clothes who made the twice-daily ascents to Leitzel's ropes, and then, just minutes later, warily watched her every move from the ground as she flew and spun. It was Alfredo Codona, the circus's newest marvel and highest-paid male performer.

Why was the show's beau ideal carrying out the menial assignment of checking another artist's equipment, especially since Leitzel already had a property manager, Frank McCloskey, who was meticulous in carrying out the same work? Alfredo's preoccupation with the trustworthiness of Leitzel's ropes and swivels struck others as the behavior of a man who believed his own life depended on the equipment.

In a way, that may have been true.

If Leitzel's equipment should ever fail, causing her to plunge through the dark chasm to the floor, it would be all over not only for her but for him, too, he now believed. He would not be able to live without her. Not again.

He had lost her before, when, at the close of a Barnum & Bailey Circus's spring visit to Madison Square Garden half their lifetimes earlier, Leitzel returned to Europe with the Leamy Ladies, and he stayed on with the show as a minor trapeze flyer. So much had happened since then.

◆ ◆ ◆

Alfredo's feelings toward Clara seemed to have soured to detestation almost overnight. She started seeing changes taking place in him almost from the instant of his reunion with Leitzel in the Garden.

Clara was stung with humiliation before the other troupers each time Alfredo drew himself up Leitzel's web to inspect her rigging. What tortured her even more, though, were the visits he made to Leitzel's private car after the evening show.

Up on the trapeze perch, Clara had always appeared to be fully in control, a confident and proud eagle at the edge of a high cliff, waiting to throw herself into the next current of wind. It was different now when she and Alfredo were alone together in their train compartment. There, she was weepy.

What happened to the plan they often discussed about having children and training them to become members of the act? she asked Alfredo over and over. It was not too late to bring back the dream, she said. Alfredo was thirty-four, she, thirty-three. He refused to engage in any discussions with Clara about any future they could have together. Now there was someone else.

Inwardly, Alfredo seemed sure that Clara would eventually agree to a divorce, and that she could be removed as an impediment to his taking Leitzel as his bride. But a greater obstacle was still in the way.

Regularly, if unpredictably, Colonel H. Maxwell Howard, Leitzel's longtime admirer, continued turning up on the circus's lots, usually staying just two, three, or four days at a time, but sometimes remaining with the show for a week or more.

It appeared to some of the other performers that Leitzel always demoted Alfredo to nonentity status whenever the colonel was visiting the show. When she was not in the big top performing, she spent all her time with Howard, either entertaining him in her private tent and train stateroom, or traveling into town with him for movies and dinners.

Alfredo was wounded by the slights from Leitzel over another man. He was not accustomed to assuming the position of a second-stringer, whether as a performer or as a lover. He told Leitzel of the hurt he suffered when she ignored him.

Leitzel took Alfredo's hands in hers. She told him that she was growing fonder of him every day, but that maybe he was trying to move too fast in their relationship. Besides, she reminded him, he was married to Clara.

As heartsick as Alfredo was during the times Leitzel shunned him to dote on the colonel, he did not receive any sympathy from his family.

"Because he treated Clara so shamefully, we all thought he was just getting what he deserved," said Anita Codona, Alfredo's sister-in-law and Lalo's wife. "Clara was a saint, absolutely the sweetest girl you could ever meet. Papa and Mama Codona couldn't have loved her more if she was their own daughter. Lalo and I loved her, too. She could not have been more devoted to Alfredo. How could he throw her out of his life after ten years of marriage? And for Leitzel of all people? Yes, she was the big star, but she liked to bounce from man to man even when she was married."

Alfredo's sister, Victoria, was similarly disapproving of Leitzel.

"No married woman would trust her with her husband," she said.

When Alfredo revealed to family members that he planned to seek a divorce from Clara, no one was angrier than Lalo.

"When he and Alfredo were arguing about it, Lalo would become so mad that I was afraid he was going to take his brother's head in his hands and squeeze it like a lemon until the pulp came out," Anita said.

A show of such fury would have been out of character for her husband. Lalo made his living by snagging his 155-pound brother out of the air and then flinging him back into space. His arms had become muscled enough to drop an ox. While he may have had the might of Samson, though, Lalo was almost always gentle. The show's other male performers passed the time between their big top appearances by pitching horseshoes and playing softball, but he usually kept to himself during free times, knitting woolen sweaters and socks or pink and blue booties, which he gifted to the circus's expectant mothers.

Although his own family withheld sympathy from Alfredo when he was suffering because Leitzel seemed to favor the colonel's company over his, ultimately he did find a friend in whom he could confide. When his misery became unbearable, he went to the sideshow tent of Clyde Ingalls, Leitzel's ex-husband.

Ingalls's expression became condolent and rueful as Alfredo poured out his heart. In a response that was automatic, the sideshow manager started playing with the stub of the finger on his right hand, remembering the night when Leitzel lopped off the missing half with a butcher knife.

"Worst thing I ever did in my life was taking up with that woman,"

Ingalls would say. "Best thing I ever did in my life was getting the divorce from her, getting her out of my life."

As for Clyde himself, he may never have been happier in life than he was then. He and his new wife, Kathleen Baines, continued to operate in separate, but side-by-side, tents, with Ingalls still exhibiting giants and dwarfs and tattooed and bearded ladies, and she still serving as caretaker to John Daniel II, the circus's stupendous-size gorilla whose daily consumption of bananas seemed so prodigious that, all on his own, the primate may have had a salutary effect on the economies of Honduras, Panama, and Ecuador.

◆ ◆ ◆

Leitzel had reigned for two decades as the circus's most widely beloved, most pampered, and most highly paid female star. Could she give all that up?

She was thirty-six, and increasingly now, there was a matter that caused her anguish. She began to wonder just how much longer she would be able to continue as a performer. Her body was starting to wear out. For more than twenty years, in twice-a-day shows, she subjected it to the most brutalizing physical punishment. An ache had settled permanently into her shoulder from the years of throwing the dislocations and stretching the tendons at her clavicle. More worrisome to her was an ugly, often infected gorge that was carved into her flesh just above the right wrist, where the loop of her rope chewed at each performance.

She had started engaging in a nightly ritual, a last act before slipping into bed. She brought out a hypodermic needle and shot caffeine into the flesh around the socket joint at the shoulder and near the open wound on her wrist. The procedure helped "quiet" the pulsating, and some nights hammering, pain.

Some physicians had already told her there was a danger the cankering sore on her lower arm might ultimately result in blood poisoning that could kill her. She lived in dread that when she had to see a doctor the next time, she might be told the flesh on her lower arm had finally become so badly putrefied that her right arm would have to be amputated below the elbow. She would rather be dead than allow that to happen, she told her closest friends, including Fanny McCloskey. That would be better than losing the arm. She tried to blank out any thoughts of ever becoming a cripple, a sorrowful woman, once the queen of the big top, whose appearance frightened young children because of a grotesque stump she had left for an arm.

Over and over in the past, doctors had pleaded with her to quit her planges and replace the feat with some new stunt that was perhaps equally sensational but less battering to her body. Leitzel remained adamant on the subject. She could not eliminate the throw-overs from her ring appearances. The planges—she regularly did one hundred of them at every show, and sometimes, when the crowds kept cheering her on, even more—were her signature.

Fanny McCloskey's husband, Frank, still serving as Leitzel's property manager at the time, said he believed that Leitzel suffered more for her audiences than any prizefighter ever did.

"A fighter steps into the ring maybe a few times a year, and, now and then, gets badly bloodied or knocked out," he observed. "Leitzel, though, appeared before the crowds twice a day, every day, and was badly mauled every time she did her act."

Besides the fear Leitzel had of her body one day finally giving out on her totally, stopping her from ever ascending to her ropes and rings again, she was becoming haunted with another terror. Often when she was performing her planges now, with the rope feeding at her wrist like a ravenous wild animal, she heard a disembodied voice:

"Why don't you let go? You're tired. It's foolish to hang on to a rope way up here in the air. The audience won't care. There's plenty more for them to look at. Let go! Let go!"

Alfredo told of sometimes being bedeviled by a similar voice when he left his trapeze and was hurtling through space. The unseen exhorter may have been the same one who hissed in Leitzel's ear, he believed. He may have been the Grim Reaper.

Alfredo used the term "casting" in talking about a change in his mental state that sometimes occurred while performing. He never fully described what he meant, but apparently he was trying to suggest that often when he was somersaulting through space, rolling like a powerfully exploded cannonball through nothingness, he was accompanied by some dark spirit trying to "cast" a spell on him. Most times, ninety-nine out of one hundred, he could ignore the spirit. Sometimes, though, the demon's plea was so insistent that he lost all concentration, lost any sense of who he was and where he was. Then, after turning the last of his somersaults, he would veer in an erratic way, miss his connection with Lalo, and plummet into the net.

He described the altering in his consciousness this way:

"The mind seems to let go, to refuse any longer to hold to the terrific burden of concentration placed on it. It's like a sharp knife stuck suddenly against a set of tightly drawn strings. The parting comes in a dozen directions. The performer sprawls hopelessly, all thought of his trick departed. And, of course, he fails. Why it happens, or how it happens, a performer rarely knows."

◆ ◆ ◆

Alone in her bed at night, her body aching everywhere, hoping to be overtaken by sleep, Leitzel must have imagined how different her life could be as Mrs. H. Maxwell Howard. Fanny McCloskey believed that for all the differences between the worlds that the colonel and Leitzel inhabited, she would have quit the circus the next day if he had been in a position to propose marriage to her.

"She could have had the life of a southern belle like Daisy Buchanan in *The Great Gatsby*," Fanny said. "A hilltop castle with maids and servants everywhere, a stable filled with Thoroughbreds, more money than she could ever spend. The colonel, a multimillionaire, could have given her all that, and more."

CHAPTER 17

The party started in the midafternoon on a Sunday and was still going strong into the night. By then a big, orange, full October moon hung in the black sky. It looked like a child's vagrant balloon. It seemed close enough to Earth to ping with an aggie-loaded slingshot.

The party, a fete, really, was intended to pay high honor to F. W. Murnau, the German-born film director. It was hosted by ringmaster Fred Bradna and his wife, Ella, inside and outside their Pullman coach. Their car, along with all the others on the Ringling train, was idled on a railroad track siding alongside the circus lot in Lynchburg, Virginia.

The Murnau reception was an invitation-only occasion, limited to the circus's top executives and the most elite of its performers, among them Leitzel, of course, The Flying Codonas, bareback rider May Wirth, wire walker Berta Beeson, and bandmaster Merle Evans. The party was received by the circus's crème de la crème as the social event of the 1927 season. It may have been the social event of several seasons.

Rarely did more than a few days pass on the circus without an appearance by at least one genuine grandee from the outside world, a matinee idol, an opera diva, maybe a Supreme Court justice. Management treated such visitors as royals. Their names and stations were announced to the crowd as they were escorted to boxes beside John and Mable Ringling.

Because of the frequency with which golden people turned up at the circus, the performers and workhands, while unfailingly welcoming and cordial, were rarely unduly impressed. Their reception for Friedrich Wilhelm Murnau was different. Everyone fawned over him.

Murnau was widely acknowledged to be the first true genius of moviemaking. Like Shakespeare, Michelangelo, and Beethoven, he was one of those far-seers who, after being drawn to an art medium, reinvented it and established new standards for elevating it to a pinnacle never before reached.

The motion picture industry was still in its infancy, barely two decades old. But more than any figure before him, Murnau showed film's malleability for revealing human drama with the complexity and emotional pitch of the greatest theater and opera. With *Nosferatu*, the first vampire movie, and others of his early movies, he developed a stylistic vocabulary that would be appropriated by almost every important filmmaker who would succeed him. Among the more revolutionary approaches he brought to the cinematic art was a subjective point of view through which the psychological makeup and inner thoughts of the characters were revealed by using the camera's lens to peer out at the world as though seeing through the characters' eyes.

Murnau was lured from Germany to Hollywood in 1926 by William Fox, head of Fox Studios. He wasted no time in starting on a new picture, *Sunrise: A Song of Two Humans*. The film, released in 1927, received the first-ever award from the newly created Academy of Motion Picture Arts and Sciences for Best Picture (Unique and Artistic Production). The movie's star, Janet Gaynor, took home the Academy Award for Best Actress.

Murnau was tall, thin, and, at thirty-nine, still boyish-looking. He may not have been totally at ease at the party the Bradnas had thrown for him. He was shy and not comfortably fluent in English. For much of the day and night, though, performers and show executives were gathered before him two and three deep. They were not truckling entirely because of his vaunted reputation. They knew the director was far along in developing the script for a second Fox movie, one to be set against the backdrop of a circus. Knowing this, many of the admirers that day viewed Murnau as a one-man job fair.

Merle Evans explained: "Everyone was having secret thoughts of worming their way into his movie. That goes for Fred and Ella Bradna, and even John Ringling. And, I'll admit it, even me. Even I thought about how grand it would be to work for the greatest film director in the world. What could be more glamorous than going to Hollywood during the off-season, getting a part in a movie, and getting paid for it?"

Murnau had linked up with the Ringling cavalcade to carry out research for his new movie. He was intent on absorbing everything he could about the circus and the lives and work of its nomads. He expressed amazement at how, within an hour and a half after the circus train and its thousand travelers had arrived in a new town, an entire tented burgh would rise up on a dusty lot, with the calliopes piping ragged tunes for the first comers and the vendors out in force, selling peanuts, cotton candy, and tiny green lizards in lapel harnesses.

"The circus," Murnau observed, "is a complete community, each member of which knows where he has to be at a certain minute and what he has to do. And he does his work quietly, speedily, and efficiently."

✦ ✦ ✦

Murnau got up with the show's earliest risers, and did not slip back into his bunk until after everyone else was asleep. He climbed the rope ladder to the dizzying height of the Codonas' trapeze rigging. There, sitting on the perch, he made sketches of Alfredo rapidly rolling head over heels through space, and the vertiginous view down to the safety net fifty feet below. He spent much of his days strolling the lots, interviewing not just the muscled acrobats and primped and talcumed equestriennes, but also the fetid men who drove the tent stakes and slept in the train's stock cars with the camels and elephants.

So deeply did Murnau fall under the circus's spell that he might have been close to staying with it forever.

"If I had remained another day," he told a reporter, "I believe that I would have joined the parade. . . . When the bugle blows for the start of a new performance, everyone says, 'There she goes,' and they join the opening parade around the arena with the same enthusiasm as if it were the first day of the circus."

After a week or ten days, though, Murnau did leave to return to Hollywood, his briefcase filled with drawings, notes from interviews, and rolls of exposed film.

For all the hopes Mister John and the circus's center ring stars had of finding places in Murnau's movie, the director did not turn out to be a grand employer. F. W. offered work to just three Ringling employees, The Flying Codonas. He may have viewed Lalo and Clara as stunt players who were mostly coming along for the ride, but he absolutely needed Alfredo's services. Alfredo was the single trapeze flyer in the world who could execute the Salto Mortale, The Triple, the feat for which the movie's antihero was celebrated.

✦ ✦ ✦

Murnau's planned film was to be an adaptation of *Four Devils*, a novella by Herman Bang, an experimental Danish writer and a friend of Henrik Ibsen. Bang's book related the misadventures of an acclaimed but ultimately tragic trapeze flyer identified in the story as Fritz Cecchi. The slim book—it was titled *De Fire Djaevle* in Danish—had been published to wide popular and critical attention in 1890.

That was three years before Alfredo was born. But he so startlingly resembled the book's protagonist inside and outside the circus world that he might have been Fritz's doppelgänger.

Like Fritz, Alfredo was born into the circus and began performing when he was little more than a tot. And also like Fritz, Alfredo momentarily stopped the hearts of almost every woman who turned her gaze his way. And just as was true for Bang's fictional character, Alfredo flirted with death in every performance. While he was famed for the perilous Triple, Bang's Fritz was hailed for the identical feat, described in his novella as "The Leap of Death."

Murnau had already cast the movie's two principals. Charles Morton, twenty years old and a new contract player with Fox, was given the part of the Fates-tempting Fritz Cecchi. He selected Janet Gaynor to portray Marion, a co-flyer in Fritz's trapeze troupe who had the name Aimee in the original Bang story. Fritz and Marion had been in love from the time both were newly orphaned children traveling with a one-wagon gypsy circus.

Morton had wavy dark hair, dashing good looks, and a physique that suggested he could have been valedictorian of a graduating class at Bernarr Macfadden's American College of Physical Education. His frame was that of a Y, moving in a straight line from his feet to his rib cage and then flaring widely right and left. As hunky as Morton was, though, he was an acrophobe. He became palsied and his teeth began chattering whenever he was directed to climb to the trapeze's perch and merely stand there and pose for the cameras. Even with Murnau's genius at using cameras to present an appearance of verisimilitude to any improbable situations, he would have been hard-pressed to trick up things enough to convincingly show Morton executing a Leap of Death from the trapeze, the maneuver key to the story. That was where Murnau wanted Alfredo to come in, to double for the leading man. Alfredo, of course, had done movie stunting before, carrying out the stunning flying for Emil Jannings's character in *Varieté*, E. A. Dupont's masterpiece.

Alfredo was a changed man after being handpicked by Murnau. He could always fly through the air. Now he gave his fellow troupers an impression that he could also walk on it.

"Alfredo was given to dark moods a lot of the time, but he was as excited as could be about going to Hollywood," Merle Evans said. "He was as bright as a new penny, a good-time Charlie, outgoing, joking, and friendly to everybody."

◆ ◆ ◆

Well, not everybody. Not Clara.

The final straw for her came November 2, 1927, the eve of the circus's final performance of its tour season. She discovered her husband in bed with another woman. It was not the first time she saw Alfredo engaged in flagrante delicto, she stated, just the last time.

Clara did not identify Alfredo's *fille de joie* by name. Nor did she specify exactly where she witnessed the pair lying together. It seems likely, though, that the other woman was Leitzel, and since Clara claimed to have witnessed "numerous" other incidents of her husband's extramarital couplings, the last pairing she saw likely occurred inside Clara and Alfredo's train quarters.

If Alfredo and Leitzel had been less than cautious in choosing a trysting place, it may have been because their libidos had completely taken control over them. They may have seen the afternoon or night of November 2 as a last chance at lovemaking for what would be a long time.

The Ringling tents were then spread in Tampa, Florida. After traveling to 119 cities in 34 states and four Canadian provinces, the circus was to present its last show of the season there the following day. Alfredo and Leitzel were then due to go their separate ways, she back to New York to resume her usual rounds of winter engagements in vaudeville, and he to Hollywood to begin the shooting for Murnau's movie, whose title he modified from Bang's *Four Devils* to *4 Devils*.

Alfredo was sick with grief at the thought of separating from Leitzel even for a short time. He was sure that once she was back in her Central Park apartment, she would be resuming her dalliances with Colonel H. Maxwell Howard. The realization was almost more than he could bear. What besides the colonel's massive wealth could Leitzel see in such an old coot? he wondered.

Clara continued to confront Alfredo about his infidelity. He refused to discuss the subject. He told her that nothing he did anymore should be a concern to her. When Clara continued to press him on the matter, Alfredo became so angry that he struck her, and, in her words, caused her "great physical pain and mental anguish."

Following the circus's season-closer in Tampa, the train traveled just thirty-five miles farther south to the circus's newly established winter quarters in Sarasota. From there, Alfredo and Lalo and Lalo's wife, Anita, boarded another train to return to Long Beach. For the first time since they had married, Clara did not accompany her husband on the trip to the Codona family home. She was on another train, this one heading for her hometown of Cincinnati.

On December 22, nine days after the tenth anniversary of his marriage to Clara, a process server delivered the court papers to Alfredo at the Long Beach home of Edward and Hortense. He did not contest any of the claims made in the document, including one charging him with "extreme cruelty" to Clara and another alleging that on "sundry occasions," he had been guilty of adultery.

Clara was granted the divorce on December 27, 1927, without a challenge.

✦ ✦ ✦

From the outside, the sprawling, wooden structure looked no more imposing than a barn, a drab, windowless cowhouse. Inside, it was another matter. Still smelling of new paint and plaster, and just-installed but yet-unused upholstered seats, its interior glimmered with the soft glow of the opulent circus theaters found in European capitals. The hall's steeply banked seats, sectioned in three tiers, surrounded an oval hippodrome. There was a great, velvet curtain at one end of the building, the entranceway for the performers, horses, and elephants.

It was January 3, 1928, the first day of production on *4 Devils* at Fox Studios off Sunset and Western Avenues in Hollywood.

The scene inside the newly slapped-up circus theater was one of outrageous chaos. In the center of the hippodrome, welders and riveters were cobbling together a massive puzzlement of steel beams that had all the actors speculating on just what it could be. Elsewhere on the earthen floor, inside a white painted wooden ring, a trainer was rehearsing a trio of elephants through headstands and two-legged pirouettes. Grips were rolling in carts, most of them piled high with lamps and coils of cable. And near the ceiling, Alfredo and Lalo, along with Edward, now sixty-nine, were jabbering in Spanish while installing the rigging for the flying trapeze.

The three, along with Anita, had motored that morning from the Codona family home, twenty-five miles away in Long Beach. They were still getting over their surprise at what they discovered on the movie lot.

"We expected to see a big top like we had on the Ringling show,"

Anita said. "Instead, we discovered a special circus building made just for his picture. It . . . must have cost a fortune."

Because the narrative for the movie mostly unfolds in Paris, Friedrich Murnau wanted to stage the trapeze performances in a setting bearing a resemblance to the Cirque d'Hiver, a four-thousand-seat circus amphitheater at 110 rue Amelot. Opened in 1852, the Cirque d'Hiver was famous not only for presenting the world's greatest circus artists but also as a haunt for such painters as Toulouse-Lautrec, Seurat, and Picasso.

For the actors, cinematographers, and lighting technicians, the first days on the set were mostly spent listening to Murnau talk about his vision for the movie, according to Anita Codona. She said a week might have gone by before any actual filming got under way.

Murnau had a reputation for being even tempered. When he was on the set, though, he refused ever to listen to any actor or technician who tried to tell him that a direction he gave could not be carried out. More than theater, opera, or dance, Murnau believed, film was an art form that had a capability of making anything that was imaginable seeable.

Among the most stunning sequences in the movie was one appearing early in the film. It introduced the quartet of trapeze artists to a Parisian audience. The Four Devils exploded through a curtain onto the hippodrome track. Each was astride a pair of galloping white horses, standing Roman-style on the backs of their mounts. Each of the Four Devils was identically costumed, wearing fleshlings, dark capes, and head caps with devil-like horns. Like gladiators who might have been entertaining a full house in Julius Caesar's Circus Maximus, they tore around the hippodrome on their tandem steeds, each with fistfuls of reins in their hands.

A *Variety* critic described the passage this way: "Murnau has given [them] a ring entrance that will set every acrobat in the world on fire when seeing it. . . . Their trapezes are lowered. As each of the trapeze flyers rides under it, they're taken aloft, their wraps falling off on the way up to the aerial pedestals."

The reviewer provided the description in 1928, but if his appraisal can still be trusted, the spectacular and richly imagined opening might draw raves even from today's film critics. Indeed, so brilliant was Murnau at conveying the pandemonium of a circus that the best scenes in such big top films as Cecil B. DeMille's Oscar-winning *The Greatest Show on Earth* of 1952 might appear pedestrian by comparison.

Murnau partly achieved his stupefying effects through a creation of his own invention, a bewildering, twenty-two-ton colossus of welded and bolted-together girders. His motor-driven invention—it was affectionately dubbed the "Go Devil" by the technical crew—was equipped with a telescoping steel strut that jutted well out into space from its center. At the far end of the strut was a large man bucket for the cameramen. Because the strut not only revolved around and around but also moved up and down like an appendage on a fairground Octopus, the cameramen could record every detail of the circus in the round.

Murnau said he had conceived the camera boom so it could "gallop after the equestrienne . . . pick out the painted tears of the clown, and jump from him to a high box to show the face of the rich lady thinking about the clown." The Go Devil did all that, and even more. Because the strut's positioning could be changed from a horizontal orientation to one that was vertical, its man bucket could be extended high into the theater's dome like the head of the long-necked Loch Ness monster. This allowed the cameramen to record the movie's heart-arresting trapeze feats, including Alfredo's Leap of Death. Not only did Alfredo carry out all of Morton's flying, but, by putting on a wig and slipping some cups under his fleshlings, he also essayed Gaynor's trapeze work.

Murnau consulted with Alfredo continually during the shooting. He wanted every detail of the film's circus to appear authentic.

Gaynor recalled one of the pair's discussions. Murnau wanted to present a scene in which Fritz would leap from the trapeze, bullet through the air, and then be caught by his legs by Marion, who was to be hanging upside down from another swinging trapeze.

"This is impossible, Mr. Murnau," Alfredo protested. "No woman can hold her weight and a man's weight with her hands. . . . This is impossible. I can't do it. No one can do it."

Murnau, though, had not asked Alfredo whether the stunt he described was possible. Of course it was possible. Everything was possible in the movies.

"This is the way we will do it," the director said curtly, and then walked away. Alfredo seemed properly chastened.

The scene, planned by Murnau for the movie's end, involved what in Herman Bang's story was a widely advertised event. Fritz Cecchi was again going to attempt the feat for which he was already famed everywhere in Europe, his Leap of Death, but now he was going to try to present it in a new way. He would not use a safety net. If he were to miss the trick now, his death would be certain.

Murnau had storyboarded the fictional Cecchi's Leap of Death as the movie's penultimate scene. In order to enact this scene for the cameras, Alfredo was called upon to execute what may have been the most daring, dazzling, and neck-risking flying maneuver of his life. Murnau wanted him to do not just The Triple but also, a split second before the turning of his somersaults, to pass through a hoop of flames.

The Go Devil was in place, with its strut high in the air, and camera and lighting men in its man bucket. After getting signals from his crew that all was ready, Murnau then cried out an order to begin the shooting.

Alfredo swung back and forth on his trapeze two or three times before reaching the right altitude in the air. Then he let go of his flybar.

He shot through the circle of fire, and, in the next hundredth of a second, with his body balled into a tight tuck, he started rising in the first of his heels-over-head, backward somersaults. Perfect. Then he turned the second of them, and then the final one. They were perfect, too. In a bat of an eyelid, he had leveled out horizontally and was streaking to Lalo at the far end of the trapeze rigging.

Afterward Murnau thanked Alfredo and told him that the spectacle he had just presented had been absolutely brilliant, everything he had wanted. Alfredo's assignment on *4 Devils* was now over, but he remained on the set to watch Murnau at work on the closing scene, one in which the photoplay fades and fades to utter blackness.

The bodies of the fictional Marion and the Great Cecchi lay on the set's earthen floor, haphazardly positioned and absolutely motionless.

Murnau was in his man bucket, high in the air and looking down at the scene with a cameraman. Through a megaphone, he kept directing the actors Gaynor and Morton to move their arms or legs just a few inches this way or that in their portrayals of the lifeless Marion and Cecchi on the ground of the make-believe Hollywood circus amphitheater.

Alfredo was on the perch of the trapeze in the building. He took in every detail of the scene below him with what may have been grim fascination.

The circus demands of its daredevils that they devote themselves entirely and irrevocably to their callings. Could Alfredo have imagined that another night might come to the circus when he met the same end as the Great Cecchi? Or, what may have been even more terrifying to him, could he have imagined a night in the big top when his beloved Leitzel could come to the same end as Marion?

CHAPTER 18

$\mathfrak{M}$ost mornings, Monday through Friday, Leitzel was ready for them at nine and stepped outside her tent. She would then start shaking a handbell and, like a Salvation Army worker outside Macy's at Christmastime, sprinkle the air with jingling. In an instant, the circus's children spilled from their family quarters on the Ringling train. Whooping, they raced in a beeline from the railroad siding to the bell ringer. Auntie Leitzel's Free Elementary School was about to begin another day.

Her school was open to all the sons and daughters of the show's performers and executives. Leitzel tried not to show favoritism, but if she had a pet, it was Dolly Jahn. She regarded the child as her protégée. She rigged up a miniature trapeze outside her tent and tutored Dolly in aerial work. She gave her private piano lessons in her train apartment.

Leitzel's attentiveness to Dolly sprang from the feelings she had for the child's father. She heroicized Hans Jahn. And she pitied him. It hurt her that so daring an artist received so little appreciation from his audiences.

Jahn was a small man, not weighing more than 140 pounds, but his arms, loins, and even his neck were ropey with muscle. His workplace was atop a forty- or fifty-foot pole held upright in delicate balance on the shoulders of his brother, Carl. There, Hans presented all manner of tricks, including, at the finish, a no-hands headstand. Hans was a perch artist, probably the best ever to appear in a sawdust ring. His was one of the most perilous acts presented in the circus, but when he completed his turns and slid down his pole, he was seldom rewarded with any more than patterings of applause.

Leitzel was always trying to shore up Jahn's spirits. She often visited his dressing room in the minutes before he was due to appear for the crowds. Sometimes she found him pacing the floor, his head down, with a rosary in his hands. Leitzel apologized at her intrusions and turned quickly to exit. Before leaving, though, a kind of handshake of their eyes took place between the two. Like fellow members in a secret coven, they seemed to recognize that they were both haunted, maybe controlled by some dark angel over which they were powerless.

◆ ◆ ◆

The towners seeing the circus's players from the seats tended to imagine them as fugitives from Scheherazade's thousand and one tales, wanderers in a rich adventure that just kept continuing on and on eternally. The wire walkers, acrobats, and clowns, though, led lives that in some ways had the metronomic regularity of the day workers who picked beans or sorted nuts, bolts, and washers on the assembly lines. They punched in for their jobs in the big top at precisely the same hours each afternoon and night. Three times a day, they filed into the cookhouse, where they took seats across the tables from the same coworkers who were there the meal before. Always they were on the move, decamping from one place every one, two, or three days to travel on to another, but almost always their peregrinations were carried on in the blankness of late night when they were asleep on the trains. When they awoke, they discovered themselves to be in a place not much different from the one they left eight or twelve hours before, almost always an overgrown field alongside a railroad siding on the outskirts of a town whose name was of no matter to them.

Because of the sameness of their days, the nomads welcomed even the most quotidian of changes in their colony—the flowering of a romance between a professional fat lady and the human skeleton in Clyde Ingalls's sideshow; the birth of lion cubs in the menagerie; the occasional death by bottle of another of those faceless animal attendants who answered to such names as Old Joe or Camel Scoop. Such changes provided them something new to talk about in the cookhouse.

One such change began evolving early in the touring season of 1928, and, because it involved the circus's queen and king, it was a doozy. Everyone on the show had cause to wonder: Just what was going on between those two now?

Alfredo started turning up at Leitzel's tent immediately following the matinee performances each day, and, at the very instant he entered her cottage, maid Mabel stepped out. She then flopped into a chaise lounge chair and, like a sentry, blocked anyone who might try to get beyond her.

Everyone on the show, of course, had known for some time that something must have been going on between the two. Just as was true the previous year, when Alfredo was still married to Clara, he was present for all her performances, always pacing the center ring far below her, and ready to try to catch her if she should ever fall. And also as was the case the season before, at least when the colonel was not traveling with the circus, Alfredo's fellow troupers often spotted him entering Leitzel's train quarters late at night.

But now, something different appeared to be happening in the relationship of Alfredo and Leitzel. When he called at her tent each late afternoon, he was carrying a rucksack that appeared to be heavily weighted.

"Because Leitzel and Alfredo were the show's biggest stars, none of the other performers were brazen enough to ask them what was going on in their late-afternoon rendezvous," said the clown, bareback rider, and trapeze flyer Freddie Freeman. "Some of us tried bribing Mabel to dish on the two, but she kept her lips zipped shut. The most popular idea was that Leitzel and Alfredo were getting together for rolls in the hay. But why was he always lugging that canvas bag?"

Weeks went by, and no one had the answer.

Practically speaking, Fred Bradna was the circus's field marshal. He had two jobs. He was ringmaster. He was also the show's "equestrian director," a title dating to the eighteenth century, when the circus's ring presentations were primarily displays of trick bareback riding. He was responsible for keeping all of the acts meshing perfectly together in the air, inside the circus's three rings and atop its two stages. At every point of the two-and-a-half-hour shows, he knew to about the quarter minute just where every performer should be in her or his act.

A onetime cavalry officer in the German army, he was as lean and tall as a Kansas cornstalk, but his most memorable physical feature was just three inches wide and was right under his nose. It was a pencil-thin mustache that bore the outline of a peaked circus tent. It looked like it could have been crayoned in black there by James Thurber.

Inside and outside the big top, Bradna was all circus business. It is unlikely he had even a casual interest in any goings-on between Leitzel and Alfredo inside her canvas sanctum sanctorum. It was Bradna, though, who finally learned the reason for Alfredo's private, between-shows calls on Leitzel, and his enlightenment came purely through happenstance.

Bradna was forever dreaming up ways in which the performers could dress up their acts. Almost instantly whenever he had such an inspiration, he sought out the performer to discuss his idea. Whether it centered on Leitzel or Alfredo is unclear, but Bradna was visited by one of his brainstorms one afternoon and, excited, immediately struck out for Leitzel's tent. As usual, Mabel was posted at its door, serving as a human DO NOT DISTURB sign. Bradna pulled rank on her. He made an end run around her chaise lounge chair and entered the tent.

Alfredo was visibly embarrassed at having been found out, but not because his boss caught him engaged in lovemaking. Bradna found him seated at a wicker table spread with children's books on social studies and ancient history. Alfredo, Bradna learned then, had been reporting to Leitzel's tent each afternoon for the same reason the circus's kids turned up there each morning. At age thirty-five, and for the first time in his life, Alfredo had started going to school.

On the trapeze, Alfredo had no peers. It was another matter when he was earthbound. When he was around others of any worldliness, he was so self-conscious about his artlessness that he sought out shadows in which to hide. He worried that his attempts at speaking would betray his lowly origins. He was, as Bradna said, "conversationally limited."

Leitzel tutored Alfredo in drama, music, and art, the areas outside the circus that mattered most to her, as well as those in the circles in which she moved outside the big top. "Her dressing tent," said Bradna, "was an ideal setting for the afternoon tête-à-tête between the two most celebrated personalities of the circus. Here Codona literally sat at Leitzel's feet . . . and caressed Lillian's two Boston terriers, Jerry and Boots, as he listened. . . . He became a virtual mooncalf in his adoration of her."

After class, Alfredo and Professora Leitzel would walk hand in hand to the cookhouse, still discussing Plato, Mozart, or the pre-Raphaelites.

Bandmaster Merle Evans remembered a distinct change that came over Alfredo:

"We'd be drinking coffee, discussing the weather maybe, and then, just like that, Alfredo would dig into his school bag and pull out a book he borrowed from Leitzel on Greek theater or whatever. He'd be as excited as could be. He'd start telling me something he just had learned about the great Greek thinkers. He'd start talking about Homer. I'd asked myself, 'Homer? Who the hell is Homer?' I thought at first it must be one of the roustabouts who hand-fed fish to the trained seals."

Could Alfredo, with ongoing tutoring from her, begin to gain new social and conversational skills? Leitzel seemed to believe so. She seemed to start valuing Alfredo as something more than the circus's prettiest male. While their joinings in the past had been carried out furtively—and, for Leitzel, perhaps, arranged mostly to satisfy certain urges—now they were open about their relationship. Just as Alfredo had always been present for all of Leitzel's performances, she was now always in the big top every time he was flying. Leitzel confided to Fanny McCloskey that she had fallen more deeply in love with Alfredo than with anyone she had ever known.

No one in the Ringling organization was more gleeful than the press agents at the signs that things had heated up between Alfredo and Leitzel. They were always looking for stories to keep the names of the circus's big stars before the public. Now they had a lollapalooza— a romance between the show's two biggest stars, its Mark Antony and

Cleopatra and Romeo and Juliet and Sir Lancelot and Queen Guine-vere. The agents were not going to let this one pass. They started leak-ing information to favored correspondents. Speculation about where the romance would lead began appearing in newspaper columns and Sunday supplements.

One Chicago writer, carried utterly away, went to her typewriter and made this announcement to her world: "The marriage of these two comets in the galaxy of circus stardom would brighten Heaven. And it will—it must—take place. It is preordained."

But what about that other man in Leitzel's life in recent years? While Colonel Howard's visits to the show had been regular occur-rences in earlier years, none of the troupers could remember seeing him on the circus lot in the first months of the 1928 season. Did Leitzel finally call things off? Or did Howard himself conclude that things could never work out, that his wife would never agree to being replaced in the Howards' Dayton, Ohio, castle?

◆ ◆ ◆

Four months into the 1928 season, in the early morning hours of July 16, the Ringling cavalcade rolled into what many of the troupers re-garded as the Promised Land. The circus raised its great tents for a nine-day stay in Chicago's Grant Park on the shore of Lake Michi-gan. The Chicago stays were always the longest for the circus any-where outside New York's Madison Square Garden and, for many of the performers and workers, also the best. A lot of them spent their mornings and late nights dunking in Lake Michigan and picnicking on the shoreline. And because they were settled in one place for more than two or three days, some of them with nagging ailments or dental problems took advantage of the time to see physicians, chiropractors, and dentists. Always, too, when the circus was in Chicago, there were ballet girls and other performers who slipped from the lot after the evening shows to see doctors who were known to perform midnight abortions.

The morning of July 21, a Saturday, dawned like those of the circus's first four days in Chicago: burnished and bright, golden and blue, sweet and good. A select group of performers that included most of the center ring stars woke up that day knowing it was going to be special.

Appearing in the big top as usual that afternoon were Leitzel and The Flying Codonas, as well as all the other performers. Instantly as the players finished their turns and took their bows, they scurried to their dressing tents. Finally, Hugo Zacchini, new to the circus that season and a big sensation, was blasted out of a cannon and soared the full length of the tent into a net. The matinee was over.

A rank of taxis was parked near the doors of the dressing tents. As the performers exited the tents, the women in their best dresses, the men in Sunday suits, they galloped to the cabs and were sped from the lot. The destination of everyone was the same, a Presbyterian church minutes from the lot.

A few people were already in the church when the first troupers arrived, among them the minister, the Reverend Harold Dozall. Also there was Leitzel's brother, Alfred Pelikan, along with his wife, Melba. After graduating from King's College in London and then receiving an advanced degree in art education at Columbia University in New York, Pelikan had settled in Milwaukee, Wisconsin, in 1925, where he held positions of distinction as both the director of the Milwaukee Art Institute and superintendent of art education for the city's public school system.

Alfred's eyes started tearing at the sight of one of the troupers who entered the church. He left his pew to embrace the man. It was Bluch Landolf, a famous clown best known for walking around the arena with a long wooden plank on his head with baskets of tomatoes balanced on both ends. Every fifty feet or so, with the plank never changing position, Bluch would do an abrupt about-face and start walking in the opposite direction.

Bluch, christened Adolph Pelikan and about fifty, was in his first season with the Ringling Bros. and Barnum & Bailey Circus, although, for decades earlier, he had been a popular auguste and trick bicycle rider in European circuses and on the vaudeville stages in America.

"I hadn't seen Uncle Adolph since I was nine or ten, and living with my mother and Edward Leamy in London," Pelikan said. "I blubbered like a baby, and my uncle did, too. How the world had changed in those twenty-five years since I had seen him last."

Everyone drifting into the church was there to attend a wedding, the wedding of Leitzel and Alfredo.

Alfredo was already in the church, but when the hour for the ceremony arrived, the bride had not yet appeared.

As was her custom whenever the circus was playing in the bigger cities, Leitzel, to get a change of scenery, had taken a room in a hotel, the Embassy in downtown Chicago. Alfredo, sensing the restlessness of the wedding guests and nervous himself, made a phone call to her hotel room. There was no answer. Had she concluded it had been a mistake for her to accept his proposal?

Another hour went by. The bride's whereabouts were still unknown.

Alfredo was now on the phone to Leitzel's room every few minutes, and still she was not answering. Some of the guests, other performers, started leaving the church, apologizing to Alfredo and explaining to him that they had to get ready for the evening show.

In 1918, at the famous Merriman's Gymnasium in Philadelphia before an audience, Leitzel did twenty-seven chin-ups with her right arm and then seventeen with her left. Some years later, before a full house at Madison Square Garden, she executed 249 of her torturous one-arm planges. Both feats were entered in the books as records for a woman.

The Guinness Book of World Records seems not to be of any help in the matter, but it may be that Leitzel chose her wedding day to establish yet another mark—this one for the longest time a bride kept a groom waiting at the altar.

Finally she did appear at the church. It was three hours later than the time when the announcement said the ceremony was to begin.

For the guests who had remained at the church, this may not have been the afternoon's most surprising event. When Leitzel did enter the church, she was accompanied by Colonel Howard.

Leitzel offered apologies to the guests for her lateness but gave no explanation for her delay. Her coworkers were left divided on the reason for her tardiness. Maybe she suddenly had come down with a case of cold feet about marrying Alfredo and just needed some toe warming from the colonel. Or maybe the colonel spent the hours trying to dissuade her from going ahead with the marriage.

Colonel Howard took a seat in the pews with the other guests. There were no other delays. The Reverend Dozall appeared on the altar in his vestments and went ahead with the ceremony. Then, after saying their "I Do's," Leitzel and Alfredo kissed. Ella Bradna, the wife of ringmaster Fred Bradna, was at the bride's side as matron of honor; Lalo was beside the groom as best man.

The postnuptial processional returning the bride and the groom to the circus lot lacked the pomp and ceremony befitting royals, but it attracted more than a little attention. The pair was ferried in what may have been the world's most freakishly fabulous automobile, a black, open-top landaulet with a large JUST MARRIED sign on its rear bumper. The car coughed like a schoolboy smoking his first cigar as it puttered over the streets and, like a rodeo horse, periodically reared up, nearly tossing Leitzel and Alfredo to the macadam. At the wheel was a uniformed chauffeur with a chalky white face and a mouth lipsticked in black. It was Myron "Butch" Baker, a producing clown for the circus. Baker had created his wonder wagon in a good-natured attempt at taking some of the shine off the ostentatious vehicle his boss, John Ringling, drove, a silver Rolls-Royce convertible.

Upon returning to Grant Park, Butch took the bride and groom on several victory laps around the tent city to let everyone know the pair had been married. There was cheering and applause from everyone. Harry A. Atwell, a prominent Chicago studio photographer, was there, snapping away. No one could remember seeing Leitzel and Codona looking happier.

As usual, Colonel Howard kept to himself, separated from the circus troupers. As the owner of a string of racing Thoroughbreds, he had known other afternoons when he finished out of the money. If his heart was unusually heavy this day, though, he took his disappointment as he took the others at the Churchill Downs, Belmont, and Santa Anita tracks, as a true sportsman. After the evening performance, he picked up the tab for a dinner of pheasant and lobster to which all the performers and executives were invited. Vintage tonics were poured from pitchers. The blowout was attended not just by circus people but also by stars from the theater and vaudeville, and by several politicians, including the governor of Illinois, Lennington Small.

◆ ◆ ◆

No one from the circus could remember another fete like it. The single attendee who did not have one of the great times of his life was Alfredo. He did not like the idea of somebody else throwing the bash, especially one of his wife's former suitors. To make matters worse, he misplaced his bride in the early part of the reception, and then spent hours trying to find her. He looked in all the tents. He checked out the train cars.

Throughout his searches, Alfredo encountered merrymakers who lifted glasses to him and offered congratulations. The groom thanked them for the good wishes, but, looking miserable, then posed a question to them.

"You see anything of Mrs. Codona?" he asked. "I know she's here. I saw her only a few hours ago at the altar."

It was the wee hours of the morning before the last of the guests, many of them zigzagging, made their way back to their nests on the train. It was about the same time when Leitzel entered the newlyweds' compartment and cheerily inquired of Alfredo whether he'd had a good time.

There were questions about whether the marriage was consummated that morning, or even anytime in the next few nights.

According to Fred Bradna, Alfredo exploded in a conniption of seismic proportions when he and his bride were finally reunited. Always thinking of the show first, this gave Bradna a lot of concern. Alfredo was left so unhinged by the humiliation Leitzel caused him,

Bradna said, that for a while, he was not sure he would ever again be the same as a trapeze flyer.

"The resultant tantrum affected his timing aloft for several days," the ringmaster observed.

The truth was that the marriage was troubled from the instant Alfredo and Leitzel looked into each other's eyes and exchanged "I Do's."

CHAPTER 19

When Alfredo entered the big top, the effect he had on the women spectators was pretty uniformly the same. Most had a sensation that a hot wind had suddenly blown into the tent, a sirocco heated by Saharan sands that in seconds caused their temperatures to shoot up. Some fumbled in their purses for opera glasses to better study the maleness that was barely concealed beneath Alfredo's white, silver-flecked tights.

Even when he was still in his teens and unmarried, Alfredo established records for conquering circus showgirls that were never broken, according to some of his fellow troupers. He likely could have had his way with at least half the single women traveling with the circus, and maybe also with some who had husbands.

As bitter as the truth must have been for him, though, he discovered that he could not have Leitzel even after taking her as a bride. Not all the time. Perhaps no man could have.

Like other women, Leitzel felt her temperature elevating at the mere sight of Alfredo. He brought on feelings of ardor in her that no man before him had ever stirred. She worshipped him. Her love for him, though, was complicated. She may have been pathologically incapable of limiting herself to one man. She may have found that by continuing relationships with other men, all of whom were admiring and were a generation older than she, she could at least partly fill a void that existed because she had never known a father and only distantly knew a mother.

The colonel appeared to be out of her life now. At least, none of Leitzel's coworkers remembered seeing him on the lot after she and Alfredo married. Other men remained in her life, though, often judges, bankers, newspaper publishers, and manufacturers, men with reputations, money, and power over others.

In most instances, Leitzel's dalliances appeared to be one-afternoon or one-night flings, and, as before she married, many of the dates were arranged by the circus's front office with an expectation that some valuable quid pro quo would be gained by the show. There is no evidence that Leitzel entered into the relationships merely for sexual gratification. Clearly, though, the liaisons must have satisfied other needs that Alfredo was unable to fulfill. His interests were almost entirely confined within the precinct in which he lived and worked, the dusty and weedy lots of the circus. Early in his courtship of Leitzel, with her urging and mentoring, he tried to extend those boundaries, but apparently he never moved them far enough outward for his wife.

Leitzel's friend Fanny McCloskey said there may have been another reason why Leitzel felt a need, even during the periods when she was married, to flutter between different men. Leitzel's need, McCloskey said, apparently grew stronger as she grew older and watched more and more of her dewy loveliness slip away.

"Probably every woman who makes a living as a performer becomes more and more sensitive about her appearance as the years go by," she observed. "This was probably especially true for Leitzel. Because of the great physical demands of her act, she sacrificed a lot of her femininity prematurely. By the time she and Alfredo married, she was nearing forty. By then, she had some of the appearance of a weight lifter. She had bulging arms and abnormally wide shoulders. She also had that ugly sore at her wrist that never healed. She was always trying to keep it hidden by covering it with ties of pretty silks."

McCloskey remembered an afternoon when she and Leitzel sat on a sofa in the star's stateroom and leafed through scrapbooks. "There were pictures from probably twenty years earlier—Leitzel's first years in the circus, vaudeville and Ziegfeld. She looked like a fairy, a tiny, delicate thing that a puff of wind could blow away like thistledown.

Leitzel got teary-eyed looking at the pictures. 'Where did she go?' she asked of the pretty young thing in the pictures. Then she put away her scrapbooks."

Whatever the reasons why Leitzel continued to carry on the serial relationships, they drove Alfredo close to near madness.

Said Merle Evans: "All of the show's married couples had quarrels now and then. But the fights that took place in Leitzel and Alfredo's car were different. They were thunder-clapping, fire-in-the-sky, the-world-is-coming-to-an-end storms. I think most of the blowups were caused by Leitzel's refusal to stop seeing other men."

The fights between Leitzel and Alfredo were also remembered by Fred Bradna. Not only did Alfredo have a furious "Latin temper," the ringmaster said, but he also had fierce pride and suffered humiliation among his cotroupers because of his wife's gallivanting.

✦ ✦ ✦

In 1928, when brand-new Ford roadsters were selling for $385, four-door sedans for $485, Alfredo's weekly salary was $500. It was a prodigious sum for the era, far higher than that of any other performer with the Ringling circus, but Leitzel. She was earning $1,200 a week.

Alfredo's lifestyle became more cushy than ever after he and Leitzel married. There were breakfasts in Leitzel's bed, served by Mabel, and Leitzel, because she had never known a love that was as exciting, observed the passing of each week of their marriage as an anniversary worthy of celebrating. Every Sunday, she gifted her husband with expensive sport coats, sweaters, silk pajamas, and jewelry. At first Alfredo felt flattered when fellow troupers remarked about his snappy dress. But as the gifts from Leitzel kept coming, he began to wonder whether she was only trying to remodel him further, to change him into someone with more refined tastes, someone like the colonel. His bride's profligate ways may also have reminded Alfredo that, as high as he had ascended in his pay grade, she was the show's only true royal, its wealthiest, most coddled star.

There was another matter that had been crumpling his ego. The Flying Codonas, as famous as they had become, still had to share the big top with other acts, usually flying troupes flanking them at either end of the hippodrome. It was different with Leitzel.

After George Denman exited the hippodrome with his herd of elephants, the house lights were extinguished for the longest time, and the people in the seats became absolutely hushed, as though they were anticipating some holy event like an apparition of the Lady of Fatima. Then, a single searchlight started playing everywhere in the house until it located Leitzel at the performers' entryway. The tiny figure appeared to be emitting a heavenly light.

Cries of adoration swelled from the crowd, and then she would start moving to the center ring, throwing kisses to every corner. Ten steps behind her, just outside the pond of light that moved with her, was Mabel Clemings, as always, holding up Leitzel's train of tulle. There were no distractions to shift the crowd's focus from the circus's biggest star for even an instant. Leitzel alone was the cynosure of all eyes. The big top was her palace entirely. In deference to the Queen of the Air, even the cotton candy and Coca-Cola peddlers stopped weaving through the stands. They moved to the aisles with their trays and, like everyone else in the house, gazed transfixedly at the slip of a woman, just ninety-five pounds. It was always that way.

◆ ◆ ◆

Because he was now regularly referred to in the press as the "Adonis of the Altitudes," Alfredo's nose, pardonably, perhaps, was sometimes in a higher position than the top of his head. And while he was generally clubby with everyone on the circus, he did show a sharpness around a few other daredevils whom he viewed as possible challengers to his status as the show's most sensational male performer.

Next to his brother Lalo, Alfredo's closest confidant may have been Art Concello. A fellow trapeze flyer, Concello was known to others as "The Half-Invisible Boy." That was because he was never fully seeable through the miasmas of cigar smoke in which he was almost always wreathed. From the time Concello was sixteen and starring with the Flying Wards trapeze troupe, he was singled out by circus experts as second only to Alfredo as a flyer. Such approbation was a matter of complete indifference to him. The boy wonder had already determined that his ambition in life was not to become a big top idol. As the son of a Portuguese railroad laborer who struggled to feed and clothe his family, Concello had another goal. He was determined to make money in the circus, real money. He aspired to be a circus boss.

"I don't care how much the biggest stars earned, it was never more than a spit in the ocean compared with what guys in the front office raked in," he declared. "Not only were they able to skim something from every ticket that was sold, but they also get a percentage on every bag of peanuts, every cup of lemonade, and every program that got into the customers' hands. That all adds up."

Ultimately Concello did work his way into the Ringling Bros. and Barnum & Bailey Circus's front office, and then, in time, became general manager of the whole shebang. It was while serving as the circus's majordomo that he brokered a deal with Cecil B. DeMille for the production of *The Greatest Show on Earth*. Charlton Heston's role in the Oscar-winning film as big top boss was said to be closely modeled after Concello.

As hard-driving as Concello could be in business matters, there was one aspect of the circus that had always brought him to tears: the performances of Alfredo Codona.

"I got goose bumps every time I saw him on the trapeze," Concello said. "Maybe you had to be a flyer yourself to realize just how great he was. It was always a religious experience for me. Maybe the feeling was like that another artist gets when he stands before a painting by Rembrandt. Codona was the absolute god."

As reverently as he spoke of his close friend, Concello conceded that Alfredo probably suffered from paranoia. He summed him up this way:

"Alfredo was not only the greatest flyer who ever lived, he was probably the greatest male performer who ever appeared in the history of the circus. Women swooned at the sight of him. In comparison with the money earned by the other stars, he was paid a fortune. He was married to the most famous circus performer of all time. You'd think a guy like that would have the world by the tail. But he was beset with insecurities. He was always looking over his shoulder, worried someone might be approaching who was going to take everything away from him."

No attraction caused Alfredo greater anguish than the Great Wallendas, high-wire walkers from Germany who became a part of the Ringling entourage in the spring of 1928.

The Wallendas' profession was an ancient one. Egyptologists have unearthed papyrus drawings recording the feats of rope dancers, or funambulists, who may have entertained the pharaohs Kheperkan and Nechtneby as long ago as 3 BC. In the passing twenty-three or twenty-four centuries, though, it seems quite certain that none of the earlier rope walkers put on spectacles that were anything like those of the Great Wallendas.

Often blindfolded, the Wallendas skipped, danced, and cartwheeled while performing on their wire sixty feet in the air without a safety net beneath them. Other times, their bodies stacked on top of one another three high, they traveled over their cable on bicycles. They made a mockery of all the laws of gravity.

Alfredo may have had good reason to believe that the quartet could bring about a reassigning of the suites reserved in the pantheon for the circus's greatest thrill acts. He might have worried that the Wallendas would eventually take over the pantheon's penthouse, forcing The Flying Codonas and even Leitzel to take quarters on a floor beneath them.

Because The Flying Codonas made regular appearances in Europe during the circus's winter off-seasons, it is likely that Alfredo had already seen the Great Wallendas perform. However it apparently was not until just days before the start of the new circus season, while the Wallendas were stringing up their rigging in Madison Square Garden, that he had direct contact with them. The first encounter was anything but pleasant, according to Karl Wallenda, the originator of the troupe.

Alfredo was on the floor, and he was livid.

"You heinie sons of bitches," he screamed up to the Wallendas. "What in hell do you think you're doing? Either you take your damned wires down immediately or I'll be up there myself to shear them."

Wallenda said that Alfredo complained that because of the way the troupe was installing its cables, their rigging would block the audience's sight lines to his trapeze.

Wallenda, twenty-three at the time, apologized. He promised Alfredo that he and the other members of his troupe would reguy their cables so they would not obstruct the view to his trapeze. Alfredo was not willing to let the matter rest.

"Maybe you heinies think you were big-time in Europe," he yelled as he angrily strode out of the arena. "But do you know what we do with acts like yours in America? We feed them to the pigs."

✦ ✦ ✦

The Wallendas were costumed in white satin sailor suits on the night of April 5 when they made their American debut. They started their turn with a series of quickly executed stunts that became progressively more mad-brained—walks, then runs, over the seventy-foot-long wire; rope skipping; headstands; frog leaps over one another. If Alfredo was watching the Great Wallendas, he may have been feeling smug. The applause for the four was polite, but nothing like the house-rocking commotions his Flying Codonas and Leitzel always detonated.

After some minutes, the air was sawed by a deep, resonant voice that perhaps bore the gravity of Moses addressing the Israelites on Mount Sinai. It was that of Ringling announcer John Stryker: "Ladies and gentlemen, the sensations of the entertainment world in all of Europe, the Gre-e-e-A-T-E Wallendas, will now attempt the most perilous feat ever presented by any circus. We beg for your absolute silence. The slightest lapse in concentration by any one of the artists could result in a terrible end for each of them."

All the lights went out except for those illuminating the Wallendas' silvery, strandlike highway near the rafters.

In a moment, one bicycle, and then another, slowly moved out onto the wire. Extending between the two cyclists, balanced on their shoulders, was a ten-foot-long pole, and standing atop the long, willowy shaft in slippered feet was Karl Wallenda. After the bicycles had traveled a quarter of the way over the cable, a seventeen-year-old girl, Helen Kreis, started walking gingerly out onto the wire. When she reached the other members of the troupe, Karl lifted her to the pole on which he was standing, and then to his shoulders, where she assumed a standing position. The Wallendas, now three bodies high, resumed the journey, moving slowly, ever so slowly.

Pandemonium exploded in the seats when the four finally came to a stop on a platform at the far end of the wire. There was shrieking, screaming, shrill whistling, the stomping of thousands of feet. There was also wailing by some spectators that verged on the hysterical. They must have been convinced that they had just witnessed a moment of spiritual transcendence, a miracle when some great power intervened and saved the four from death.

One after the other, the cyclists Joe Geiger and Herman Wallenda, Helen, and finally Karl descended their rope ladder to the floor. Over and over, they were pummeled by blows of noise that were more deafening and terrifying than any they had ever experienced at the conclusion of any of their performances.

The Great Wallendas bowed disconsolately. Then, with their heads down, they quickly exited the floor.

Karl slumped into a chair inside the troupe's dressing room. The words Alfredo Codona screamed at him a few days earlier came back, and now they stung more than ever: *Do you know what we do with acts like yours in America? We feed them to the pigs.*

The din that the Wallendas had set off was continuing unabatedly. It rattled the locked door.

In Europe, such unrestrained outbursts were received by the performers as derision from the audience, the equivalent in the United States of boxers in a fixed fight being peppered with rotten fruit.

Karl was still looking fretful.

"Well, we really stunk up the place tonight, didn't we?" he said to the other members of the troupe.

Minutes went by, and there was pounding at the door. It was Fred Bradna. The ringmaster's face was ashen.

He ordered the four to return immediately to the floor. He explained that the audience was not going to permit the circus to continue unless they reappeared to resume their bowing. He escorted the four to the center ring, and at least another five minutes went by before the crowd ended its cheering. Tears of joy ran down the cheeks of each of the Wallendas.

"I shall never forget their debut," Bradna said. "They made the biggest hit of any death-defying feat ever displayed. . . . In forty-two years [as ringmaster], I never heard another ovation of half the decibels."

Billboard summed up the Wallendas' inaugural American performance this way: "Easily the best act the circus ever had, and the most daring."

Just as Alfredo had warned the Wallendas, a great feeding did take place following their first performance in Madison Square Garden. The feeding, though, did not involve any sows and hogs, but rather Alfredo himself. He found himself eating all those bilious words he had spat out to the Wallendas a few days earlier.

◆ ◆ ◆

Leitzel's love for Alfredo continued to intensify after their marriage.

"She never really seemed to have left the honeymoon stage even after she and Alfredo had been married for some time," said Fanny McCloskey. "She was happier than I had ever seen her before. She said she would rather be in Alfredo's arms than anywhere in the world."

More and more, she declined the invitations that continued to come her way from partisans from the outside world who wanted to see her, but she seemed unable to wean herself entirely away from them. As infrequent as they had become, her after-show alliances remained a matter of soreness with Alfredo, especially since, during this same period, Leitzel was insisting that he rid himself of a woman who still remained in his life.

That woman was his ex-wife, Clara Curtain Codona. She had continued as a member of The Flying Codonas even after she and Alfredo had divorced the previous year. Alfredo had no interest in reestablishing a romantic relationship with Clara, but he still valued her as being almost indispensable to his flying troupe. Because she had been with the act for a dozen years, she could gauge the timing of each of the troupe's stunts to split seconds.

Leitzel, though, not only persisted in her demand that Alfredo eliminate Clara from the troupe once and for all, but she also insisted on having final say in the selection of her successor. After considering the personalities and big top talents of all the young women touring with the show, Leitzel settled on an Australian-born showgirl, Vera Bruce, as Clara's replacement.

Bruce, twenty, was tall and thin, but also statuesque. She wore her brown hair in a modish bob with finger waves. She would be striking on the trapeze perch, Leitzel assured Alfredo.

Bruce had been touring with the circus for three or four years. Her principal assignment with the circus was that of a bareback rider. She was lovely to look at, but she was never a performer who distinguished herself with the razzle-dazzle of many others in the equestrian displays, among them her brother, Clary Bruce. Vera also appeared as an extra in several of the circus's other displays. She was one of a dozen or so women and men who struck different poses in the Living Statues, and also appeared in the aerial ballets, showy fillers in which the show's shapeliest chorines performed on webs that were strung from the rafters.

It is unlikely Leitzel pushed for Vera as Clara's replacement because she was unusually impressed with her performing talents. Rather, she may have felt some empathy for Vera because, like her, she was orphaned as a child. Immediately after her birth, her father, a circus bandmaster, and her mother, a trapeze artist, placed her in the care of Catholic nuns in an Australian convent. Vera remained there until she was sixteen. In the mid-1920s, she traveled to the United States with her mother, Annie, and Clary to join the Rieffenach family riding troupe.

Vera was unlike the show's other single younger women. Most of the others had but one thing on their minds, and for many of them, that involved someone who wore the snuggest white tights to work every day. Vera was chaperoned everywhere by her mother, then widowed and retired from the big top. She was also serious in manner, a loner, and had few friends on the show.

Alfredo was resentful that Leitzel would even presume to suggest that he fire Clara and replace her with someone she, not he, had recruited. He was the originator of the troupe and believed he had always done just fine managing it.

Annie Bruce, along with Vera and Clary, shared quarters on the train near those of Leitzel and Alfredo. Annie said she often heard blowups between the two over Leitzel's insistence that he hire her daughter. The disturbances did not involve only shouting, Annie said, but also the exploding of teacups and dishes hitting the walls. "Sometimes Leitzel's temper got the better of her," Annie explained. "Objects flew from her hands to Alfredo's head."

As was true of almost every battle the couple ever fought, though, Leitzel emerged triumphant in this one. Alfredo, beaten down, finally surrendered to her. Vera was on her way to becoming a member of the greatest flying trapeze act of all time. He agreed to take her in as an apprentice. Clara was on her way out.

The good feeling that Leitzel had over her victory would not last. In time she would come to view her sponsorship of the young, pretty Australian as the most ruinous move of her life. It would take somewhat longer for Alfredo, but ultimately he, too, would come to rue the day he had agreed to try transforming an unknown, barely noticed extra into a big top star, a Flying Codona.

*P*atches of gray and rust-colored snow still littered the streets, but finally after a harsh winter, signs of spring were starting to appear in New York City. Central Park was greening and birds were feathering nests in the trees lining the streets. The windowsills outside the tenements were crowded with clay pots from which scallions, daisies, and daffodils were beginning to push up.

It was 1929, early March. As was true every year at this time in New York, the sides of auto shops, stores, and fences blazed with luridly colored, newly broomed-up posters. The Ringling Bros. and Barnum & Bailey Circus was returning.

The paper murals, some of them twenty, thirty feet wide, twelve, sixteen feet high, transformed the city into an outdoor museum. There were pictures everywhere with the most improbable sights—a human missile, Hugo Zacchini, shot from the smoking barrel of a giant cannon and soaring two hundred feet through space; a sea lion that the poster artists suggested was greater in size than *Tyrannosaurus rex*; the white faces of one hundred laughing, leering, weeping, and lusting clowns.

Of all pictorials, the most ubiquitous of them advertised the circus's biggest star of the last fifteen years. THE DAINTY MISS LEITZEL, THE WORLD'S MOST MARVELOUS GYMNAST. She looked a bit coquettish on the posters. She wore an expression that could be read as come-hither. She was wearing high heels, the briefest of bloomers, and ankle socks.

The circus was due to play the New York Coliseum in the Bronx from March 21 through March 30, and then move to Madison Square Garden in Manhattan on April 1 for a three-week stay. But New Yorkers who were set on seeing Leitzel this year would have to settle for only her likeness on the posters.

The news had not been made public, but there was grave concern among John Ringling and the show's other executives about whether Leitzel would ever appear in a circus ring again. There was even concern about whether she was going to live, and, if so, whether it would be with both her arms.

Leitzel was weak from double pneumonia, an ailment she contracted abroad while she and The Flying Codonas were performing in Paris and London late in 1928. But double pneumonia may not have been the worst of her troubles. After years of being gnawed at by her ropes, her right arm was now dangerously diseased. She had phlebitis, an infection of the vessels in her arm.

She had been hospitalized for a short time, but then released with orders that she suspend all physical activity and spend all her time in bed. Physicians warned her that if the blood clots inside the arm vessels broke away and traveled to her lungs, the effect would likely be fatal. Her days as a performer were over, they said. Mabel Clemings, Leitzel's devoted maid, housekeeper, secretary, and confidante, now assumed an additional role, that of a nurse. She saw to it that Leitzel regularly took her prescribed medications. She applied compresses to Leitzel's arm day and night.

It surprised the medical specialists, but after suspending performing for months and withdrawing the daily feedings she gave to her ropes, her cankered arm started to show improvement. Still, doctors advised her against resuming her performances or the infection would return.

Leitzel likely smiled wryly at the warnings. What she had not told the physicians was that she had already begun preparing for a comeback. Late each night in the Coliseum, and then in the Garden, after the audiences had gone home, she worked at slamming her muscles back into shape, "twisting, turning, bending nearly one hundred feet in the air on her rope."

She could never give up performing. It was what she breathed for.

One doctor with whom she consulted during this time suggested that if she absolutely refused to retire from the spotlight, maybe she could alter her act in a way that would not return her right arm to a running sore. He asked if she could perform her planges with her left arm.

"Easily," she said.

The doctor appeared relieved.

"Then it seems to me the matter is solved."

Leitzel shook her head. She would perform her act with her right arm as always, she said.

"All right." The doctor sighed. "The slightest increase in the infection will cause blood poisoning. You know what that means? Amputation. . . . Don't you understand?"

Leitzel studied her left arm appraisingly, and then moved it closer to the doctor's gaze.

"I understand," she answered, "but you don't. My right arm is scarred. I've become accustomed to seeing the burns on it. But my left arm is still pretty. After all, doctor, I am a woman."

✦ ✦ ✦

Because she had to recover not only from pneumonia but also from her infected arm, Leitzel was unable to appear at any of the six weeks of shows the circus presented in New York at the start of the 1929 season, but she was able to rejoin the show on April 25 for the first of its six days of performances in Boston.

Because he had always viewed the demands that she made on the circus to be extortionate, Mister John had never been one of her greatest fans. At the same time, though, he recognized that her name resonated with the public as widely as those of such other contemporary idols as Babe Ruth, Valentino, and Clara Bow. He was aware, too, that he could thank Leitzel, more than any other single attraction, for all the Cranach, Tiepolo, Rubens, and Gainsborough masterpieces he had in his art collection, along with one or two of the twenty-one galleries that had been constructed in his massive new John and Mable Ringling

Museum of Art on his property in Sarasota, Florida. She generated far more money for the circus than any other performer in its history.

✦ ✦ ✦

Leitzel was disbelieving at first. Then she started stewing.

How could Mister John do this to her? She made up her mind that somehow she was going to make him rue his decision. She would show him once and for all.

While the circus had been playing Boston, she had learned that he had reduced her weekly pay from $1,200 to $1,100.

Even with the cut, her pay was still well more than double that of any other single star with the show. It was also far more than the per capita income for working-class families at the time, which was $750 a year. Certainly the reduction would not necessitate any scrimping on her part, but, again and again, she kept asking herself how Mister John could have done this to her. Since joining the circus, there had never been a year when she had not gotten a sizable raise.

Did he now see her as a star whose light was beginning to fade? Did he not see how she was received in Boston? A standing ovation when she appeared before the audience the first night of her comeback. An even longer standing ovation after she completed her performance and took her bows.

John's decision to cut Leitzel's pay likely had nothing to do with a feeling that her star was losing some of its glimmer. He was beginning to worry. For the first time ever during the 1920s, the circus's business had been down in New York, and there were other indicators that the nation was heading for an economic downturn. In almost every sector of the economy, manufacturers were reporting that their inventories were up and that consumer spending was decreasing. They were starting to lay off employees.

Leitzel was not the only one in the show having her salary pared. Everyone started getting smaller pay envelopes, including Alfredo Codona, whose weekly earnings dropped from $500 to $400.

Still, Leitzel took it all personally. She continued to brood over the cut. She saw it as a sign that Mister John was devaluing her importance as the show's star attraction and leading ambassador with the press.

✦ ✦ ✦

Lewis Perez and James Evans had just been welcomed into Leitzel and Alfredo's apartment on the train. Both appeared to be bedazzled. Their gazes bounced off the furnishings in the long, narrow quarters—the grand piano, the Atwater Kent radio, the RCA Victrola phonograph, and the silver services and china cups that a uniformed maid had just placed on a table before them. The two might have been having the same thought: so this is how stars, really big circus stars, live and travel.

Lewis Perez and James Evans, both thirty-three, were performers. They were perch pole artists and jugglers, and had been a team for thirteen years. Mostly their appearances had always been made at small-time venues—county fairs, firemen picnics, and on high school football fields. But the two were now about to present the most important performance of their lives, and they would have an audience of just two—three, if maid Mabel could be counted.

Perez and Evans sought out Alfredo and Leitzel because they had a proposition, a proposition that they were confident was wired and cinched, can't-miss, and absolutely surefire. They wanted to partner with them in the creation of a new circus, a railroad circus.

They addressed Alfredo and Leitzel deferentially, but also with earnestness. They were frank in stating they themselves would not have a lot of money to invest in the venture. As entertainers who tramped the small-time, they had never been able to salt away much money. As small as their savings were, though, they were willing to bet everything they had on the show. They were also willing to assume whatever roles Alfredo and Leitzel might see for them in the circus. They had no doubt that the show would be a major success. How could it be otherwise? It would be headlined by Lillian Leitzel and The Flying Codonas, the two greatest big top attractions in the world.

Perez and Evans probably could have ended their pitch right then and there.

Alfredo's expression had changed to one of rapture. He saw the picture the two men had painted. The circus would include a sleek train and big top. In gold letters so big they could be read a block away, both the train and the tent would be emblazoned with the title *THE GREAT CODONA CIRCUS.*

Like her husband, Leitzel, too, appeared to have been transported to another place. She had not stopped chafing since that day in Boston a couple months earlier when she learned Mister John had cut her pay. She had vowed then that she would get even with him somehow. The two guests in their train quarters were now showing her the way. She and Alfredo would operate their own circus. They would make all the decisions concerning its operations. Best of all, they would no longer have to content themselves with whatever Mister John chose to dribble out to them.

It was somewhere in Ohio and sometime in June when Alfredo and Leitzel had their first meeting with Perez and Evans. Within a month or a month and a half, the quartet had advanced so far with the plans that they were ready to reveal the first details to the entertainment press.

The Great Codona Circus would be a one-ring, European-style show, presented inside a round big top 160 feet in diameter. The new circus was already booked to present its premiere performance in the border town of Laredo, Texas. From there, it would travel south, moving through Mexico and then through Central and South America. In all, the Great Codona Circus would feature twenty-one different acts, including The Flying Codonas and Leitzel and, of course, the perch pole artists and jugglers Lewis Perez and James Evans.

◆ ◆ ◆

When the telegram from James Evans reached Alfredo and Leitzel on the Ringling lot in Alexandria, Minnesota, on August 9, 1929, Alfredo and Leitzel were overtaken with shock, and then with dread that left them sick.

Lewis Perez was dead. He had broken his neck when, along with the perch pole that had been balanced on Evans's shoulders, he crashed twenty-five feet to a stage inside the grandstand at the Tri-State Fair at Burlington, Iowa.

There had been no way of preventing the accident. Just as Perez had done in hundreds, maybe thousands, of performances before, he had put his feet into the stirrups at the top of the pole and then, like a flag atop a staff, extended his body out horizontally. In the next instant, a great gust of wind appeared and swiped at him. Evans tried to keep the pole upright. He moved this way and that way on the stage, but then the pole started its downward lean and there was no way for him to stop Perez's crash.

Everyone had tried to assure Evans that he was blameless, but he remained knifed with guilt. If only he had had the strength to overcome the force of the wind.

The dream of having roles in the management of a circus was one Evans and Perez shared from the time they had become a team more than a dozen years earlier. Evans told Alfredo and Leitzel that he no longer thought he could continue in the plan to create the Great Codona Circus.

"'Laugh, clown, laugh,'" he said bitterly. "That's all right for the movies. But just try it."

Perez was dead, and now it sounded like Evans was abandoning the venture. Were these omens? Was the Great Codona Circus now dead, too? Leitzel and Alfredo had already made a sizable investment in the enterprise. Their purchases included a small train, a big top, seating, and a power generator. They had also entered into contracts with most of the circus's performers. Alfredo and Leitzel were queasy but decided they would go ahead with the plan anyway.

✦ ✦ ✦

Within a week after the 1929 Ringling tour ended in October, Alfredo and Leitzel were in Nuevo Laredo, Mexico, just across the Texas border, and carrying out dress rehearsals with the other performers.

Leitzel apparently was confident that she would never be returning to her old employer. She had been given headline billing in all the ads that started appearing daily in the *Laredo Morning Times* and the Spanish-language *Tiempo de Laredo*, and was described this way:

Miss Leitzel

The Queen of the Air
Former Star of the Ringling Bros.

When flying on the trapeze, Alfredo's sense of timing was as exquisitely precise as the orbital moves of the planets, but it utterly failed him choosing the date for the grand opening of the Great Codona Circus. He scheduled the premiere for November 16, 1929, a Saturday night. That day Nuevo Laredo was slammed by a blizzard, an event not likely to happen there at that time of year more than once in a century or two.

"It was a disaster," remembered Edna Antes, who was trying to sell tickets the night of the opening. "Icicles were hanging from the big top. We went ahead with the show, but it was pretty much a dry run. Hardly anybody ventured out. Mexicans won't go anywhere when it's freezing and snowing."

In addition to Leitzel's aerial act and The Flying Codonas, the show featured about twenty attractions, many of them poached from the Ringling circus, including The Arleys, another perch pole act; Bluch Landolf, Leitzel's uncle and producer of the clown acts; the Sabots, a bareback riding troupe; Charlotte Shives, who performed on a single trapeze; and Vera Bruce, who appeared as an equestrienne as well as the third member of Alfredo and Lalo's flying trapeze act. After initially telling Alfredo and Leitzel that he was too brokenhearted after the death of his partner, Perez, to ever perform again, Evans had a change of mind and decided to become a part of the new circus, after all. As a small investor in the show's creation, he took on some of its management tasks, and also appeared in the ring as a juggler.

A *Billboard* correspondent, on hand for the premiere of the Great Codona Circus, described its attractions as "extensively entertaining," but enthused even more about the classy impression its canvas theater made. The show, he wrote, was a creation of "unusual splendor, attractiveness and comfort [with] no expense or trouble . . . spared by management to provide the show with the most modern equipment." Among the features that attracted the writer's eye were the circus's "large, spacious boxes" and its "specially built electrical plant [that] brilliantly lighted the 160 feet [in diameter] top." The circus was scheduled to remain in Nuevo Laredo for "only a few days," according to the newspaper ads, and then start on the southward tour that would eventually take it to South America. The attendance picked up in Nuevo Laredo after the snow melted, but only slightly.

"We had four or five clowns with the show and one of them was George Harmon, a midget who went by the professional name of Yo-Yo," said Edna Antes. "Families with eight or ten kids came to the lot, trying to steal a free glimpse of Yo-Yo and drink in the band music drifting through the tent walls to the outside. Then, without leaving behind so much as a peso with the show, the families returned to their homes."

Not only had Alfredo opened his circus on a night of hateful weather, but, more broadly, he launched the show during the worst economic period in twentieth-century history. On October 29, barely two weeks before his circus opened for business, the Great Wall Street Crash of 1929 occurred, ushering in the deepest and darkest depression of the twentieth century. Almost overnight, the unemployment rate in the United States soared to nearly 25 percent. In cities across America, colonies started to sprout up with shacks made from scavenged box wood, sign tin, straw, and cardboard.

From the beginning of the planning, Perez and Evans and even Leitzel tried disabusing Alfredo of his belief that it would be a good idea to travel through Latin America with the circus. The three suggested that because of the prominence of the Codona name with American circus audiences, and also those of Leitzel and other Ringling performers traveling with the show, the enterprise figured to have its greatest success in the States. Alfredo, though, remained insistent in wanting to carry out the tour south of the Rio Grande. Three and a half decades earlier Edward Codona, the family patriarch, had traveled through Mexico with his small family circus, the Gran Circo Codona, and it was there in 1893, while the family was in Hermosilla, Sonora, that Alfredo was born. Alfredo's urge to return to Mexico may have been impelled by the same impulse that sends millions of humming-birds migrating from North America to Mexico each fall.

"Alfredo was my brother-in-law, and I loved him dearly," said Anita Codona, "but he could be as stubborn as an old mule. He was still con-vinced he could make a go of the circus in Mexico even though our ex-perience in Nuevo Laredo was awful and the world was in a depression."

The caravan set out on the first leg of its journey south of the bor-der, a trip of 325 miles to Victoria.

"The train was nothing like the one we had become used to while traveling with Ringling," Anita recalled. "There were three or four baggage cars for the big top, the seating, the electrical plant, and the Sadots' horses. There was just one passenger car. There were no beds. It was miserable, especially for married couples. All of us had slept on wicker seats. To make matters worse, there was a family traveling with us that presented a trained dog act in the show, the Millers. They were always yipping and running everywhere in the car, and scrapping with a dog Bluch had brought along."

In the plans for the new circus that were outlined in the first stories in the trade papers, it was reported that the show would be making ap-pearances of one or two weeks in most cities and, in Mexico City, likely have a stay of a month or two. But because the Great Codona Cir-cus tent was nearly empty for the performances in Victoria, the show pulled up stakes after a day or two and traveled farther south to the port city of Tampico.

"All the time we moved through Mexico, we were hearing about how terrible the Depression was in the United States—the soup lines, the Hoovervilles, the millionaires jumping from skyscrapers because they lost everything," said Anita. "As bad as things were in the States, though, they couldn't have been nearly as awful as they were in Mexico.

Most people there always worked for low wages, and now there was no work for them. About the only people we saw in our tent were town officials—mayors and police chiefs and the like, and they were given free tickets for themselves and their families."

The entire troupe was on the brink of mutiny by the time the circus got to Tampico.

"We were afraid we were going to be left stranded in Mexico with no way to get back to the States," said Paul Arley, who with his wife, Loula, and Fanny McCloskey presented the perch pole act. "The show was hardly even taking in enough money to feed us. Bluch was our cook. He'd go to the markets and try to trade tickets for groceries. Mostly he came back to the lot with nothing but some bags of rice and beans. Sometimes, though, he was lucky enough to get some live chickens and fresh vegetables. He'd throw everything into a pot on a campfire. These were the only times we enjoyed decent meals."

The show had been scheduled to head from Tampico to Mexico City, where, according to the original plan, Alfredo had expected it to settle in for a month or longer. Alfredo, though, instructed the train's engineer to reverse the show's course and travel north to Monterrey. There, Alfredo, Leitzel, and James Evans handed everyone letters typed on stationery printed with the title "Great Codona Circus— Touring Mexico and South America."

Monterrey, N. L., Dec. 2nd, 1929

Dear Sir:

As per contract and owing to the general conditions of the country, we regret very much to advise you that we are compelled to close our season at this time and hereby serve you with two weeks' notice.

We will ship the outfit back to the States at the end of the engagement here, and if you care to ride back with the show on the train and have your baggage go as far as Laredo, we will be very glad to take it.

Sincerely yours,
Great Codona Circus

His store of hope almost gone, Alfredo joined with the show's men in raising the tent in Monterrey, Mexico's third largest city and an important business and industrial center.

As was true of all their stops elsewhere, the performers and musicians found themselves putting on shows where they outnumbered the spectators in the seats.

After a day or two, the circus train was on the move again. Everyone was beaten up, beaten down, bedraggled. Because the show had never been in one place long enough for them to take care of personal matters, like laundry, everyone was smelling as rankly as their co-tenants inside the stuffy passenger car, the Millers' dogs. All the travelers ached for a night of uninterrupted sleep, something impossible in a car with hard, upright seats, yipping dogs, and crowded with two dozen other travelers. More troubling to everyone, though, was their uncertainty about what was ahead. They had signed on with the circus with an expectation of having work for a year or more. What were they going to do now? The world had become a different place. They were funnymen, head standers, bareback riders, rope swingers, drum pounders, and horn tootlers with talents that no longer seemed merchandisable.

As despairing as the troupers were, a day did come in the second week of December when, at least for a little while, the attachés of the Great Codona Circus rejoiced. The cavalcade of the Great Codona Circus had just crossed the Mexico border and had rolled to a stop in Laredo, Texas.

"We were home again, back in America," said Fanny McCloskey. "We felt like prisoners of war who had just been airlifted to the United States after having been in a strange and hostile country. We all kissed the ground."

A few of the troupers immediately bought train tickets to start on trips back to their homes in Minnesota, Kansas, and Arkansas, but most of them stayed behind in Laredo.

The Great Codona Circus had a final stand to make, its only one on American soil. A first matter of business for Alfredo was to go to the *Laredo Morning Times* to arrange for advertising. Meanwhile others in the show fanned around the town of forty thousand to hang posters in the stores, barbershops, and bars.

✦ ✦ ✦

The Great Codona Circus, "The Show Beautiful," as it was subtitled in the advertising, opened in Laredo at nine forty-five the night of December 31, 1929.

Leitzel, "The Queen of the Air . . . Former Star of Ringling Bros.," as she was billed, and likely the most prominent entertainer ever to appear in the town, presented a show that was as dazzling as any she had ever given in Madison Square Garden or Ziegfeld's New Amsterdam Theatre. Alfredo, Lalo, and Vera were flawless on the flying trapeze. Anita Codona, all in red and clicking castanets, did a flamenco dance in a reprisal of those she did in vaudeville when she and Lalo first met. Bluch, his face smudgy with burned cork and wearing a hobo's outfit, absurdly walked around the ring with his eight-foot plank on his head, bushels of tomatoes balanced at its ends.

The show ended just minutes before midnight. At the stroke of twelve o'clock, the bells of Laredo's churches began pealing everywhere in town, signaling the beginning of a New Year.

Its seats had only been about half filled, but the Great Codona Circus had just performed to the biggest audience of its forty-five days of life. The performers, all of them still in costume, gathered as one inside the sawdust ring and then the band resumed its playing. Leitzel and Codona, along with the troupers that had remained with the troupe, started singing, many of them with tears streaming down their cheeks. The audience, immediately recognizing the song, joined in. The band was playing "Auld Lang Syne."

PART FOUR

A COMBINATION IMAGE SHOWING MEMBERS OF THE FLYING CODONAS
PERFORMING ON THE TRAPEZE (ABOVE) AND LYING ON THE SAFETY NET.
ALFREDO CODONA IS ON THE LEFT, VERA BRUCE IS IN THE CENTER, AND
LALO CODONA IS ON THE RIGHT. (AUTHOR'S COLLECTION)

CHAPTER 21

Before the end of January 1930, Leitzel and Alfredo were resituated in her lustrous, richly furnished New York apartment. Both may have been wondering how long they could remain there.

Without providing specific figures, the newspapers reported that Leitzel and Alfredo had suffered huge financial losses in their attempt at starting their own circus. Leitzel's brother, Alfred, believed the pair might have been on the verge of bankruptcy at this time.

"My sister never told me how much they lost," he said. "It could have been $100,000, the equivalent of millions today. And while she made a lot of money in the circus and vaudeville, she really never saved that much. She always lived the high style—fancy apartments, diamonds, furs, big cars, chauffeurs, maids. She was also very free about handing out money, whether it was for family members, friends or down-and-outs on the circus. Alfredo, too, made more than a comfortable living, but nothing close to my sister's pay. Whatever money he invested in the circus, it was likely just a fraction of Leitzel's investment."

The egos of both Leitzel and Alfredo were so outsize that there had never been a lot of room left in their psyches for humility. They were out of work now, though, and maybe also almost out of money. They had to try to get their old jobs back with the Ringling show.

Initially they approached Pat Valdo, the show's personnel director, although they were aware that ultimately it would be John Ringling who would make any decisions about whether there was a place for them in the circus. Valdo, though, was clear on one matter: if there was any chance that they could regain employment with the circus, they would have to agree to sharp cuts in their pay from their earlier years. Because of the Depression, there had been a great downturn in the circus's gates in the last months of the 1929 tour, and Mister John was on pins and needles about what the season ahead would be like.

He, along with his sister-in-law, Edie Ringling, Charley's widow, now owned every railroad circus of significance in America. Months earlier, just before the crash on Wall Street, Mister John had signed a note for nearly two million dollars to buy the American Circus Corporation, a conglomerate with five other shows—the Al G. Barnes, Hagenbeck-Wallace, John Robinson, and Sells-Floto Circuses, and Buffalo Bill's Wild West Show. With these added properties, Mister John's circus empire had now grown to forty-five hundred employees, and another two hundred railroad cars.

Pat Valdo was an affable man, and one who particularly admired Codona and Leitzel. The circus's personnel manager went back and forth with Mister John on behalf of the pair, pleading with him to reinstate them.

John may not have been even casually interested in hearing about the reverses Leitzel and Alfredo suffered. The tens of thousands of acres of undeveloped land he owned in Florida, Montana, and elsewhere were now worth but a small fraction of his original investment in them. Likewise, the fat portfolio of stocks and bonds that he had amassed over the years was now bleeding like a slaughtered pig. He was probably wondering at the time how he was going to write a check for his next Titian or Rubens, but, at Valdo's urgings, he agreed to take back both Leitzel and The Flying Codonas, the biggest attractions in the six decades of The Greatest Show on Earth.

❖ ❖ ❖

New York's circus fans were no less rabid than its Yankees crazies. For a segment of the city's population, opening day of a new Ringling Bros. and Barnum & Bailey season was always regarded as a holy day, a second Christmas or Easter. They would not miss the observance of such an occasion for anything, not even, apparently, for a Great Depression.

Some of the spectators may have bought the tickets with money raised by spending the year hunting for empty So-Da-Licious and Coca-Cola bottles and turning them in for the refunds. A few others might have pawned gold teeth removed from the mouths of grandfathers moments before their caskets were lowered into the ground. Surprisingly, as bleak as the times were, every one of the fifteen thousand seats in the New York Coliseum was occupied the night of March 27 when the Ringling Bros. and Barnum & Bailey Circus opened its 1930 season.

The most sensational feature of the new circus was not a ring act but a sideshow attraction, seven women from a village of grass huts in equatorial Africa. The women were topless and wearing see-through raffia skirts when, along with two of their chieftains, they stepped down the gangplank of the boat that brought them into New York. Some in the harbor may have remarked that the septet appeared underdressed for such a cool and breezy day, but it probably was not their brief costuming that many were studying. Each of the women had lips that, like the bills on ducks, cantilevered off their faces into space a full six or eight inches. The ladies—they were Ubangi tribeswomen—gained their prodigious-size lips during their growth years when, like their mothers, grandmothers, and great-grandmothers before them, they had series of progressively larger disks placed into their mouths, permanently stretching the flesh around them.

Posters of the Ubangi women were everywhere in the city. THE EDUCATIONAL FEATURE OF ALL-TIME! the bills all screeched. Such a claim was excessive, surely, but maybe a case could be made for the instructional value of the circus's new sensation. The women seemed to add credence to the observation that beauty is in the eyes of the beholder. It was said that the men in the Ubangi women's village were affected by the sight of the lips in the same way that men in other parts of the world were moved by exposed female body parts north of the waist and south of the shoulders.

The 1930 show was among the strongest Ringling shows ever. The Great Wallendas were returned for a third year; Hugo Zacchini, the human cannonball, for a fourth; and Leitzel and The Flying Codonas were also back, and, as before, still holding positions as headliners.

Leitzel and Alfredo were ebullient at having been restored to The Greatest Show on Earth. They were back among friends. They again had paying work. And now when they were performing, they again were appearing in front of thousands, not the small handfuls before which they appeared when their star-crossed and short-lived Great Codona Circus rolled through Mexico.

For Leitzel, though, the rejoicing lasted for but the first two days of the new season. The third was among the bleakest she had ever known.

◆ ◆ ◆

Hans Jahn had already essayed most of his routines atop his forty-foot wooden pole, balanced upright on the shoulders of his brother, Carl.

So far, everything had gone smoothly for him in the Coliseum in the Bronx on this night of April 29, 1930, the third of the new Ringling season.

Hans had but one more stunt to show the crowd, his act-finishing, no-arms headstand. Then he could shimmy down the pole, take his bows with Carl, and call it another night.

He slid a cushioned, disklike headrest at the top of the pole. Next, he gripped the pole with his powerful hands, placed his head into the cushion, and, with no apparent strain, lifted into the headstand. In another moment, he loosed his hands and was balancing on his head, his arms and legs akimbo.

No one knew what happened next. Hans seemed to have been suddenly possessed by a demon. He appeared to be suffering some torture. The flesh on his face became lopsided. His arms first and then his entire body started to shudder violently.

And then Hans was falling.

He slammed into Carl a little more than three-quarters of his way down, knocking his brother unconscious, and then crashed headfirst onto the stage.

Leitzel inside her private tent circa 1920. *(Author's collection)*

Lillian Leitzel in her dressing tent, with her longtime maid, Mabel, who is attending to her hair. *(Courtesy of Circus World Museum, Baraboo, WI)*

Nellie and Leitzel in Paris in 1921. By this time Nellie had reinvented herself as "Zoe, the Aerial Venus," a striptease aerialist, and had been appearing for several years in cabarets throughout Europe, as well as at Coney Island in New York. Leitzel, during the same period, was comfortably settled into being queen of the big top, the highest-paid, most coddled, and most beloved star in the history of the circus. *(Author's collection)*

Clyde Ingalls, manager of the Ringling Bros. and Barnum & Bailey sideshow, and Leitzel's second husband, circa 1920. *(Author's collection)*

Leitzel with two pupils in her traveling school, Auntie Leitzel's Free Elementary
School, circa early 1920s. *(Courtesy of Circus World Museum, Baraboo, WI)*

Papa Edward Codona, flanked by Lalo and Alfredo, mentored his sons for years before the two mastered The Triple, the big top's most glorious trapeze maneuver in their time, and the most perilous. *(Author's collection.)*

Aerial view of The Flying Codonas. Lalo Codona swings from the trapeze and reaches out to brother Alfredo Codona, who is in flight. *(Courtesy of Circus World Museum, Baraboo, WI)*

Leitzel poses for the camera on a circus back lot, standing on the hood of a Packard automobile. Several circus tents can be seen in the background. *(Author's collection)*

Alfredo Codona sitting on a trapeze. *(Courtesy of Circus World Museum, Baraboo, WI)*

Leitzel performing in an open-air arena, swinging one-armed from a rope. *(Courtesy of Circus World Museum, Baraboo, WI)*

The Flying Codonas, mistakenly renamed "The 3 Codonas" in this poster from the early 1930s, often traveled to Europe at the conclusion of the Ringling Bros. and Barnum & Bailey Circus's annual summer touring seasons. There, they appeared in such major venues as the Cirque d'Hiver in Paris, the Wintergarten in Berlin, and the Circus Schumann in Denmark and Germany, which toured widely on the Continent. *(Courtesy of the Circus World Museum, Baraboo, WI)*

Alfredo Codona and Vera Bruce stand on a suspended platform, ready for a performance under the big top. *(Author's collection)*

Alfredo Codona and J. A. Westmoreland of the Circus Fans of America stand before the flower-adorned monument *Reunion*, in Inglewood Cemetery, Inglewood, California. Alfredo commissioned an Italian sculptor to create the stone memorial after Leitzel plunged to her death while performing in Copenhagen in 1931. *(Courtesy of Circus World Museum, Baraboo, WI)*

Forty clowns spewed onto the hippodrome floor, trying to divert the crowd's attention from the gruesome scene. Then the Jahn brothers were carried from the arena by attendants with stretchers.

Leitzel learned of the accident while in her dressing room. She raced to the room of the Jahn brothers. Hans's wife, Gretchen, was already inside, and so was Dolly, the couple's eight-year-old daughter. Both were looking down at Hans's broken head and mangled body.

Gretchen was pleading with her husband to start breathing again, to open his eyes, to move a finger, anything.

Leitzel embraced Gretchen and then took eight-year-old Dolly into her arms.

Carl revived in a few minutes. He tried to leave his stretcher to see his brother, to try to talk to him. The attendants struggled to hold him down on his mattress. An ambulance was on its way for him.

But it would be a hearse that carried Hans from the Coliseum.

"What could have happened?" Gretchen sobbed. "He did that trick thousands of times before."

Leitzel was shaking. Her face was the color of paraffin. She may have been wondering if Hans had been stalked this night by the same ghost that still sometimes appeared when she was on her rings, pleading remorsefully: "Why don't you let go? You're tired. . . . The audience won't care. There is plenty more for them to look at. . . . Let go! Let go! Why go through all this effort when you can just drop to the ground and rest?"

There was no other family on the show to whom Leitzel felt closer than the Jahns. She wanted to do or say something to comfort Gretchen and Dolly, but felt helpless.

Maybe she thought she was only thinking the words, but they came out of her mouth all the same. Gretchen and Dolly heard them, and were startled at her pronouncement.

"I will be next," Leitzel said. "I hear Hans calling me."

It was a day or two after the funeral when Leitzel saw Dolly again.

She was the first of the circus children to enter Auntie Leitzel's Free Elementary School.

Dolly was wearing a crepe, ash-colored mourning dress with black trim at the collar, wrists, and hemline. The dress was way too big on her. It was bought that way to allow for her growth over the year she would be wearing it.

Leitzel's breath was taken away. She had to excuse herself from Dolly. She stepped outside the tent to cry.

Dolly continued to appear in the dress each day she came to school.

"Some mornings when I was in Auntie's tent, I'd look up from a book and catch her staring at me," Dolly remembered. "Her eyes were always brimming with tears. I was too young to understand why she appeared to be so sad, or maybe I knew but didn't want to think about it too hard, or I would start crying, too."

Gretchen wore a mourning dress, too, one identical in style to that of her daughter. She also wore a veil whenever she stepped out on the lot or entered the big top, although now she tried to avoid circulating among the ticket holders. The big top was supposed to be a church of gaiety. It would be wrong, she thought, if some of the circus-goers had their holiday mood broken because they saw all the sorrow that was on her face.

Dolly almost never missed Leitzel's performances. She positioned herself in the darkness at the performers' entranceway in her way-too-big gray dress, a small shadow inside a larger shadow, hardly seeable except for her light brown hair. She wanted to grow up to be just like her aunt, the brightest star of the big top. Leitzel tried hard to help make that happen. She continued to rehearse her daily on the small, low-slung single trapeze that was hung outside her private tent. Before the summer of 1930 was over, though, Dolly was sent away from the circus to attend a Catholic boarding school in Pennsylvania. Leitzel's heart ached like that of a mother who loses a child. She wrote her letters every week and sent her books and dolls.

◆ ◆ ◆

In part because Leitzel no longer saw Dolly in her school in her mourning dress each day, the fissure that had opened in her heart after Hans died began to close by the fall of 1930. Now, though, there was another gash in Leitzel's heart, one that was deeper, wider. She did not think it would ever go away.

There was another woman in Alfredo's life now, one younger and prettier than she was, and while certainly it had not been Leitzel's intention, she had put her there. Alfredo was now besotted with Vera Bruce, whom Leitzel herself, after engineering the ouster of Clara, had handpicked for The Flying Codonas.

When they were interviewed by newspaper and magazine writers, Leitzel and Alfredo, now married for more than two years, conveyed an impression that they were still all lovey-dovey. They held hands. They answered questions about how puppy love stirred in each of them when they first met on the circus as teenagers. They told journalists about their dreams of settling someday in Long Beach, California, where they would be close to his family and their friends in Hollywood. When Leitzel and Alfredo were alone together, though, in their apartment on the train or a room in a hotel, it was another matter.

Alfredo had become withholding, aloof. Leitzel had already gone through the coming-apart of two marriages. She fretted now that this one could be coming to an end, too.

Alfredo was thirty-seven, a dozen years older than Vera. If he initially felt dislike for her because Leitzel, not he, had chosen her for The Flying Codonas, his antipathy may have started dissolving soon after he began training her two years earlier. Alfredo found her to be an able pupil for the flying trapeze. She had no fear of heights and was strong and athletic.

Leitzel, along with The Flying Codonas, had performed in Paris, Berlin, and London in late 1928 and early 1929 during the Ringling off-season. Vera accompanied them on that trip abroad. By then she had already become rehearsed enough on the flying trapeze to appear in one of the flashiest and most dangerous of the Codonas' maneuvers, the "passing leap." In this stunt, she was tossed into the air from Lalo's hands, and then, while Alfredo was cannonballing just inches above her while en route to his brother, she caught the flybar he had just vacated and returned to the perch.

Often The Flying Codonas and Leitzel appeared as separate acts with the same circuses during their European sojourns. But there were also times when the two attractions performed at different circus venues. It was during these partings that he began making his most aggressive moves on Vera, according to Annie Bruce, Vera's mother.

Her daughter, the older Bruce insisted, never would have knowingly assumed a role where she would be interfering with Leitzel and Alfredo's marriage. There was no one to whom Vera felt a greater indebtedness than Leitzel, she said. Leitzel had picked out her daughter from the ranks of the circus's nameless performers and arranged her placement with one of the world's greatest big top attractions. Her daughter, Mrs. Bruce said, always tried to be gentle in rebuffing Alfredo's overtures for romance, but at the same time she was resentful that he continued his attempts at arranging trysts with her.

"Vera was always scrupulously honest, and possessed an innate fairness . . ." she declared.

While not discounting Alfredo's reputation for skirt chasing, Alfred Pelikan, Leitzel's brother, presented a different picture of Vera's positioning in the triangle.

"My sister had taken in Vera as a protégée and had given her a place in The Flying Codonas," he said. "Apparently that wasn't enough. Vera was cold, and she could be calculating. Maybe she didn't really have a serious romantic interest in Alfredo, but I think she plotted to take him away from Leitzel. She was angling to replace Leitzel as first lady of the circus. Always an opportunist, she thought she could do this by stealing her husband. Her betrayal of my sister was almost Shakespearean."

◆ ◆ ◆

The Ringling circus raised its tents for the last time of its 1930 season on October 10 in Birmingham, Alabama, and the next day the train started on its way for winter quarters in Sarasota. Mister John glumly told the troupers that it had been necessary to quit the tour four or five weeks earlier than originally planned because of the still-worsening economic conditions.

The collapse that began on Wall Street a year earlier spread across the ocean. As bleak as the conditions had become in the United States, with the shutting down of factories and the idling of a quarter of the country's work force, they were even harsher in Europe.

As gloomy as the managers of Europe's circus halls were about what the 1930–1931 winter show season might be like, they pleaded with Leitzel and The Flying Codonas to return to the Continent. The two American attractions had been powerful audience generators in their past appearances abroad.

Leitzel may have had reservations about sailing overseas again. She was nearing forty, old for continuing in employment that was so brutally punishing to her body. There was something else that was now weighing increasingly on her thoughts. After the deaths of Lewis Perez and Hans Jahn, she had become more preoccupied with thoughts of her own mortality.

She told George Brinton Beal, the Boston newspaperman, critic, and her friend, that now every time she ascended her web to present another performance, she worried more than ever that it might be her last.

"Someday," she remarked, "something will happen . . . and there won't be any more Lillian."

Beal did not note whether Leitzel seemed unusually morose when she made the pronouncement. But after cavorting in the big top's stratosphere from the time she was a child, she must have wondered how much longer she could continue taunting the fates. The thought of coming to her end before an audience in the manner of Perez and Jahn seemed hideous to her, like being a martyr led onto a platform for public execution.

◆ ◆ ◆

Whatever uneasiness Leitzel might have felt about once again returning to Europe to perform during the winter months of 1930 and 1931, ultimately she did decide to go. She may have been holding out hope that the sojourn would provide a chance for her and Alfredo to start mending their marriage. Late in October, she and Alfredo, along with Lalo and Vera and her maid, Mabel, and rigger, Frank McCloskey, shipped for France. By November 14, they were settled for six weeks into Paris's Cirque d'Hiver.

In the past, Leitzel and Alfredo had always looked forward to the late-year trips abroad. In comparison with their tours with the Ringling circus, when its cavalcade picked up and moved to a new town every one, two, or few days, the European engagements were almost restful. They were put up for a month or more at a time in the same venues, and stayed in the finest hotels. Because they gave but one performance a day instead of the two required in the Ringling circus, they were free to take in movies, museums, and the variety theaters almost daily. What they loved most about traveling in Europe, though, was the esteem they enjoyed with the public. Even more so than in America, they were ranked with the noblest artists of ballet, theater, and opera.

During Alfredo and Leitzel's stay in Europe this time, though, he either turned down her requests to visit the theaters and museums, or invited Vera to accompany them on the outings.

Leitzel felt she was on the verge of a crack-up every day.

She and Alfredo, along with their entourage, had taken rooms at a hotel near the Cirque d'Hiver, and met as a group for breakfast and dinner each day. Leitzel saw Alfredo's gaze soften each time he looked at Vera. She suspected at times that Alfredo was reaching under the table for Vera's knee. Her cheeks were pinking. Sometimes Leitzel had to excuse herself from the table midmeal and return to her room. Her heart now always felt like her right wrist, rubbed raw, lacerated, softly bleeding.

The engagement in the Cirque d'Hiver of The Flying Codonas and Leitzel ended on Christmas Day 1930. The Codonas were scheduled to shift almost immediately to the Wintergarten in Berlin, but Leitzel was free of any bookings until February.

◆ ◆ ◆

She had a lot of things to sort out but could not spend another day of carrying on a pretense that she and Alfredo were still a couple. She packed her bags, checked out of the Paris hotel, and had a porter place her luggage at the curb. She was alone when she stepped into a taxi and directed the driver to deliver her to the train station. Mabel, usually her constant companion, was unable to accompany her. She had come down with the flu and was too sick to even get out of her bed at the hotel. Leitzel may have felt it was just as well that she was unaccompanied this time.

In not many minutes, she was at the station, and then was ushered into a private compartment on a train. There, she could cry the whole trip if she wanted. No one would see her tears.

The train started moving out of the station. Leitzel's anxiousness may have risen. For a long time, she had felt a need to fall into the arms of someone whom she had not seen in years, someone now a day and a country away. Maybe she would find that this someone yearned to be with her just as much.

She hoped. She prayed.

CHAPTER 22

The apartment was just one room, small, almost claustrophobic. For Leitzel, who had just come in from the cold of Berlin's streets and climbed the flights of stairs to the sanctum, it must have seemed almost airless. And, like most everyone else who stepped into the dimly lit space for the first time, she may have been momentarily startled.

There were small, handmade dolls everywhere, dozens of them. They were arrayed side by side atop a dresser, ten or fifteen of them. Others of the tiny figures were crowded together in sitting positions on the room's two or three chairs. They were spread everywhere on the bed that dominated the space, and overhead, suspended on strings from the ceiling and dangling by their arms from tiny trapezes and ropes, there were more. All the little people were female, and all of them were in costume, leotards, and short skirts of white and apple-blossom pink.

Leitzel had a similar collection of dolls, although not one nearly so large. They had kept arriving at her New York apartment for years. Always they were delivered in cardboard boxes plastered with orange and purple and green and blue postage stamps from France and Germany and Belgium and Spain. And, almost always, they were brought to her door a few days before her birthday, Christmas, or Valentine's Day.

The room's walls were also covered with framed photographs. Many were pictures of the apartment's sole occupant, overprinted with the lettering MADAME ZOE, THE AERIAL VENUS. They showed her just feet below the high domes of circus halls. She was posed on crescent moons of wood, or hanging by her teeth from the grip of a parasol. There were other photographs, pictures of Leitzel, also in costume, and dangling from a single trapeze or pinwheeling on her rings.

Nellie Pelikan, still unmarried and alone, was now retired to her memories and scrapbooks thickly pasted with brittle newspaper clippings celebrating her years as the star of the Leamy Ladies and later as Zoe. She was at a stage of life when some referred to her as *die alte Jungfer*, "the old maid." At fifty-two, though, she was still a woman to whom men tipped their hats when they passed her on the street. Her waistline still appeared to be only about half the circumference of her shoulders, and gray had not yet crept into the tower of chestnut-colored hair atop her head.

✦ ✦ ✦

Now and then, in some of her earlier trips to perform in Europe, Leitzel had had brief reunions with Nellie, and on these occasions, she presented her with gifts such as hats and colognes, bought from the finest milliners and perfumeries. This time, Leitzel brought her only her pain.

Leitzel had always revered Nellie as a creature out of a fable, so eternally childlike, so lovely, so empowered with so much magic that a handsome prince might have picked her as his bride from a crowd of thousands. From the time Leitzel was a girl, she had tried imitating her. Her feelings for her were never those of a child for a mother. Those were reserved for Grandma Julia, who not only suckled her, but also cared for her throughout her infancy and childhood when Nellie was almost always countries away, traveling with circuses.

From the moment Leitzel entered the apartment that day, Nellie must have sensed she was weighted with sorrow. She led her to the bed, made her sit, and wrapped her in her arms. It was a moment of intimacy between the two that neither had ever known. Leitzel started shuddering, and then began quaking so hard that Nellie could barely hold her.

"I never before had a chance to have her so much to myself," Nellie said.

Through her sobs, Leitzel told her that Alfredo had fallen in love with Vera Bruce, a woman far younger than her, far prettier. She hardly knew how she could go on another day.

Nellie tried drawing her even closer.

There, there, Nellie said. There, there.

There was nothing Nellie could do to make Leitzel's pain go away. She could only hold her, cry with her, assure her that from then on, she would always be there for her, telling her she wanted all bygones to be bygone, and asking if they could be mother and daughter.

"She loved Alfredo perhaps too much. . . ." Nellie would later say in remembering their embrace.

Throughout Leitzel's stay, mother and daughter slept in the same bed, waking up mornings to the sight of the tiny circus figures floating above them like wingless angels. Nellie did not want their time together ever to end. She remembered these days as the most precious of her life. She felt almost happy that Mabel Clemings, Leitzel's maid and constant companion, had taken sick and had not been able to accompany her.

"It was a bad wish," she said, "but I wished Mabel would stay away longer so I could stay with my dear Leitzel [alone]. She told me so many things—all her troubles."

The two often left the apartment on strolls and visits to cafés and theaters. Nellie loved showing off Leitzel.

"Do you know who this woman is?" she would ask neighbors, waiters, and shopkeepers. "This is Lillian Leitzel, the center ring star of Ringling Bros. and Barnum & Bailey in America, the biggest circus in the world, The Greatest Show on Earth. She's my daughter."

◆ ◆ ◆

After being together four or five weeks, a day came when Nellie and Leitzel had to part again. Mabel Clemings turned up at the door of Nellie's apartment a week or so into February 1931. It was time for Leitzel to go. She had been engaged to appear in Copenhagen, at the Valencia Music Hall. Frank McCloskey, Leitzel's property manager, would be joining the two there in a few days, Mabel said.

Nellie and Leitzel embraced for a long time before separating, and each was crying. The bygones, all of them, were bygone now, and they were closer than they had ever been. They were mother and daughter.

It was not until Mabel and Leitzel were on the train, traveling to Denmark, that Mabel presented her with a letter that Alfredo had asked her to deliver.

Leitzel whimpered as she read the letter. She had to keep blotting her tears with a handkerchief as she read it over and over.

He said he had been miserable since the day she left him in Paris to see Nellie. He said he never again wanted to be away from her for so long. He begged for her forgiveness. He said he knew he had been cruel to her. He loved only her, he assured. She was the only woman he ever loved. Vera meant nothing at all to him. She never really did. He told Leitzel that he sometimes flirted with Vera because he wanted her to feel jealous but now knew this was wrong. He could not wait until they were together again. He would try to make up for everything.

Did Alfredo really mean that she was the only woman he had ever loved? Leitzel may have wondered. Or had Vera finally made it clear to Alfredo that there could never be anything more between the two than a working partnership in the flying act? Of course Alfredo was speaking from his heart in his letter to her, Leitzel concluded. He meant every word of it. In all of time, there were never two other lovers who were more destined to be together forever. They were the circus's queen and king.

After receiving the letter, Leitzel's spirits soared like a stringless kite. Her mood was still bright when she and Mabel checked into a suite at the Grand Hotel Copenhagen that provided a view of the city, including the famous Tivoli Gardens. It was in that suite a few days after arriving in Copenhagen that she sat down for an interview with Erna Milde, editor of the women's pages for the daily *Ekstra-Bladet*.

Leitzel told Milde she had been overcome with nostalgia from the moment she arrived in the city. She had been there once before, perhaps twenty-five years earlier, when, along with her mother and her aunts, Tina and Toni, she performed there with the Leamy Ladies.

"I still remember the Tivoli Gardens and the beautiful tulips, and I have a vague memory of a marvelous ride along the coast," she said. "I am just waiting for a similar sunshiny day to repeat the trip. A repeated trip will most likely wake up a lot of memories almost forgotten."

Milde joked with Leitzel about her reputation for expensive "hobby horses." The reporter asked if she still had such indulgences.

"Well, for a while it was diamonds," Leitzel said. "I was obsessed . . . and searched everywhere for large, precious stones and simply had to own them. . . . Now I couldn't be bothered to even look at a diamond. Then came my manias for fur coats and cars. The last craze reached its climax when I had a specially built, black and platinum Packard which I brought to Paris two years ago. . . . You can hardly think of something more difficult than to get this car and a driver into France. The . . . government is still holding five thousand of my dollars for this joke. . . . It's doubtful I'll ever get the money back."

"What are you interested in at the moment?"

Leitzel beamed at the question.

"Only my husband. . . . To see his act is the most exciting and wonderful thing in the whole world."

"Are you ever nervous?"

"I can wake up in the middle of the night scared to death. . . . But during the act, it comes naturally. I'll continue my act two or three years, then stop. . . ."

"And then what?"

"A wonderful house in California. . . . My husband has his family there, and both of us have good friends [there]. Harold Lloyd happens to be one of [our] best Hollywood friends. He's the nicest fellow. . . . In Hollywood, a lot of people are getting megalomania, but Harold . . . has always kept his balance, although he's one of the wealthiest men in Movie City."

◆ ◆ ◆

The Valencia was located in Copenhagen's Vesterbrogade section near the gateway to Tivoli Gardens. The music hall regularly featured world-famous entertainers, but it was almost equally renowned for the high-class prostitutes that trolled its bars and the tables surrounding its first-floor ballroom.

The hall's interior had the appearance of having been decorated by the same designer who conceived the look of Marie Antoinette's apartment in the Palace at Versailles. The walls were covered with Gobelin tapestries with gold and silver threads that glinted in the sconce lighting, and hanging over the center of the ballroom was a massive chandelier with hundreds of pieces of crystal.

What was most remarkable of all, though, were the Valencia's gilt-framed mirrors. They seemed to be everywhere on the ballroom's walls, so if a dandy placed a hand on his escort's thigh, his action could be seeable to almost everyone in the house, reflected in the looking glasses. Not since the years in the 1910s when Leitzel appeared in Ziegfeld's *Midnight Frolic* in the rooftop garden theater atop New York's Amsterdam Theatre had she been booked into a hall quite so glossy.

Leitzel was always jittery before performing in halls in which she did not have a lot of familiarity, but her engagement at the Valencia made her even more jumpy than usual. She wanted the audiences to see her at the top of her form. She worried that the weeks-long layoff from performing while staying with her mother could have taken some of the sharpness from her act.

There was something else that troubled her. She did not discuss it with the Valencia's management, but over and over she talked about it with Frank and Mabel. She was a bit anguished by where in the Valencia's lineup of entertainment her act was listed. She was also feeling some uneasiness about the date and day of the week for her premiere in the Valencia. Finally, she decided she was only being silly in her concerns over these matters, and, besides, her premiere appearance had already been advertised in all the Copenhagen papers

✦ ✦ ✦

Leitzel stood behind a curtain at the entranceway to the hall's floor, peering out through a slit at the crowd in evening dress. The braided scents of Cuban cigar smoke and expensive perfume were so thick that the air inside the Valencia seemed almost chewable.

On the floor, The Stroganoffs, Russian dancers, were in the final moments of their performance. Up until now, all the entertainers in the night's show had been dancers—tangoists, fox trotters, adagioists, even one or two strippers. The audience seemed to be growing a little restive, perhaps bored by the sameness of the fare. The applause was tepid when The Stroganoffs took their bows.

Speaking in Danish, the *konferencier*, Julius Reger, announced the next act, the evening's headliner. Leitzel picked out only some of the words:

"America . . . Ringling Bros. and Barnum & Bailey . . . Mademoiselle Lillian Leitzel. . . ."

When she parted the curtains and appeared on the floor, the applause swelled to a storm. Almost always Leitzel appeared in white or pink for her performances, but this night was different. Days earlier, while shopping in Copenhagen, she fell in love with a tutu of crème de menthe green. She was wearing it when she appeared before the crowd, with Mabel, as always, eight or ten feet behind her and holding up her train of tulle.

Near the center of the floor, Leitzel curtsied to all sections of the house and slipped from her mules. Next, with McCloskey tugging at her web to keep it taut, she began her ascent. Because she needed to get well beyond the hall's chandelier so the great lamp would not block the audience's sight lines, her upward journey was about twice the distance she usually ascended in American theaters.

She was now a month and a half beyond her fortieth birthday, but she was still as graceful as she had been twenty-five years earlier. She ascended her web weightlessly, almost floated upward, with her body and legs remaining perpendicular to the cord. As impossible as her manner of levitation may have appeared to the audience, the exercise seemed to take nothing from her. Finally she was almost four stories in the air and then transferred from the web, reaching off for her trapeze bar.

Without a moment's pause, she started her routine, standing on the bar, and, with her legs pumping it, driving it out into space. In seconds, she was flying in an ever-higher arc. Two hundred degrees. Two hundred and twenty degrees. Two hundred and fifty degrees . . .

She sank into a crouch on the furiously swinging bar. In another instant, she was hanging upside down, her legs folded over the bar at her knees. Her golden hair started to become unbound, flying every which way. Her flight was reflected in the hall's great mirrors and could be seen in almost whatever direction the spectators turned, as if it were being projected on a dozen movie screens.

She pulled herself up and momentarily assumed a sitting position on the bar. Next, with the trapeze still moving in a great arc, she lay on the trapeze at the small of her back. Her arms and legs were turned outward, spread beyond the ropes.

There was more.

As the trapeze began to slow in its back-and-forth tracings of a half circle, Leitzel once again assumed an upside-down position, this time dangling from the bar with only the upper parts of her feet. She appeared to be as much at peace as a sleeping bat. There was a faint screaking in the air as the trapeze moved forward and backward, but otherwise the hall was without a sound.

When she finished her performance on the trapeze, everyone in the balconies and at the tables on the ballroom floor was standing, applauding, and crying out *bravas*. The tumult was so great that the crystals on the chandelier tinkled reverberantly.

Leitzel, now seated on the trapeze, pushed the hair from her face and buried it in her hands. She was chuckling to herself. She had never been able to quite believe that she, that anyone, could do the things she did in the air.

Her time for basking in the crowd's adoration was brief. She was only halfway through. She reached out for one of the silver hand rings at the ends of two white ropes tethered to the ceiling and transferred from her trapeze bar.

✦ ✦ ✦

How many of her wild, sensational, propellerlike full-body revolutions would she turn this night? Fifty? Eighty? Would she break one hundred? The matter always drew speculation among the crowds that turned out to see her. Some in the audiences even made wagers on the number she would achieve.

Now, almost forty feet above the floor, she was hanging from the rope with her right hand alone. Few could watch the first moments of her exertions without grimacing. Over and over, she threw her short legs forward and then backward, building the momentum that would enable her to start her revolutions. She writhed. She resembled a great, hooked game fish, putting on the fight of its life, trying everything to avoid being boated and added to a stringer. Finally, with an audible groan, she threw her ninety-five-pound body over her arm.

A snare drum in the orchestra was rolling in a paradiddle and snapped sharply at the first of her full revolutions. At the same time, a cry rose from the crowd.

"*En . . . !*"

Then, the drum resumed its roll.

Coming a little easier this time, Leitzel completed a second revolution. The drum barked again, as it did for each of her full-circle turns, and spectators continued their count.

"*To . . . !*"

"*Tre . . . !*"

Soon her turns were coming quickly and with less strain. A swivel attached to the hand ring clicked with each of the revolutions.

"*Twenty-en . . . ! Twenty-to . . . !*"

"*Twenty-fin . . . ! Twenty-seks . . . !*"

Momentum alone swept her upward halfway through another revolution. Her feet were now at twelve o'clock in her revolution.

Then, when her toes were pointing to two o'clock and then three o'clock, something happened, something terrible.

She was falling away from her rigging with the silver ring still in her hand.

In the instant when she realized what was happening, she made a desperate attempt to grab the bar of her nearby trapeze. She batted it, sent the rod swaying, but was unable to grasp it.

The Roman ring remained in her hand for a split second more during the fall, but then dropped away.

Coming down, Leitzel looked like a mallard that had been blasted out of the sky while flying over a hunter's blind. Just feet from the bottom, she managed to position herself horizontally with her back to the floor.

Her shoulders hit first, and then her head snapped back, pounding the thin rubber mat covering the flooring.

Mabel and McCloskey rushed to her.

She was still conscious.

She rasped, "It's what I told you I was worried about. Thirteen."

Her act been listed on the Valencia Hall's program as No. 13. The night of her premiere appearance in the Valencia Music Hall was February 13, Friday the thirteenth.

Two attendants shot through the performers' curtained entranceway, carrying a stretcher. When they got to her side, she tried waving them away with a slow, fanning movement of her hand, signaling she did not need them.

"I'm all right," she said. "I can go on."

Her first thought was with the audience. McCloskey and Mabel laced their arms with hers and managed to get her to her feet. She started moving wobbily back to the entranceway. She got only halfway. She traveled the rest of the way on the stretcher. Within ten or fifteen minutes, she was lifted into an ambulance. With its bells clanging, the conveyance rushed her to the Copenhagen Municipal Hospital.

+ + +

Mabel sent a wire to Nellie and Alfredo, who received the news in Berlin where, after completing their run at the Cirque d'Hiver, The Flying Codonas had started an engagement in the Wintergarten. They traveled together by plane and appeared at the hospital the next morning at about six o'clock. There, along with Mabel and McCloskey, they were ushered into an office where they received a report from the attending physicians.

Leitzel's skull had been cracked everywhere, like the shell of a dropped egg. Her vertebrae were shifted every which way.

Nellie ran from the room into a hall and then sank to the floor. She had never felt as complete as she had when Leitzel came to stay with her in Berlin. Now, after having felt largely estranged from Leitzel all her life but the last month and a half, she felt she might be losing her again. She sobbed hard and gasped for air.

A doctor injected Nellie with a sedative to help calm her. Even so, she could not have been prepared for what she saw upon being admitted to her daughter's room. The flesh on Leitzel's face was yellow and blue. Her hair was shorn to the scalp.

"Poor Leitzel hardly recognized me," Nellie said later. "Her poor head. She was in terrible pain. How I suffered at not being able to help her."

Alfredo moved to kiss Leitzel on her lips. When he was within inches of her and saw just how badly swollen and bruised every inch of her face was, he withdrew, concerned that even his slightest touch would cause her more pain. He took her right hand and kissed it for a long time.

"My doll." He wept. *"Mi muñequita. Oh, mi muñequita pobre."*

The pupils of Leitzel's eyes seemed hardly larger than pinpricks. She gave Nellie, Alfredo, and Mabel signs that she knew who they were, but she was unable to speak. She was heavily sedated with morphine. Her wakefulness was brief. She sank back into a deep sleep.

Once or twice more in the morning hours when Nellie, Alfredo, and Mabel were in her room, she woke for a minute or two, and again seemed to show some signs of having a connection to the three.

By the afternoon, things had changed. Now and then, her eyes fluttered open like those of a mechanical doll, but they did not appear to be seeing anything. Nellie, Alfredo, and Mabel were left terrified by these awakenings. She was delirious during each of them. She shrieked in pain and fright. The figure with the broken head had changed into someone who was no longer a daughter, wife, and dearest friend.

The physicians told Nellie, Alfredo, and Mabel that Leitzel could lie in a coma for days or even weeks, or possibly she could go anytime. All the three could do was to pray and wait.

Alfredo was tormented with self-reproach.

"Why hadn't I been with her when she fell?" he asked. "She could have fallen into my arms. I would have caught her. . . . Leitzel never knew how to fall. I never taught her. She never fell in her life."

Nellie, Mabel, and Alfredo had been at Leitzel's bedside sixteen or eighteen hours. The best thing any of them could do, they were told by the nurses, was to get some rest—that, and pray and wait. If there was any change in their loved one's condition, the three were assured, they would be notified immediately. Nellie, Mabel, and Alfredo left the hospital.

Alfredo was mindful that The Flying Codonas were still under contract with the Wintergarten for a long engagement, and that the theater would suffer great losses the longer he was gone. He caught the last train of the day for Berlin.

Nellie and Mabel returned to their room at the Grand Hotel. Nellie could not stop crying. She stayed up for a couple more hours, and finally, after having gone without sleep for more than twenty-four hours, slipped into bed.

The hospital rang up Nellie and Mabel's room at two o'clock on the morning of February 15. Alfredo received the news after getting off the train in Berlin.

She was gone. Leitzel was gone.

✦ ✦ ✦

Before the day was out, the news of the death of the circus's queen was on the front pages of newspapers everywhere in the world. The circus had lost the most glamorous, most widely beloved royal in its history.

But was Leitzel really gone, or had she somehow just entered into another realm?

Such was the claim made by some of the dancers and other entertainers with whom she had appeared in the Valencia Music Hall that night on a Friday the thirteenth, forty-eight hours earlier. Some of them insisted Leitzel had returned to the music hall in time for the start of the evening show of February 15, eighteen or twenty hours after it had been reported she had died. She was there the next night, too, and the next and the next. They saw her, as clear as could be, with their own eyes, the performers said. They would swear on stacks of Bibles.

She was wearing the same crème de menthe–colored tutu she had on the night of her debut in the Valencia. When they saw her, the entertainers claimed, she said nothing, but smiled at them. Her eyes had a sadness now that was not there before, but her smile was warm, like spring sunshine on the face.

◆ ◆ ◆

The first of the public tributes was held two nights later in New York's Madison Square Garden, the place where she had made her American debut as an aerialist and a place where at the beginning of the new Ringling Bros. and Barnum & Bailey Circus season each spring, she was the cause of massive adoration.

Before the start of a hockey game between the New York Rangers and the Ottawa Senators, as thousands stood with their heads bared, the great arena was darkened. A single spotlight played on a white rope that was slowly lowered from the ceiling. Then, when the rope stopped moving, another spotlight disclosed Joe Humphreys, a well-known announcer at the Garden. He was standing at the center of the ice rink.

"To the memory of Lillian Leitzel," Humphries said. "God rest her soul."

As the rope was slowly drawn upward, a drum corps sounded the roll that always marked the finale of her Garden appearances. Next, an orchestra started playing "Nearer My God to Thee." When the hymn ended, the Garden lights went on and the rival teams swarmed out on the ice.

Colonel H. Maxwell Howard was in Havana, Cuba, wintering at the Sevilla Biltmore Hotel, when he learned of Leitzel's death. As a gentleman who was always elegant in his manners, he may have felt that, as a paramour of Leitzel's, it would be indecorous to express his condolences to Alfredo. He did send a wire to her brother.

ALFRED PELIKAN=

  CIVIC ART DIRECTOR, MILWAUKEE (WIS)=

  I AM BARREN OF WORDS. . . . LEITZEL GAVE HER LIFE TO THOSE

SHE LOVED. THE UNPARALLELED HAPPINESS SHE DISTRIBUTED TO

THE WORLD WILL NEVER BE MATCHED BY ANY WOMAN. STUNNED AT

SAD NEWS. LOVE TO MELBA AND CHILDREN=

  COLONEL.

Alfredo remained in Berlin, fulfilling the terms of the long engagement The Flying Codonas had at the Wintergarten. Then, in March, he, along with Lalo and Vera, boarded the SS *Mauretania* in Southampton, England, and started on their return voyage to the United States. Alfredo was carrying a copper urn with Leitzel's ashes

As the ship steamed into New York Harbor late in the morning of April 3, the same day the circus was opening its 1931 season at the Garden, four wreaths were dropped onto its deck by planes flying overhead. One of the wreaths was from John Ringling. There were others from the Circus Saints and Sinners Club of America, a fraternal organization of theater and circus people, and Tina Burroughs (née Pelikan), an aunt to Leitzel and a coperformer with her in the Leamy Ladies. The biggest of the wreaths, though, and the most elaborate, laced with long-stemmed white and red roses, bore the simplest of cards, a small, white square that was simply signed "Colonel."

◆ ◆ ◆

In her lifetime, one well before television, Leitzel had appeared live before more people than any other entertainer in any medium, or even any United States president. She had been cheered by untold tens of millions, most of them spectators inside the tents of the Barnum & Bailey and then Ringling Bros. and Barnum & Bailey Circuses with which she toured for twenty years. For these adorers, her story, as sad as its ending was, was over.

This was not so for great dozens of the dancers and other entertainers who would perform in the near and far time ahead in Copenhagen's Valencia Music Hall, where the circus's royal queen had fallen—or so they would claim.

The reports of Leitzel sightings by the dancers, magicians, acrobats, and jugglers in Valencia Hall would continue for years. None of the entertainers ever claimed to see her directly, but rather, they said, they glimpsed her in the large, ornamentally framed mirrors that were everywhere in the Valencia, either on the walls of its ballroom, or in the looking glasses at their makeup tables in their dressing rooms. Always she was costumed in the same mint green tutu she was wearing on the night of her fall, these witnesses said, and always she was smiling.

Heinz Saxburger, a Danish magician and illusionist of wide fame in Europe, was among the Valencia entertainers who told of having such a sighting.

"It was a night sometime around 1960 or 1961, and I was making my very first appearance in the Valencia," he said. "I was in a dressing room, putting on my makeup, when, appearing in the dresser mirror before me, was a beautiful woman with golden hair. The door of my dressing room was open, and she was leaning against its frame. She was wearing a performer's tricot of light green, and she was smiling. I only saw her for a few seconds in the mirror before I turned from my chair to look to the door. There was no one there. The door was still closed."

Saxburger said his first thought was that one of the Valencia's dancers had entered the room, and then, discovering her mistake, instantly vanished. Later he carefully looked over all the dancers appearing in the evening's program. None of them bore any resemblance to the beautiful, smiling woman in green.

Saxburger said he was still puzzling over the incident the next day when he met a representative of the talent agency that booked his appearance at the Valencia. The agent then told him the story of an internationally famous circus performer, an American, who had taken a fatal fall in the music hall on a night three decades earlier.

"You saw her, Heinz, you saw her," the booker said. "You're a lucky, lucky man. You will be blessed as all others who have seen her have been blessed. You will have great success as an entertainer. You will have a long and happy life."

Saxburger was eighty and still working as a professional magician when he recounted the story of his encounter with the ghost of Leitzel.

The Valencia Music Hall was razed in 1980. There apparently have been no reports of Leitzel sightings since.

Alfredo saw it in a dream the first time. It was towering, all in white, and emitted the glow of a winter moon. It was the most beautiful sight he had ever seen, or could even ever imagine. The dream of white came to him just days after Leitzel died. When he awoke from it, he could not get it out of his head.

He talked about his vision with Lalo and with some of the other performers at the Wintergarten in Berlin. Someone told him of Professor Escoli, and on a day off from the circus, Alfredo boarded a train for Italy.

The leather-aproned man who answered Alfredo's pounding at the wooden door looked like a ghost. He was silted head to toe in white dust and invited Alfredo in. His studio was a place of daily sandstorms. There was not a tabletop or a tool that was not, like Professor Escoli, frosted in white. He was a stonecutter, a sculptor.

The two sat at a table, and Alfredo told the professor of his dream in white. He showed him some crude pencil sketches, his attempts at recalling what he saw in the dream, then handed him a small collection of photographs, some of them showing himself, others showing Leitzel.

Escoli looked at the photographs, and then at Alfredo's sketches. With a sure hand, he started refining Alfredo's drawings.

"*Sì? Sì?*" the professor asked as his pencil and eraser moved swiftly over Alfredo's rude conceptions.

"Yes, yes," Alfredo answered. "Oh, yes, yes. Exactly so."

Before Alfredo left to return to Berlin, Escoli brought out a large caliper. He took careful measurements of his caller's head, neck, chest, waist, and thighs. He carefully recorded all of the dimensions in a ledger.

✦ ✦ ✦

When Alfredo saw his dream in white a second time, it was ten months later.

The dream was seventeen feet high, chiseled from vein-less, Carrara marble, and weighed several tons. It bore a $38,000 price tag. Alfredo had commissioned the work by Professor Escoli with funds from Leitzel's estate.

The wood-crated monument was unloaded from the SS *President Pierce* in Los Angeles harbor on December 3, 1931, and then moved on a flatbed truck to a place atop a grassy knoll in the Inglewood Park Cemetery.

The cemetery, southwest of downtown Los Angeles, already had an impressive collection of grandiose creations in granite and marble that marked the last earthly addresses of Hollywood directors, screen stars, and world-class boxers. Even so, Codona's dream out-rococoed all the other stone follies in the 340-acre park.

The monument's most conspicuous features were its full-length, life-size likenesses of Leitzel and Alfredo. The two royals were embracing, and they were nude except for some skeins of carved drapery that Escoli had discreetly situated over their private parts. This was not all that was astonishing about the Italian sculptor's conception. While huge, seraphlike wings sprouted from Codona's back, not even a trace of feathery fluff appeared on Leitzel's shoulders. Had Codona directed the professor to represent him as a divine, and his beloved wife as a mere mortal?

The figures were posed in a manner suggesting that Alfredo was trying to cling to Leitzel, trying to keep her earthbound. What was surprising in Professor Escoli's representation of the lovers, though, even startling in a way, was that some force seemed to be drawing

Leitzel upward. She appeared to slipping from Alfredo's hands, levitating, perhaps on her way to heaven to receive wings, too.

Carved in relief beneath Leitzel's feet were two Roman rings, a symbol of her act. Each was attached to a rope, but the rope on one of them was severed. Escoli had gotten this detail wrong. Clearly he intended for the snapped rope to represent the cause of Leitzel's fatal plunge, but, in fact, her fall had resulted not from a severed rope but from the shattering of a metal swivel that was attached to her ring.

◆ ◆ ◆

The Ringling Bros. and Barnum & Bailey Circus presented the final performances of its 1931 season in Atlanta on September 14.

By the time Alfredo, Lalo, and Vera wound up business with the show and returned to Long Beach for the off-season, it was eight or nine days later. That was not quite soon enough for the Codona brothers to see their mother alive a last time. Hortense died on her sixty-second birthday, a day or two before the pair arrived back home.

The nation was in the third year of the Great Depression, still felled on the mat, groggy and hardly moving. The 1931 Ringling tour had been the shortest of any in its history. The abbreviated season meant that all its performers and laborers had to give up a month and a half or two of pay. Most of them were paralyzed with fears about not only how they could ever survive the winter but also whether there would still be a circus to report to in the spring.

This, though, was not an immediate concern for Alfredo, Lalo, and Vera. Metro-Goldwyn-Mayer had signed The Flying Codonas to do the stunting for two major pictures, *Tarzan, the Ape Man*, the first of six Tarzan movies in which Johnny Weissmuller and Maureen O'Sullivan were to be paired, and *Polly of the Circus*, costarring Clark Gable and Marion Davies. Both pictures were scheduled for release in 1932.

The filming for *Tarzan, the Ape Man* got under way in mid-October in Sherman Forest, a densely wooded area of mountains and a lake twenty miles from downtown Los Angeles.

Alfredo and Vera did the vine swinging for Weissmuller and

O'Sullivan, and Lalo doubled for Cheeta, a chimpanzee appearing as Tarzan's confidant in many of the scenes. Unlike Lalo, who had to suit up each day in a hot, itchy, and heavy ape suit, Alfredo's costuming requirements were minimal.

"Nothing on but a fig leaf and some paint," he said in describing how he appeared for the shoots each day.

Alfredo brought Papa Edward to Sherman Forest to help string the trapezes into the treetops. The family patriarch was still grieving over the loss of his wife of fifty years, but he enjoyed having a role in the moviemaking.

"Dad and I have a nice tent and Vera lives in a very pretty cottage with all the comforts of modern life," Alfredo recounted. "There are 150 people out here and we have a wonderful camp—showers running hot and cold water, and everything. There is a beautiful clubhouse where we eat and spend our evenings until 9:30 P.M., then to bed. Regular farmers."

The Flying Codonas' work on the Tarzan film continued for eight weeks, and then, after a short break, Alfredo, Lalo, and Vera started work on *Polly of the Circus*.

All the time that Alfredo was engaged in the movie work, he was also carrying out plans for a final tribute to Leitzel. The memorial services were to be held on December 10, ten months after her death. The *Long Beach Press-Telegram* predicted the occasion would be "the most elaborate affair Long Beach has witnessed." And so it was.

✦ ✦ ✦

Hours before the services started, locals began massing outside Mottell's Chapel and Mortuary; many were clutching autograph books in hopes of gathering signatures from the celebrities who were expected to appear. In an attempt to impose order, police organized the horde into a double file leading to the chapel door. Then the mourners started arriving and moved through the double rank of townspeople. As the *Press-Telegram* had forecast, the memorial services brought about the largest concentration of picturesque figures ever to appear in the city.

Among the first to file into the chapel were Harold Lloyd, the film comedian and producer, and his wife, actress Mildred Davis. They had been ferried to the services from their forty-four-room mansion in Beverly Hills in a chauffeur-driven car. Also turning out were Janet Gaynor and Charles Morton, for whom Alfredo, Lalo, and Clara Curtain had doubled in the trapeze scenes in *4 Devils*.

Not surprisingly, numerous other big top stars were also present for the final tribute to the circus's greatest female star ever, among them Mabel Stark, the renowned tiger and black panther trainer, and Minnie "The Human Top" Fisher, a retired aerialist who had been a sensation at the turn of the century when, with a rope gripped in her teeth, she whirled like a dervish high in the big top. Numerous Ringling executives were there, too, although not Mister John, who, as was usual for him during the winter months, was in Europe, scouring the Continent for new center ring attractions as well as more masterpieces for his John and Mable Ringling Museum of Art in Sarasota.

Inside the chapel, Alfredo had reinstalled a shrine to Leitzel similar to the one he'd earlier created inside a bedroom of the Codona family's Long Beach house on Cherry Street. The shrine's centerpiece was a silver urn filled with Leitzel's ashes, some of which were still in the simple copper container in which he had carried her remains back from Europe. Some of the mourners knelt before the urn and said prayers.

After the services inside the chapel, presided over by the Reverend Perry G. M. Austin, a great rainbow-colored and waxed cortege of mostly Pierce-Arrows, Bentleys, Duesenbergs, and Stutz Bearcats motored to the Inglewood Park Cemetery.

There Alfredo led the mourners to the knoll where, a short distance from the park's Lake of Memories, the cemetery workers had sited the monument he commissioned for Leitzel. The stone memorial was still entirely enshrouded beneath a large tarpaulin when the mourners first arrived, and a great gasp rose from them when, a short time later, a couple of gray-suited cemetery employees removed the canvas to reveal Alfredo's dream in white.

The plinth below the towering and glowing statuary of the embracing, near nude Leitzel and angel-winged Alfredo bore a simple identification:

QUEEN OF THE AIR

Works of art, especially creations that are intended to last forever, almost always are given titles, and the monument that Alfredo had commissioned for his beloved bore one that suggested he foresaw a day when the two of them would again lie together. He titled it *Reunion*.

He was sobbing audibly, and his hands were shaking as he inserted a key into the small bronze door near the base of the monument, unlocked it, and then placed Leitzel's silver urn inside.

Afterward, one by one and two by two, the mourners approached Alfredo, shook his hand, and embraced him. No spouse could have presented a grander, more lasting, and more affecting tribute of love to a lost mate than he did, everyone told him. *Reunion*, they all said, was a masterpiece, the most beautiful work of art they had seen anywhere.

After pleading with Vera day after day after day for months, Alfredo finally received the answer he wanted to hear.

Vera's answer came on a July night of 1932, a year and a half after Leitzel's death and a little more than a half year after Alfredo had placed her ashes inside the bronze-doored vault of *Reunion*. It likely followed along this line:

Well, okay, Alfredo. Okay, okay. If that's what you want, if it will make you feel better, then, all right, fine. I'll marry you.

It likely was the most tepid and diffident response Alfredo had ever heard from any woman in his life, but he was deliriously happy.

As though he felt the action might help bond her word, the first thing Alfredo did was contact the news wire services and such magazines as *Time* to announce that he and Vera had become engaged to marry. Next, he contacted the Gunther Hotel in San Antonio, Texas, to book its grand ballroom for the afternoon and night of September 18, 1932. The Ringling show would be playing in San Antonio on the day he had chosen for the wedding. Also in the city at the same time, holding their annual convention, would be the Circus Fans of America, an organization of hundreds of big top enthusiasts from throughout the country.

Alfredo seemed to have been anticipating a wedding celebration that would approach the scale of a British coronation. He was crazy in love. He wanted everyone in his world to share in his joy.

Whether she was strolling a sidewalk or going through the racks of dresses in a couturier, Vera probably never appeared anywhere in public without causing strangers to wonder if she was a movie star. She was that stunning. Her eyes, both light and dark in their gray chiaroscuro, were penetrating. Her skin was creamy and flawless, she had a slightly aquiline nose, and she was always fashionably coiffed and dressed. What may have been even more striking about her, though, was her air. She seemed almost sphinxlike in her mystery. She had always withheld from others any real sense of who she was. She was also guarded in revealing how she felt about anyone else.

At twenty-seven, Vera was a dozen years younger than Alfredo. No one who knew her, though, not even her mother, believed that she said yes to Alfredo's marriage proposal out of love. Annie Bruce remembered receiving a letter from her daughter during the time Alfredo was begging her to become his wife.

"Mother, Alfredo wants to marry me," Vera had written. "I don't want to marry him, but he keeps pleading and pleading. He treats me beautifully, and gives me everything I want. But I don't love him."

Bruce said that Alfredo always brushed aside her daughter's words when she told him that while she admired him beyond anyone else as an artist and was honored to have a place in The Flying Codonas, she did not feel ardor for him. On these occasions, Bruce said, Alfredo took Vera's hands in his and responded, "You'll learn to love me. I'll make you love me."

✦ ✦ ✦

As large as the Gunther Hotel's ballroom was, it was not so capacious that it could accommodate all the invited guests at one time. The circus had arrived in San Antonio with sixteen hundred people.

All afternoon and all night, the well-wishers came to see the newly marrieds in shifts. Not only were all of the circus executives and Alfredo and Vera's fellow performers invited to the blowout, but so were the canvasmen, the pony grooms, and the camel attendants. For some of the roustabouts, the trip to the Gunther may have brought them into contact with flush toilets for the first time in months.

The feasting and revelry continued until dawn, but sometime before midnight, the new Mr. and Mrs. Alfredo Codona said their good nights to the wedding guests and made their way to hotel's bridal suite.

Fourteen hundred miles away, beneath the lid of the silver urn locked inside the white marble shrine in Inglewood Park Cemetery, there may have been some stirring of Leitzel's ashes.

Alfredo had long been regarded as a first royal of the circus. Now, through marriage, Vera had become a princess, although few of her fellow troupers would have ceded her the honorific wholly on the basis of performing skills. She looked luminous on the trapeze platform, but there were at least a half dozen other women flyers touring with circuses who soared through the air with greater bravura. As adoring as Codona was of Vera otherwise, it bothered him that she seemed completely incapable of exuding any warmth to the people in the seats. "The more she practices, the worse she seems to get," he once confided to Frank McCloskey.

While Vera seemed not to grow any closer to Alfredo in the first months of their marriage, she did enjoy the new associations she gained by being Mrs. Codona. One of them was with the celebrated painter John Steuart Curry, who, along with Grant Wood and Thomas Hart Benton, was a leader of the American Regionalist movement. Like numerous great artists before him, among them Daumier, Toulouse-Lautrec, Léger, and Picasso, Curry viewed the circus's *saltimbanques* as godlike, artists who consecrated their entire beings to their calling, and in some cases, even risked their lives for it.

Through arrangements made by Alfredo, Curry had received approval to travel with the Ringling Bros. and Barnum & Bailey Circus for a two-month period in 1932. It was during this time that the bald, moon-faced man from Kansas produced the working drawings for some of his most widely known paintings, including those of the horseback-riding Rieffenachs, the jungle cat trainer Clyde Beatty, and Irma Ponticio, an eight-hundred-pound fat lady who was better known to the public as "Baby Ruth" because of a prodigious appetite for candy bars of the same name that she ate by the twenty-four-count box.

Curry dined with Alfredo and Vera each night, and, in the morning hours, often gave his new circus friends guided tours through the art museums in bigger cities like Washington, D.C., Boston, and Philadelphia. Curry revered the Codonas, especially Alfredo. He spent so much time on their trapeze perch, making sketches, that many in the audiences may have thought he was a fourth member of the troupe. He painted at least two major canvases of the Codonas. One was titled *The Missed Leap* and showed Vera falling through space to the net. Another of the paintings, this one called *The Flying Codonas*, provided a dramatic view of Alfredo cannonballing through the air while in transit to Lalo's hands. *The Flying Codonas*, regarded by some critics as Curry's most successful painting, was acquired by the Whitney Museum of American Art in New York even before its oil was dried.

✦ ✦ ✦

Alfredo and Vera sailed for Europe soon after the Ringling circus finished its 1932 tour in October. The newlyweds spent their first weeks abroad visiting with friends, motoring through the countryside, and honeymooning. By November, they were joined by Lalo for the first of their winter engagements on the Continent, an extended return appearance in Berlin's Wintergarten, where, as always, The Flying Codonas were the headliners.

After spending six months in Germany, France, Spain, and England, Alfredo, Vera, and Lalo returned to the United States just in time for the start of the Ringling circus's 1933 season in the Garden.

Alfredo was nearing his fortieth birthday. There have been professional baseball pitchers, ballet dancers, and even a few prizefighters who remained close to their top form in their middle years, but, except for Alfredo, this was never true of flyers. Most of them reached their peaks around their twenty-fifth year, and then, like cheap watches, started losing their timing. Alfredo still performed The Triple, and also his blindingly rapid, three- and four-turn pirouettes.

There was never any dispute among circus critics or even other trapeze artists about his place as the greatest flyer ever, but what surprised everyone was that he seemed to get ever better every year. So many thousands of times had Alfredo performed on the trapeze over the last twenty-five years that soaring into space and then getting safely back to his platform appeared to be as day to day for him as a spring robin's morning departures from the nest to shop for night crawlers to take home to the hatchlings.

It continued for him this way during the first two and a half weeks of the new season in the Garden in the spring of 1933, and then something changed one night. He moved through the first parts of his act as smoothly as ever. Then, it was time for him to throw The Triple and call it a night.

He had rounded out a third somersault and was streaking to Lalo when he did something queer, something he had never done before. Instead of extending his hands to Lalo's, he raised them up over his head, as though he was trying to clutch those of someone other than his brother. He soared right by Lalo, missing his connection with him altogether. In the next fraction of a second, he smashed headfirst into the uplifted apron of the safety net, and then, springing backward from the recoil, caromed into a guy wire stretched to the trapeze rigging. He moved grotesquely through the air for another second or two and then slammed onto the Garden floor.

Alfredo lay unconscious for some time. When he came to, he had a sensation that knives were plunged everywhere in his upper back. He was carried from the arena on a stretcher.

◆ ◆ ◆

Alfredo's upper torso was tightly bound with tape when, an hour or two later, Lalo was admitted into the room of the hospital where his brother had been conveyed. The ligaments in his back were torn everywhere.

"You did something that was strange for me tonight," Lalo said. "What was the matter?"

Alfredo turned his gaze from his brother and, as though still trying to figure things out, stared blankly at a wall for seconds before replying.

"I saw Leitzel's hands reaching for me," he finally answered. "I tried grasping them."

A new Ringling season had hardly started, but for Alfredo, it already was over.

He began consulting with doctors. When he asked them how long it would be before he could rejoin the show, he always received the same crushing answer: he might never fly again.

Alfredo went to see Paul Arley, a Saraosta chiropractor who earlier had been a circus perch pole artist. Arley had a reputation for ridding other big top athletes of cricked backs, pulled muscles, and other injuries of their trade. He assured Alfredo he could help him nurse his shoulder back into shape. He massaged Alfredo's back daily. He fashioned an upper-body corset that was intended to keep Alfredo's shoulder muscles stabilized. Within three or four weeks, Alfredo was pitching horseshoes and playing tennis.

By November of 1933, six months after being grounded, Alfredo was ready to start a comeback. He rented an abandoned chemical factory in San Pedro near the Codona family home in Long Beach, and he, Lalo, and Papa Edward laced the barnlike building with his flying trapeze and net. His goal was to rejoin the Ringling circus the following spring when it opened its 1934 season in the Garden.

Alfredo was surprised at how swiftly he was able to reclaim the more fundamental of his flying maneuvers. Even after his layoff of more than a half year, he was soon able to spring into the air from Lalo's hands and then turn two or three pirouettes while moving through space to his trapeze bar. It was evident, though, even after several weeks of practicing, that it could be some time before he could recover his signature stunt.

A circus expert had once calculated that when Alfredo came out of the third somersault of The Triple and caught the hands of his brother, the shock to his body was equivalent to that of someone grabbing a fence post from the open door of a car traveling at sixty miles an hour. Now, even when he threw a single somersault and was caught by Lalo, the pain that ripped through his back was so great that he sometimes seemed close to passing out.

Alfredo damned the gods for reclaiming The Triple from him, but

he conceived another stunt that he was sure would be equally spectacular, one that no one had ever accomplished before, a Three and a
Half. His idea was to turn three and a half somersaults in midair and
have Lalo catch him not at his wrists, but at his ankles. The brothers
worked on the trick hundreds of times. Now and then there were times
when Lalo's hands grazed Alfredo's ankles, but he was never able to
lock them in his hands.

One day, though, after trying for weeks, Lalo managed to keep his
clasp on Alfredo's ankles. Elated, the brothers came down from their
trapeze and hugged each other. Alfredo had spent ten years searching
for The Triple before he could accomplish it. Because the brothers had
succeeded once in executing a Three and a Half, they now knew that
the laws of physics and gravity would allow the stunt. Their challenge
now was to so precisely calibrate their timing to each other that they
could carry out the feat with consistency.

Over and over, they tried retrieving the Three and a Half. There
were times when they seemed to get within a hairsbreadth of docking,
but because one brother or the other was a quarter second too early or
too late in being where he was supposed to be, they could never quite
relocate the feat. In the end, Alfredo always tumbled to the net. Because of his own feelings of powerlessness, he often took out his frus-
trations on Lalo, cursing him and blaming him for the failures.

After a series of botched attempts one day at calling back the feat,
Alfredo climbed the rope ladder to try yet again. He was angry, not
fully in possession of the sharp concentration and control he usually
regained the instant he stepped onto his platform.

He catapulted into space, whirled heels over head three and a half
times, and then in the final stretch of his flight, shot beyond Lalo.
He collided with the net's upswept apron, sprang backward, and then
started dropping to the net. After hitting the roped body catcher this
time, he geysered upward ten or fifteen feet back into the air, and then,
with his arms and legs flailing wildly, moved beyond the perimeter of
the net below and crashed to the floor on his back.

When Alfredo regained consciousness, he felt the same pain in his
back that he had suffered eight or nine months before, after the acci-

dent at the Garden. The ligaments had again snapped from his shoulder muscles. This time there were also broken bones. Alfredo must have known it even as he lay on the floor. This time it was over, his flying days were really over. Mercifully, Papa Edward was not a witness to the final disintegration of his creation. The Codona patriarch died a few months earlier, age eighty-one.

And what about Vera? Were her days as a flyer with The Flying Codonas over now, too? And what about her assignments on movie sets, doubling for some of Hollywood's brightest stars? Were they gone as well? The questions may have started troubling her from the moment she saw her husband on the ground in the practice barn, writhing and moaning in agony. As distant as her feelings for Alfredo may have been, she understood that the glamorous life she had been enjoying was a trapping of being married to the circus's greatest male star.

◆ ◆ ◆

As they had been for decades, The Flying Codonas were back with a circus in the spring of 1935, but this time it was not with The Greatest Show on Earth, and this time it was not Alfredo that the crowds saw somersaulting in the big top's empyrean. He was now being held together with tape and an upper body brace.

Alfredo chose his own replacement for the act. Twenty-one-year-old Clayton Behee was a capable leaper, even a good one, but not one with Alfredo's dovelike gift for flying.

Mister John had relegated the reconstituted The Flying Codonas to the Hagenbeck-Wallace Circus, one of his smaller properties. Even there, the act was denied star billing. The new Codonas were given air space at a far end of the tent. Appearing over center ring were The Behrs, a group of fifteen- and sixteen-year-olds who earlier had performed with a Boy Scout circus.

Probably as much out of pity for the broken Alfredo as for any other reason, Mister John included Alfredo on his payroll. He hired him as the Hagenbeck-Wallace equestrian director, a top position, one giving him primary responsibility for the look and pacing of the tent productions. But Alfredo was miserable in the role. He was not a manager.

He had been a performer since he was a child. His heart ached every time he looked to the big top's ceiling and saw another flyer carrying out his work on the trapeze. His unhappiness must have been evident to the front office. When the Hagenbeck-Wallace season finished, his contract was not renewed.

Alfredo was bitter. He had worked for the Ringling brothers since he had been in his teens and now Mister John could not find a place for him anywhere in his empire.

He prevailed on a longtime friend, Tom Mix. The "King of the Cowboys," then fifty-six, had gotten into the big top business in 1933, buying a $400,000 stake in an existing show, the Sam B. Dill Circus, which was renamed the Sam B. Dill Circus and Tom Mix Wild West Show. After a single season, Mix bought the enterprise kit and caboodle. The renamed Tom Mix Circus did not travel by train but in a large caravan of red, white, and blue trucks and buses. Because of Mix's popularity with cinema audiences as America's number one western star, the circus was greeted with turn-away crowds almost everywhere.

Mix put Alfredo on the payroll as assistant equestrian director. His circus already had a strong flying act, though, The Flying Arbaughs, he reminded Alfredo. He said there just would not be a place in the show or its budget for the remade Flying Codonas. Alfredo's expression turned saturnine at hearing Mix's decision in the matter. He nodded that he understood why the circus could not use a second flying act but then pleaded with his new employer to give Vera work as an additional member of The Flying Arbaughs. Mix, probably again acting out of charity, agreed to Alfredo's request. Vera's placement in the Arbaughs troupe was largely ornamental.

Because maintaining high morale among the performers was critical to the success of any circus, it was an important function of equestrian directors that they regularly assume priestly roles. Their duties might involve refereeing disputes between two feuding clowns one day and, on the next, getting the okay from the front office to advance train fare to a performer with a mother on a deathbed in Keokuk, Iowa. There were complaints from the troupers that Alfredo was ineffective in this part of his job. Because he was so consumed with self-pity over his own wrecked career as a performer, he found it difficult to be consolatory to others' troubles. The Mix Circus presented its last performance of the season on November 5, 1936, in Anniston, Alabama. Mix wished Alfredo luck and shook his hand. He did not say "I want you back next spring when the show moves out again."

Alfredo had never known any world other than the circus. He had been born into it, traveling at first with the forever starved-out Gran Circo Codona with which his father and mother toured Mexico, and eventually rising to the highest place in its pantheon. Now, after giving more than forty years to the big top, after risking limb and life for it almost daily, there was no longer a place for him in it. All the glory and heart-in-the-stomach thrills that he had once been able to give to the audiences were used up. The circus, which is born anew every spring, retired him, cast him out, just as it did every year with once-radiant showgirls who, over time, gained just too many pounds or wrinkles.

◆ ◆ ◆

He and Vera hardly spoke after they left the Tom Mix Circus in Alabama and then started on the long train ride to Long Beach. He was being eaten inside by both anger and disgrace.

Within a few weeks after resettling into the family home on Cherry Street, Alfredo, already starting to feel time long on his hands, took work in an auto garage in nearby Walteria. The garage, W. K. Adolph & Codona Co., was operated by Billy Adolph, a former professional race car driver and husband of his sister, Victoria, now long retired from the circus. Years earlier, in fact, Alfredo had put up the money to get Billy started in the garage, and thus the inclusion of Codona in the shop's name. Now his brother-in-law would be signing his paychecks. The W. K. Adolph & Codona Co. specialized in servicing luxury cars and catered to many Hollywood stars, among them Al Jolson and Alfredo's friend Harold Lloyd.

Alfredo tried to convince Vera that the time had come to start a family. Long Beach was a good community. They could have a good life. Vera was thirty-three, not yet willing to trade the glamour and adventure of the circus for a life in a quiet neighborhood with crying babies and a crippled husband who was employed as a . . . a grease monkey.

"Maybe in another year or two," she said.

Vera and Alfredo had only been back in Long Beach for a few months when she was offered an opportunity to return to circus life. Her brother, Clary, a trick rider, phoned her from the Ringling winter quarters in Sarasota, Florida, where he was putting together a new bareback riding act for the 1937 season. Vera had begun her circus career in Australia as a member of May Wirth's famous riding act. There would be a place for her in the new act he was assembling, Clary assured her.

Alfredo begged Vera not to leave. He would not be able to live without her, he said. She had to go, she answered. She could not disappoint Clary. He was her brother.

As excited as Vera was at the prospect of rejoining the Ringling circus, there likely was a bigger reason why she felt she had to leave. Alfredo was sinking ever deeper into depression. There were days when he came home from the garage and never got out of his coveralls until bedtime. He smelled of axle grease. She found him weeping much of the time.

Maybe even more disturbing to her was a shrine to Leitzel that Alfredo maintained in their bedroom. The copper urn, along with photographs of her, was on its linen-draped surface. Sometimes, when Vera was in another room, she heard Alfredo talking and even singing to the remains of Leitzel he kept.

❖ ❖ ❖

Alfredo begged and blubbered even as Vera packed her bags. When it was clear to him that her mind would not be changed, he drove her to the train station. She promised to write him every day, and phone at every opportunity. He kissed her. Then she was on the train, beginning the cross-country trip to Sarasota.

After a few days, Alfredo received a first letter from Vera, and then, as she promised, her letters and postcards started arriving every day. She talked about the Florida sunshine and inquired about the weather in Long Beach. She went on and on about how well Clary's riding act was coming together, and how easily she had been able to regain her old skills at pirouetting and somersaulting on the backs of cantering horses. Always she told Alfredo she hoped he was doing fine but said nothing about missing him. She signed off all her letters the same way, not with "Love always, Vera," but "Cheerio, Vera."

She phoned him, too. Alfredo cried throughout all the calls. He told her how miserable he was. He told her he was tormented with thoughts that she was going to fall in love with someone else. He would take his own life if that ever happened, he vowed.

Then Vera's letters and phone calls started to become spaced further apart, although his letters and attempts at phoning her continued uninterruptedly. Some days, she found three or four of them in her mailbox. Each was a plea for her to return to Long Beach.

"Dear Wife Vera," he wrote in one letter. "In front of your picture I have two beautiful roses, one white as snow which stands for your character, mind and beauty, and also your pure heart, the other, red, which stands for my love for you, and my fierce jealousy for all the things you are, and which are mine only."

In another letter, apparently penned moments after Alfredo had received a phone call from Vera, he wrote, "At seven twenty-five your sweet voice came across 3300 miles, and it made me so happy I almost cried. . . . After our little three minutes together, I lay down on the davenport, and, lonesome and blue, fell asleep thinking of you. Maybe something will happen over there to make you fed up with it, and you'll come home to the one who loves you more with every breath he draws."

Despite Alfredo's hopes, Vera did not become "fed up" with her ambition to resume her career as a big top performer. When the hundred-car Ringling train left the show's Sarasota winter quarters late in March, on its way to New York to open the 1937 season, she was aboard, along with thirteen hundred other performers and workers.

CHAPTER 25

Alfredo's foot was crunched to the floorboard for much of the three-thousand-mile trip. Even then, he worried that his brand-new, canary yellow, four-door Studebaker President sedan would not get him there fast enough. Maybe it was already too late for him to do anything about it, but he had to try. He drove for three or four days and nights, making stops long enough only for refueling, meals, and roadside catnaps. He kept pounding the Studebaker ahead, and over and over rehearsed in his head what he was going to do when he got there, what he was going to say. It was early in April 1937.

At first, Alfredo was disbelieving. Before long, he was red-faced and screaming. He had just finished the cross-country trip from California to New York and was outside the performers' door at Madison Square Garden. The security guards there had been given a photograph of Alfredo. They had been ordered not to admit anyone into the Garden who matched the man on their picture.

Alfredo tried explaining. His wife was a performer with a bareback riding act in the Ringling circus. She was inside the building, along with other members of the circus, rehearsing for the show. It was important that he see her right then and there.

Vera apparently had forewarned the circus's management that her husband might try to get into the building and cause a disruption. Alfredo started yelling in anger at the security policemen, but they held him back. Their orders were orders, they explained.

If the guards would not let him enter, could someone at least locate his wife on the Garden's hippodrome floor and bring her to the door? The guards shook their heads again and this time closed the door on him. The circus's biggest male star of just a few years earlier was now banned from even getting into the Garden. Alfredo was left to pace the sidewalk outside. His anger continued to rise.

The Ringling Bros. and Barnum & Bailey Circus of 1937 was a different enterprise from the one that Alfredo had been forced to retire from after his crippling fall four years earlier. The show's general manager now was Samuel Gumpertz, the former operator of the Dreamland Circus and Side Show on Coney Island. John Ringling, the last of the great circus's founding brothers, had died five months earlier. Although Mister John had managed to retain possession of his art collection and the John and Mable Ringling Museum of Art, along with a palatial home there and another on Park Avenue in New York City, he had lost virtually everything else he owned in the Great Depression, including thousands of acres of undeveloped land throughout the United States, his short line railroads, and his once bulging portfolio of stocks and bonds. There was but $311 in his bank account at the time of his death at age seventy on the second day of December, 1936.

◆ ◆ ◆

Vera was with her brother, Clary, and other members of the bareback riding troupe when, some hours later, she exited the Garden. Alfredo rushed to her and began rebuking her for leaving him. Things had gone far enough, he told her. It was time to end all the games, he said. She was his wife and was traveling home with him.

Vera had known for a long time that this day would have to come. She was grateful Clary was at her side when it did. Her eyes were filled with pity as she looked at Alfredo. He may have mistaken her expression as regret at having hurt him. He tried to embrace her. She shrank back.

"Alfredo," she said firmly, "I'm not happy with you. Honestly, I don't even like you to put your hands on me. This can't go on. The only thing to do is to get a divorce."

Alfredo's threatening manner dissolved. He now looked contrite, as if he had just been punished.

"I tried to make you love me," he answered. It might take longer, but it could still happen, he said. He pleaded with her to give him more time.

Vera started walking away from him, with Clary still at her side.

"Good-bye, Alfredo," she said.

Alfredo resumed his letter writing to Vera even as he was returning on his long trip to Long Beach, posting his declarations of love for her from towns along the road. He continued to send her letters when he returned home. In one, he might accuse her of seeing other men and threaten to take her life and his own. In the next, sometimes posted the same day, he would beg Vera for her forgiveness, telling her he had threatened her only because he loved her so much and could not think clearly.

Vera's letters and phone calls to him had stopped altogether after the encounter outside Madison Square Garden.

✦ ✦ ✦

It was late in June before Alfredo heard anything more from Vera, and then the communication was carried out indirectly. He was served with papers from the Superior Court of Los Angeles County. Without his knowledge, Vera had taken a leave from the circus and returned to California to begin divorce proceedings.

In her affidavit, Vera testified that "during the past year, the defendant has, without cause, become very jealous. . . . That on numerous occasions, the defendant has threatened to kill the plaintiff. That the defendant is possessed of a violent temper, and on many occasions has struck, slapped and abused plaintiff, and has subjected plaintiff to such a course of cruel and inhuman treatment, coupled with threats of violence, as to cause plaintiff to fear for her life and safety." In petitioning the court to sever her bonds of matrimony with Alfredo, Vera requested that it order her husband to award her alimony of $200 a month, along with a lump sum payment of $3,500 to cover her attorney fees.

The lawyer Alfredo hired to represent him in the lawsuit, Chris

Wilson of Long Beach, warned him that his reputation could be forever sullied if Vera's lawsuit proceeded to trial. Because he was still remembered everywhere in the world as one of the circus's greatest artists ever, the attorney advised, the press would treat any courtroom proceeding in which he was involved as a cause célèbre. He told Alfredo further that if Vera testified in open court that there had been times when he had "struck, slapped and abused" her, and had threatened her life, he, the Great Codona, could be viewed by much of the public as a madman.

Alfredo's attorney, along with James E. Pawson, the lawyer that Vera retained, arranged to meet before the first hearing that was scheduled in the case. During their meeting, the opposing attorneys codrafted a document that they planned to present in court and have Alfredo sign. It was spelled out in the document that Alfredo, of his own free will, was agreeing to all of the conditions, including the financial terms, that Vera requested in her petition for a divorce.

The document was presented for review to the presiding judge, Joseph M. Maltby, in Los Angeles Superior Court on July 1, 1937. The judge approved the terms of the settlement, as they were detailed in the document drafted by the attorneys, but also ordered an addendum to the agreement: Alfredo was to be legally "restrained and enjoined from visiting, molesting, or in any manner whatsoever, disturbing the plaintiff." Alfredo signed the amended document before Judge Maltby. The jurist then entered a decree for an interlocutory divorce, with the provision that neither Alfredo nor Vera could remarry before a year passed.

Alfredo left the courthouse with the humiliated appearance of an aging but once world-class prizefighter who had just had much of his life pounded out of him by some palooka. How much more could he take? Now that he was crippled and used up as a performer, his wife was leaving him. Not only that: he was legally bound to continue supporting her.

✦ ✦ ✦

George Lait, an occasional screen actor, a publicist for United Artists films, and a correspondent for the International News Services, found

Alfredo to be badly beaten down a couple of weeks later when the two met for lunch at a Hollywood restaurant. Because Lait was a man with connections, Alfredo asked if he could help him out.

"He was a man living in the past," Lait said. "He had . . . a leather folder containing notes, photographs, and newspaper clippings—in all, the story of his life and career. Could I advise him or assist him in arranging the publication of the story of his life? Surely everyone knew the Great Codona, the greatest aerialist who ever lived. Everyone would like to read his story. Or would they? Would they refuse his story because he was now a patchwork of broken bones?"

Lait said Alfredo expressed great bitterness toward Vera during the lunch. "He seemed to resent . . . the consummate professional skill he had imparted to Vera, but which he was now unable to employ."

Lait was traveling to New York on business the following day. He promised Alfredo he would do what he could to get his story told.

✦ ✦ ✦

Annie Bruce was the first to be awakened by the rapping at the window. Startled, she roused Vera, who was sleeping in the same bed with her in a motel room in Livermore, California. It was in the predawn of July 26 or 27, 1937.

Vera switched on a table lamp. There were boxes and bags everywhere on the floor, all of them filled with clothing and other items that she had hastily gathered from the Codona house. She threaded her way through the maze and to the window. Her heart was pounding. She pushed the curtain just far enough away from the window frame to investigate. Alfredo's face, inches from the glass, was backlit by the headlights of his yellow Studebaker, parked directly in front of the motel unit with its motor running. There was a crooked grin on his lips. He appeared crazed. He was waving a revolver.

Vera made a call to the motel's desk, awakening the owner. She pleaded with him to contact the police. Then she and her mother locked themselves inside a bathroom. In minutes, they heard a spraying of gravel from Alfredo's car.

Alfredo's behavior had become increasingly bizarre, unpredictable, and occasionally menacing toward her at least since the time he had been cast from the big top world the year before. Even though the two were now divorced, Vera must have continued to feel threatened by him. Vera and her mother had taken sanctuary in the motel room right after the divorce was granted. Livermore was four hundred miles from Long Beach. Until he had turned up at the motel that night, waving a revolver, she must have thought that she had traveled far enough away from him.

When the police arrived at the Livermore motel in the early morning hours after Alfredo had traveled there and terrorized Vera and Annie, they discovered that all the tires on their car had been slashed. After arranging for their replacement, Vera and her mother checked out of the motel and traveled to Long Beach. There she sent a note, written on the back of an automobile repair order, to Frank McCloskey, who, along with Fanny, was living in the Lenora Apartments in Los Angeles.

> *Frank,*
>
> *Am in plenty of trouble. Would like to see you as soon as possible. I am registered at the Hotel Alexander, Long Beach, Locust St., as Verna Bowen. Alfredo and I are divorced, but he is making life a hell for me. Sorry I did not call you today. Hope to see you or telephone the hotel.*
>
> *Cheerio, Vera*

There remained yet one final legal matter to be resolved before she could leave California to return to Clary's bareback riding troupe and the circus. She and Alfredo had been directed by the court to meet on August 1 in the Los Angeles office of her lawyer, James E. Pawson, to work out an agreement on how the common property of the two should be divided.

♦ ♦ ♦

Except for the ashes of his beloved Leitzel, kept in a regularly polished copper urn atop the shrine he had erected in his bedroom, Alfredo was now isolated in the family house without another human presence.

July was almost at its end, and now the days lay on Long Beach like a barber's steamed shaving towel. Whether because of the broiling heat or his profound loneliness, Alfredo often found it unbearable to stay at home nights. Sometimes he would leave the house on Cherry Street at eleven o'clock or midnight and cruise the streets of Long Beach and Los Angeles in the yellow Studebaker. Sometimes he brought along the urn with Leitzel's ashes and carried on one-sided conversations with her during the nighttime meanderings.

He did not return to the house after all the nighttime wanderings. Sometimes an hour or two before daybreak, he would pull the Studebaker into the driveway of the W. K. Adolph & Codona Co. garage in Walteria. There, he would sleep in his car until it was time to put on his coveralls and go back to greasing axles.

On the morning of August 1, though, Alfredo awoke in his bed in the house on Cherry Street. Those who would talk to him later that day, including Lalo, concluded he must have had a rare night of untroubled sleep. He seemed cheerier than he had been and gave others an impression that he had finally started to figure things out and was ready to put his life with Vera behind him.

Always when Alfredo opened his eyes in his bedroom in the morning, his attention was first drawn to the urn on the bedroom shrine. He would call out a greeting of the new day, *"Buenos días, mi muñequita."* On this morning, because he had awakened in unusually good spirits and was excited about the new day ahead, he may even have sung the song he often sang to Leitzel, one of her favorites:

> *Mexicali Rose, stop crying.*
> *I'll come back to you some sunny day.*
> *Every night you know I'll be pining,*
> *Every hour a year while I'm away.*

He fixed himself breakfast and afterward made telephone calls to Lalo and Victoria. Neither had heard from him much since the divorce was granted a month earlier, and when they did, he was usually sullen and complained about how Vera had already taken him for almost everything he was worth, and still wanted more. Both Lalo and Victoria were surprised when they heard from him that morning, though. He sounded cheerier than he had in months. He said nothing about Vera, nor, for that matter, anything at all that had to do with the present.

His talks with his brother and sister that morning were long and winding, bumping on topics from the long-ago past when the three were young children, moving through Mexico with Papa and Mama in the family Gran Circo Codona.

"Those were the days, weren't they, Lalo?" Alfredo said to his brother. "No cares in the world. What I'd give to be able to start them all over."

Before ending the calls, he told Victoria and Lalo how much he cared about them.

❖ ❖ ❖

When Alfredo stepped outside the house that day, he was snappily dressed in a cream-colored linen sport coat, blue trousers, and a panama hat. Those who knew him might have guessed he was resuming one of the activities in which he frequently took part before he had sunk into depression—an outing on a yacht with friends, maybe, or perhaps a lawn party at Green Acres, the Beverly Hills home of his friends Harold Lloyd and Mildred Davis.

There was not likely to be much that was to be festive for Alfredo about this day, though. This was the day he was scheduled to meet in the office of Vera's attorney to arrive at a binding agreement with her on how the two should divide their personal effects. The relationship between the pair would be over once this last bit of legal housekeeping was finished. Then each would be free to go their separate ways.

Alfredo remained bright as he rode an elevator to the offices of

Attorney Pawson on the sixth floor of the Security Building in Downtown Los Angeles. Vera and her mother, Annie Bruce, were already in the reception room when he entered.

"Hello, Mother," he chirped. "Good afternoon, Vera."

Vera, as always, looked stunning. She was wearing a dress that looked like it might have been selected from one of the shops on Rodeo Drive. It was knee length, a powdery blue, and was printed with what seemed to be a hundred small white flowers. Her hair was cut in a bob that partly covered one eye and fell to her chin.

Alfredo complimented Vera on her appearance. Next, he took his mother-in-law's right hand and kissed it. Vera instantly folded her arms in front of her and tucked her hands behind them.

In minutes, a secretary appeared and led the three into a conference room. Vera's attorney was already seated at a table with papers all around him. He directed them to take seats.

Alfredo did not raise any objections as the lawyer read from the sheets listing the jewelry, furs, clothing, and other personal effects that Vera was claiming. Many of the items were gifts Alfredo had made to her, among them some expensive rings, bracelets, necklaces, and hats that had once belonged to Leitzel. All of the articles were still back in the Long Beach house that he and Vera once shared.

Alfredo eyes were lighted throughout the meeting. He was smiling. He made small talk about the birthdays, anniversaries, Christmases, and other occasions during their nearly five-year marriage when he had presented her this ring or that pair of earrings. Vera had worried earlier that this meeting with Alfredo could turn out to be especially rancorous. She was surprised, but grateful, that Alfredo remained civil throughout the proceedings. He seemed subdued, maybe even a little sad, but did not challenge a single one of the claims she had made for the items listed on the inventory sheets.

Finally the lawyer ended his recitation of the articles recorded on his sheets and looked up from his papers. He asked Alfredo if he wanted to dispute the ownership of any of the articles Vera said belonged to her. He said no. Pawson then asked if he was ready to sign the papers that spelled out which articles would be going to Vera. He nodded his assent. The attorney pushed the forms to Alfredo's side of the table, and he reached into his coat for a pen.

When Alfredo finished with the signings, he asked Pawson if it would be all right if he had a private moment with Vera. The attorney looked to her. Vera may have thought Alfredo wanted to apologize for the incident a week earlier when he tracked her to the motel in Livermore, and, after rapping at the window of her room, pointed a revolver at her. Or maybe, Vera may have thought, Alfredo simply wanted to wish her well in the future. She and Alfredo had been wife and husband, and though it had not worked out, she may have wanted to express the same wish to him.

Vera nodded to her lawyer, signaling to him that she thought it would be okay for her to hear what Alfredo wanted to say to her.

Pawson thanked Alfredo for not contesting any part of the afternoon's proceedings. He shook his hand, wished him luck, and left him in the conference room with Vera and her mother.

Alfredo calmly locked the door behind the attorney. Next, he knelt before Vera's chair and locked his arms around her lower legs. In an instant, beginning at the hemline of her dress and then moving upward, he started kissing the small, white flowers on the garment, one after another. Vera was startled, disarmed. She sprang to her feet. She opened her purse and fished out a cigarette. Her hands trembled as she fitted an Old Gold into a long-stemmed holder.

Alfredo drew a lighter from his trousers and held its flame to her cigarette.

"Vera," he said, "you've left nothing more for me to do."

In the next moment, his hand disappeared into his coat. When it was visible again, he was holding a revolver, the same one that Vera had seen that early morning outside the window of the motel room in Livermore.

Alfredo fired four slugs. One entered Vera's jaw and another went into her chest. He fired two more into her abdomen.

The air was acrid with smoke from the revolver's bursts. Annie Bruce was shrieking in terror. Alfredo looked at his mother-in-law for a moment, then positioned the revolver's barrel against his temple, and fired a fifth round. His legs crumpled under him, and he apparently died instantly.

Vera was still alive but unconscious. Blood streamed from her head, and from her chest and stomach. The bodies of the pair were just feet apart on the floor, positioned in a manner curiously similar to the way F. W. Murnau had carefully arranged those of Marion and the Great Cecchi in the love-death scene at the very end of his *4 Devils*.

Vera was rushed by ambulance to the Seaside Hospital in Long Beach. She remained unconscious for sixteen hours. Then she opened her eyes and saw her mother sitting beside her bed.

"Are you all right, Mother?" she asked.

Vera closed her eyes again, and then she was gone.

✦ ✦ ✦

She was buried three days after the shootings in the Calvary Cemetery in Westmore, California. Only her mother, brother, Clary, and Fanny and Frank McCloskey were present.

The services for Alfredo were held the following day at the Mottell Chapel and Mortuary in Long Beach. So many mourners clogged the chapel that dozens of others had to remain outside. A minister said a few words about Alfredo. He mentioned Alfredo's siblings, Lalo, Edward, and Victoria, along with the nieces and nephews who survived Alfredo. He mentioned that Alfredo had traveled with the circus for years and more recently was employed at an auto garage. He could have been talking about a man who spent all his working years driving a milk truck. He said nothing about the Great Codona's worldwide renown as the big top's greatest male artist ever.

As the mourners filed out of the chapel, an organ pealed "The Blue Danube Waltz." It was Alfredo's favorite song, one that was often playing as he soared on the air.

Edward Codona Jr., a member of the Long Beach Police Department and a younger brother to Alfredo, had arranged for a group of uniformed motorcycle officers to lead the cortege to Inglewood Park Cemetery just outside Los Angeles.

It was far from the biggest audience before which Alfredo had ever appeared, but it was in the hundreds. Movie producers, circus impresarios, powerful talent agents, aerialists, wire walkers, famous animal trainers, clowns, and film and stage actors were gathered in the cemetery when pallbearers brought his casket out of the hearse. Men removed their hats. Women drew veils over their faces.

A note had been found in Alfredo's coat after the shootings.

"I have no wife to love me," he had written. "I am going back to Leitzel, the only woman who ever really loved me."

His casket was lowered into the ground, within feet from where Leitzel's ashes lay, inside the locked vault of *Reunion*. The circus's queen and king were together again.

Afterward, the mourners broke into different groups of two, four, six, or more people.

Those from the worlds of the movies and the theaters talked about how hard it was to understand what drove the Great Codona to close his life that way, and also to take Vera Bruce's. The sorrow he must have suffered after losing Leitzel and then becoming a cripple, unable ever to fly again, must have been bottomless. Surely this all drove him to madness. It was all so tragic.

The bareback riders, tight wire dancers, midgets, and clowns who were present listened to all this, but at least some of them thought there could be a different explanation. The circus exists apart from the ordinary world, they believed, and it is one that is governed by its own divines. When Leitzel dropped from the air that night in Copenhagen, it may have been foreordained that Alfredo and Vera would come to their ends, too. Black luck always comes in threes in the big top, the *saltimbanques* have always held. It is the way of the circus. Because Alfredo and Vera were the two people most intimately involved in Leitzel's sphere at the time of her death, their sacrifice may have been necessary. It might have been the only way that the planets over the circus could become properly realigned, the only way for the big top's order to be restored.

One side might have been right in the matter, or maybe both sides might have been partly right and partly wrong. Who can ever know in cases like this?

Only this much might be certain: as an institution, the circus has been around for a long time, maybe almost from the moment a few far-dreamers started wondering about what lay beyond the boundary of what others thought was the absolute limit of the humanly possible. As long as there continue to be such dreamers, the circus, in one form or another, will likely continue to go on and on. In what were just two snaps of the fingers in time's flow, though, the big top lost not only its two most surpassing artists ever but also its queen and king. The great canvas cathedral was never again quite as magic, wondrous, and even as holy a place as it was when they were its rulers, and, it seems almost sure, it never will be again.

ACKNOWLEDGMENT*S*

⁋ was the art critic and also an entertainment and feature writer at the daily *Milwaukee Sentinel* (now *Milwaukee Journal-Sentinel*) when I first set out to write the story of Leitzel and Alfredo Codona. More punctilious then than I am today, I set a strict deadline for the book's completion.

I missed it, but only by thirty-plus years.

Actually, except for the last chapter or two, I had completed a first draft of the book by the early 1980s. And I hated it. Every word. I felt back then, as I do today, that the story of Leitzel and Alfredo was the greatest one the big top has ever had to tell. They presided over an ever-relocating sawdust-and-rainbows-made Camelot where, one after another, wonderments kept occurring. Their love story was epic. Had it played out in the ancient world instead of the first third of the twentieth century, it might have been presented on the stage by Sophocles. Their story moved in the arc of a Greek tragedy, and, I believe, was complete with mischievous fates and vengeful gods.

And yet nothing of this radiated in that initial draft of the story I produced. I stowed that effort in a desk drawer, believing I needed to rethink everything. I thought then that I might return to the pages in six months or a year. But at about this same time, my life started changing in a lot of radical, but good, ways. In 1981, I took a position as a guest curator at the Milwaukee Art Museum. In 1982, I married the love of my life. The academic year of 1985–86 was spent at the University of Michigan in Ann Arbor where, with funding from the W. K. Kellogg Foundation, I had been recognized for my critical writing with a Journalists in Residence fellowship. Then, in 1987, I fulfilled a long-held wish: I opened a gallery of contemporary art in Milwaukee, the eponymously named Dean Jensen Gallery that I continue to operate today.

Around 2009, I decided to revisit the Leitzel and Alfredo Codona story. I never took a second look at my first telling, but did regather my research materials, including notebooks, envelopes plump with letters and yellowed newspaper cuttings, and many dozens of tape-recorded interviews, most of them with Alfredo and Leitzel's fellow travelers with the Ringling Bros. and Barnum & Bailey Circus and also members of their families. Soon, I was stabbing at the letters of a keyboard on a new first chapter. For another year and a half or so, in slivers of time stolen from the gallery, I continued to write. Then, *Queen of the Air* was finished. I do not know if this book is a good one, but I know it is many times better than my early attempt at telling the story of the two greatest stars that ever appeared in the canvas cathedrals.

I was immediately exhilarated when, after so many years, I finally I finished the story. But I also felt a sadness, one that still abides. While engaged in research, I interviewed more than a hundred of the circus's nomads, among them such legendary figures as Karl Wallenda, patriarch of the great and still-performing family of wire-walking daredevils; Merle Evans, bandmaster of the Ringling circus for about a half century; May Wirth, the dazzling, Australia-born equestrienne; and Victoria Codona, Alfredo's sister and the princess of the high and low wires. All the troupers were retired and in their advanced years when I started my visits with them, and they are all gone now. How I wish they were still here to let me know if I got anywhere close to accurately describing their world.

My thanks go first to Eileen Cope, the agent who represented me in the sale of *Queen* to The Crown Publishing Group. At the time I contacted Eileen, she was with the Trident Media Group, LLC, and was still with that agency when she negotiated the sale. She has since started her own New York agency, MCM, Mark Creative Management. Whether in her phone calls or emails, Eileen tends to be stinting about giving out a lot of words—or so it has always seemed to me. She seems to value them at about a hundred dollars each. But she gave me three hundred dollars' worth all at once after I wrote her a short letter, telling her of the Leitzel–Codona story. "This sounds fabulous," she responded immediately. My heart soared. And what a glorious ride it has been since she agreed to represent the book.

I am equally adoring of Crown's Jenna Ciongoli. She was acquisition editor for the book and then took on the role of its working editor. Jenna never gave me an impression that she was anything less than over the moon about my creation, and the suggestions she had for fine-tuning the narrative's musicality—its idyllic passages as well as those that are more somber and grave—were so numerous that she could almost be credited as the book's coauthor.

I am also indebted to another Crown editor, Domenica Alioto, who ably took over the stewardship of *Queen* during a short period while Jenna was on maternity leave. I am beholden, too, to the mighty triumvirate that Crown assembled to design a campaign to bring the book to attention in the marketplace. This team was made up of Dyana Messina, publicity manager; Julie Cepler, associate marketing director; and Danielle Crabtree, marketing department.

Queen of the Air benefited enormously from help that was provided by some of the world's most distinguished circus scholars. First and foremost in the august group was a longtime friend, Fred Dahlinger, Jr., curator of the Circus History, John and Mable Museum of Art, Sarasota, Florida, Florida State University, and before that, director of the Robert L. Parkinson Library and Research Center at the Circus World Museum in Baraboo, Wisconsin. There may hardly be a movie or significant book on the circus of the last twenty or twenty-five years that does not have Fred's handprints all over it. How many times did I call on him while producing this book? Any figure lower than fifty would be too low.

I would have been absolutely at a loss in writing about Europe's late-nineteenth- and early-twentieth-century circus landscape had it not been for the considerable help I received from Dominique Jando, former associate artistic director of the Big Apple Circus and today the editor of Circopedia.com.

The book's evocation of the early lives of Alfredo and Victoria Codona, when the brother and sister were touring Mexico with their father Edward's tiny circus, would have been impossible to develop without help from Greg Parkinson. A former executive director of the Circus World Museum and now deputy director of the Wisconsin Historical Society, Greg generously turned over his files on the Codona family to me.

David Kinchen, once a colleague at the *Milwaukee Sentinel* and later a writer at the *Los Angeles Times*, also had a major role in the book's development. He ferreted out numerous old newspaper stories that filled in blanks about Alfredo's life and death in California, and also provided me with a place to stay while I carried out research in Long Beach and Los Angeles.

Also contributing importantly to *Queen* were Maureen Brunsdale, rare book and special collections librarian at the Milner Library at Illinois State University, one of the country's richest repositories of circus reference materials; Peter Shrake, current director of the Circus World Museum's library, along with a staffer there, Ralph Pierce; Fred Pfening III, editor and publisher of *Bandwagon*, the bimonthly journal of the Circus Historical Society; Prof. Vanessa Toulmin, director of the National Fairground Archive at Sheffield University, Sheffield, England; and Ole Simonsen, Copenhagen, vice president of Danish Circus Fans Association.

I must extend thanks, too, to Janet Bergstrom, professor of Cinema and Media Studies at UCLA. She is not a circus specialist, but rather a distinguished scholar of émigré film directors of the early twentieth century, among them F. W. Murnau. The book's pages describing Alfredo's part in the making of the now-vanished movie, *4 Devils,* could not have been developed without the help Janet gave so freely.

Finally, but really firstly, too, I extend my gratitude and love to Rosemary Arakelian Jensen, my wife of nearly thirty years. It should be well more than enough for anyone to have a partner who is as loving and constantly encouraging as mine always is. But Rosemary has also always been a partaker in every important project I have undertaken in the past three decades, including the creation of *Queen of the Air*. She is a librarian by profession, and a marvel at carrying out difficult research work. She is also a master at indexing books, and, of course, carried out that work on this one. Finally, she is talented as an editor, one whose natural gifts in this regard have likely come to her through a long habit of devouring about one new book a week. Could any other writer be more blessed than I am? I have a live-in editor, one who is beautiful, and one who regularly spreads the table with divine Armenian dishes.

NOTE*S*

PROLOGUE

The description of the circus's appearance in Boston, along with many of the direct quotations, were drawn from a feature article on Leitzel that appeared on the front page of the *Boston Sunday Herald's* Sunday Magazine Section of June 13, 1920. The article carried the byline of Janet Mabie, and, in fact, was based on a visit Mabie had with Leitzel in 1919 when the Ringling Bros. and Barnum & Bailey Circus appeared in Boston from April 14 through 19. Leitzel had saved the article in a scrapbook that came into the author's possession, a gift from Leitzel's late brother, Alfred G. Pelikan, of Milwaukee.

4   *"How splendid you were tonight"*: "How Folk Work and Live Under the Big Top," *Boston Sunday Herald*, June 13, 1920.

4   *"Look out for the mud:"*: Ibid.

5   *"Beautiful dreams for honorable little lady"*: Ibid.

CHAPTER I

Most of the descriptions presented in this chapter were related to the author by Alfred G. Pelikan, the son of Nellie Pelikan. Alfred was not a direct witness to the events described, but learned of them through Nellie. She lived the last several years of her life in his Milwaukee home. Alfred had a great interest in recording his family's genealogy. He interviewed his mother at length about her girlhood in Breslau, Silesia, along with her travels as a child circus performer, first with her father's show, Eduard Pelikan's Family

Circus, and then with the Willy Dosta Circus. Many earlier accounts published about Leitzel and Alfred identify their father as having been a "Hungarian army officer" with the name "Edward J. Eleonore," whom Nellie supposedly married in Prague. These accounts are false. Both Leitzel and Alfred were fathered by Willy Dosta, the operator of the gypsy circus with which Nellie toured. At no time were Nellie and Dosta married to each other.

Alfred Pelikan was director of the Milwaukee Art Institute, a predecessor institution of the Milwaukee Art Museum, and also director of art education for the Milwaukee Public Schools. The author came to know him in 1976 while employed as an art critic and feature writer at the daily *Milwaukee Sentinel.* Because of the author's fascination with circus performers, and especially with Leitzel, the big top's greatest artist ever, he visited Alfred on numerous occasions in the late 1970s and early 1980s to interview him and pore over his large collection of family photographs, letters, scrapbooks, and other materials that came into his possession after the deaths of Leitzel and Nellie. Over time he presented the author with numerous items from his collection. He also gifted many items to the Circus World Museum in Baraboo, Wisconsin, an institution maintained by the Wisconsin Historical Society, which has the world's largest archive of important circus research materials.

9   *Nellie Pelikan was twelve:* Copy of church birth record now maintained in Wroclaw, Poland, which, at the time of Nellie's birth, was Breslau, Silesia, a part of the German Empire.

9   All of the author's searches to find any published accounts of Willy Dosta or the Willy Dosta Circus failed. This does not seem unusual. Small, one-horse circuses of the kind Dosta operated were rarely recorded in the press. A partial copy of an article that appeared in London's *World Pictorial News* identified Leitzel and Alfred's father not as a Willy Dosta, but rather as "Willy Dehosta." This variation may have resulted from a misspelling by the reporter who wrote the article. The article was in one of Leitzel's scrapbooks, and was headlined "Romantic Search by a Circus Queen/Heroine of a Thousand Thrills, and Giant Scottish Father She Has Never Met." Like many of the newspaper cuttings Leitzel saved, the date of the publication had been clipped away, presumably to accommodate the size of the scrapbook's pages. The clipping's content suggests the article was probably published sometime in December 1921, when Leitzel was in London, headlining Captain Bertram Mills's International Circus and Christmas Fair.

12 *Almost from the time:* Frances Stover, "Aunt Tina Tells the Story of Little Pelikans of Circus Days," *Milwaukee Journal*, June 1, 1939.

12 *She had been an equestrienne:* A. J. Leibling, "Here Comes the Clowns, profile of clown Bluch Landolf," *New Yorker*, April 15, 1939, 25–26. Landolf was an uncle to Leitzel.

12 *Often the nun:* Alfred Pelikan.

12 *"This will be your forever":* Ibid.

13 *Once the circus came upon:* Stover.

15 *"I used to be able to throw down":* Pelikan.

16 *"I'd like Nellie":* Ibid.

17 *"No. No. No":* Ibid.

19 *"Arghrr. . . . Arghrr . . . Arghrr. . . .":* Ibid.

21 *A few months:* Copy of Leitzel's birth certificate, church record now maintained by Poland in Wroclaw (formerly Breslau, Silesia).

CHAPTER 2

23 *"Oh, if any man could do":* Victoria Codona, Palm Springs, CA. Interviewed by phone at her home in Palm Springs, CA, by author, October 2, 1976.

23 *Edward arranged:* Ibid.

23 *Though the show had no printed programs:* Letter to the author from Victoria, dated November 8, 1976.

25 *The Buislays appeared:* Parkinson, 11.

27 *"I only wanted a home":* Parkinson. Recorded interview conducted by Marilyn Parkinson with Victoria at her Palm Springs home, February 1979, cited in Greg Parkinson's "Poster Princess—Victoria Codona."

27 *By the time Alfredo:* Phone interview with Victoria, October 8, 1976.

CHAPTER 3

29   *Even though Eduard and Nellie:* Alfred G. Pelikan.

29   *She told Nellie:* Ibid.

31   *When Nellie moved to the wagon's:* Undated article from one of Leitzel's scrapbooks, identified as being from a publication titled the *News of the World*, presumably the London newspaper. The article, which quotes both Nellie and Leitzel, is believed to have been printed sometime in December 1921 when Leitzel was engaged at the Bertram W. Mills International Circus and Christmas Fair, a show Mills presented annually at London's Olympia for many years.

34   *"My mother had been born":* Pelikan.

35   *Possibly because his wife: True Story* magazine article, quoting both Leitzel and her mother, circa 1921, p. 56, from a Leitzel scrapbook.

35   *"His methods were so cruel":* Ibid.

CHAPTER 4

38   *The man Julia admitted:* Toni Rainat (née Pelikan). Letter received by Alfred Pelikan from his aunt, Christmastime, 1914.

38   *White cuffs fastened with diamond: New York Times*, August 2, 1914.

38   *As imposing a figure:* Ibid.

39   *Prof. Edward J. Leamy, Mgr.:* Leamy business card, author's collection.

39   *"The cross at his neck":* Rainat.

39   *After taking a seat:* Ibid.

39   *The drawings:* "Tricks of the Trapeze: How Aerialists Are Taught to Perform Graceful and Sensational Acts," *Dublin* (Ireland) *Telegraph*, April 14, 1894, 1.

39   *The inner part of its frame:* E-mailed description of the trapezone rotaire to author from Dominique Jando, author, circus historian, and, for many years, associate director of the Big Apple Circus in New York City.

40   *Eduard looked at Leamy:* Rainat.

40   *The trapezone rotaire was entirely Leamy's invention: Dublin Telegraph.*

42   *"I was only months old":* Pelikan.

43   *"Big clubs only develop": Dublin Telegraph.*

43   *"The worst accident":* Ibid.

44   *The Blackpool Tower also had something else:* Willet.

45   *Nellie and Emma dangled: Dublin Telegraph.*

45   *By and large, though:* Ibid.

46   *An agent representing Oscar Hammerstein:* Sheen, 85.

46   *Opening night at the Olympia:* Ibid.

47   *Nellie also sent home money:* Pelikan.

47   *"She was in the same classrooms":* Ibid.

48   *"He was so good and generous":* Ibid.

49   *"It was quite a scene":* Ibid.

49   *"Someday it will be different":* Ibid.

49   *"These get-togethers":* Ibid.

CHAPTER 5

50   *"She has long, silky . . . hair":* Pelikan.

50   *"Oh, and did I tell you":* Ibid.

51   *"There's no two people":* Ibid.

52   *"It's not her":* Ibid.

54   *Nellie and Leamy lived:* "Lillian Leitzel: Abolisher of Gravity," *Ekstra-Bladet*, Copenhagen, Denmark, February 13, 1931. Translated by Ole Simonsen, Copenhagen.

54   *Leamy had already rented:* Pelikan.

55   *"Stop! Stop!":* Ibid.

56   *"Show off!":* Ibid.

56   *"She was just having":* Ibid.

56   *"I was circus crazy":* Ibid.

CHAPTER 6

57   *It was May of 1902:* Pelikan.

58   *"There were Indians":* Ibid.

59   *None in the quartet:* Ibid.

61   *Nellie was still in high dudgeon:* Ibid.

61   *Edward Leamy was beaming:* Ibid.

CHAPTER 7

62   *"Did you see her again":* Pelikan.

62   *"She makes me feel so bad":* Ibid.

63   *"You're La Belle Nellie":* Ibid.

64   *"The yearning that ever existed":* Cooper.

64   *"He had a strict rule":* Pelikan.

66   *"Oh, he was there":* Taylor, "Star I," *New Yorker,* April 21, 56.

66   *"The Wintergarten's show":* Pelikan.

69   *"They found the business in the hands of vagabonds":* Fox quoting Ade in *A Ticket to the Circus,* Bramhall House, New York, 1959, 107.

70   *One sister piloted:* Pfening Jr., "Sisters La Rague," 20.

70   *"He appeared to be analytically gauging":* Pelikan.

71   *"My mother, sister, aunts, and I":* Ibid.

71   *He so wanted:* Ibid.

NOTES

CHAPTER 8

74 *Mister John had arrived . . . with every confidence:* Phineas Taylor Barnum, born 1810, partnered in 1888 with James A. Bailey to create Barnum & Bailey's Greatest Show on Earth.

78 *"He watched those girls like a hawk":* Fellows, 229.

CHAPTER 9

80 *Then, in an instant:* Author's phone interview with Victoria Codona, October 8, 1976.

80 *"Papa couldn't stop":* Ibid.

80 *"Papa was a broken man":* Ibid.

80 *Maybe their house:* Ibid.

81 *"Oh, did we awaken you?":* Ibid.

82 *They started rummaging:* Ibid

82 "Bonita, bonita": Ibid.

83 *"All those years":* Ibid.

83 *"The circus was the only life":* Ibid.

84 *"We all believed":* Ibid.

85 *Of all the daredevils:* Accosta.

86 *Edward, in a black tuxedo:* Beekman.

86 *One of these circuses:* Parkinson, 11.

86 *It was the largest circus:* "Olympians of the Circus," compiled by William Slout for *Bandwagon* online, Circus Historical Society.

87 *So great was the tumult:* "Big Show Coming: High Wire Queen One of the Features of the Show." *Lowell* (MA) *Sun,* June 5, 1912, 12.

87 *Among those on their feet:* Ibid.

CHAPTER 10

89   *After Leitzel descended:* Victoria Codona.

89   *"After seeing Leitzel":* Ibid.

89   *"Alfredo was in love":* Ibid.

90   *The position he had been given:* Davis, 33.

90   *An agent for the big show:* Ibid.

90   *"Give her the moon":* Ibid.

91   *CAN OFFER YOU:* Otto Ringling telegram, Victoria Codona collection.

92   *"You would have thought":* Shives.

92   *"For one thing":* Ibid.

93   *Charley Ringling, who was in charge:* Brann.

93   *"Nothing is quite so frustrating":* Bradna, 14.

94   *"Every town had a post office":* Brann.

95   *"Over and over, Papa warned":* Author's phone interview with Victoria Codona, October 2, 1976.

96   *"I think this was all a game":* Shives.

96   *"What Leamy didn't know":* Brann.

97   *Alfredo could be moody:* Ibid.

97   *"He even talked to me":* Ibid.

98   *There were accounts:* Fraser, 28, and C. G. Sturtevant, "The Clarke Family," *The White Tops* (December–January 1938–39), 12.

98   *"If he could perform":* Author's phone interview with Victoria Codona, October 2, 1976.

98   *"No," he said:* Ibid.

99   *"Nothing in the entire list:"* George Brinton Beal, "They Lived the Greatest Circus Love Story of All Time, Codona and Leitzel, the King

and Queen of the Aerialists," *Boston Sunday Post*, color feature section, May 3, 1931.

100 *"Alfredo could always throw":* Brann.

100 *"I think she saw":* Shives.

101 *"He would get teary":* Brann.

101 *Their romance:* Ibid.

CHAPTER II

103 *From the time:* Pelikan.

104 *"My mother always felt":* Ibid.

104 *Nellie sailed to Berlin:* Ibid.

106 *"She was elegantly attired":* Leontini.

106 *"In Europe, at least":* Ibid.

113 *Edward Leamy lay near death:* "Silver King's Hurt, $2000 Pin Gone, Friends Believe Edward Leamy, Old Showman, Was Beaten to Death," *New York Times*, August 2, 1914.

114 *George DeFeo, a theatrical producer:* Deposition taken April 24, 1915, introduced at divorce proceeding in Cook County Court, Chicago.

115 *"She wanted him to go to work":* Ibid.

115 *"My wife and I visited":* Ibid.

116 *"People got the idea":* Taylor, *Center Ring*, 221.

116 *Standing before Leitzel:* "Lillian Leitzel," Ringling Bros. and Barnum & Bailey Circus website.

117 *The circus could offer:* Ibid.

CHAPTER 12

123 *It looked like a municipality:* "Here Is a Study of Circus Contrasts," *Mansfield* (OH) *News*, June 24, 1915.

124 *"Do you know":* Wirth.

124 *"Oh, forgive me":* Ibid.

124 *"With all due respect":* Ibid.

125 *"Our jaws had dropped":* Ibid.

125 *"The three met":* Ibid.

127 *"We have always had a rule":* Telegram sent to Leitzel, a copy of which is in collection of Circus World Museum, Baraboo, WI.

128 *Colonel Howard was the founder: National Cyclopedia of American Biography.*

128 *Several of his ponies:* Hillenbrand, 178–80.

128 *The colonel was not just a millionaire: Literary Digest,* April 26, 1927.

129 *"Now I just took the liberty":* Taylor, *Center Ring,* 233.

129 *"Money, money," she snapped:* Ibid.

129 *Always unaccompanied:* McCloskey.

129 *"Leitzel never answered":* Ibid.

133 *"Because of the show's rules":* Brann.

CHAPTER 13

134 *"Come in, please":* Leitzel in a letter to her brother, Alfred, Christmastime, 1918.

134 *"My arms turned to gooseflesh":* Ibid.

135 *"Like a god and goddess hugging":* Ibid.

135 *"I'll never forget it":* Ibid.

136 *"I had to keep pinching":* Ibid.

137 *According to one magazine writer:* Taylor, "Star I," 58.

138 *She had spent much of her girlhood:* Hayter-Menzies, 17.

142 *"Lillian Leitzel, 'Aerial Frolic' ":* New York World, December 10, 1918.

142 *"What a grand, grand night"*: Leitzel in letter to Alfred.

142 *As she rolled:* Ibid.

CHAPTER 14

143 *"The pairing of Clyde and Leitzel"*: Evans.

144 *Ingalls, in the words of Merle Evans:* Ibid.

146 *"His voice was so booming"*: Freeman.

146 *"I looked at these tunes"*: Evans.

147 *"One early morning"*: Ibid.

147 *"Zip was lying"*: Ibid.

147 *"On the circus"*: Ibid.

148 *The* New York Mail, *for one: New York Mail*, February 1, 1920.

148 *The* New York Sun*: New York Sun*, February 1, 1920.

149 *On average, Leitzel fired:* Cooper.

149 *"Where were you, Mabel?"*: Ibid.

150 *"Leitzel and Clyde appeared cold"*: Wirth.

150 *"Flo and Billie"*: McCloskey.

151 *"He must be ever there"*: Leitzel, quoted in Mary Rennel's "What Type of Men Make Best Husbands?" *Thomson Features*, 1923, a newspaper clipping in a Leitzel scrapbook.

152 *"Oh, they were at it again last night"*: Evans.

152 *During one especially pitched battle:* North, 156.

152 *"Leitzel and I got so seasick"*: Evans.

153 *Mills's International Circus:* The *Times* of London, December 17, 1921.

154 *"There'd be times"*: Jahn.

154 *"She considered my drummers"*: Evans.

154 *Evans was paid twenty-five dollars:* Ibid.

155 *"Here's a tenner":* Taylor, "Star II," *New Yorker*, 61.

155 *Leitzel was awarded a divorce from Ingalls:* Divorce decree, Shreveport, LA.

CHAPTER 15

159 *Sometime after midnight:* "Sells-Floto Circus Has Auspicious Opening," *Billboard*, April 26, 1919, 3, 14.

160 *There was another distinctive subculture:* Ibid.

161 *Alfredo was married now, too:* James L. Adams "She Flew through the Air . . . with Tragedy," *Cincinnati* (OH) *Post*, May 23, 1964.

163 *He wormed himself into a gunnysack: Boston Globe*, May 27, 1919, 9.

165 *She had become:* "Big Circus Day, Tuesday, Aug. 3," *Fort Wayne* (IN) *Journal-Gazette*, August 3, 1915, 18.

166 *Alfredo found:* Farmer, 56.

167 *"I had adopted a fatalistic attitude":* Codona, Cooper, 76.

167 *He experienced, he said:* Tait, 27.

169 *"If any other people":* Anita Codona.

CHAPTER 16

171 *When Alfredo turned up:* Anita Codona.

171 *Ernie Lane, the flyer who had been competing:* At least a few circus scholars have made the claim in writing that Lane had begun performing The Triple before Alfredo was able to accomplish it. This was absolutely not true, according to trapeze performer Mayme Ward, who, with her husband, Eddie, headed the Flying Wards, the troupe in which Lane flew. Ward told Charles Philip (Chappie) Fox, former head of the Circus World Museum and the author of numerous circus books, that Alfredo began performing the feat "well before" Lane. Fox's undated written record of his interview with Mayme on the subject

is currently in a file identified as the "Tom Parkinson Papers" at the museum.

171 *He was pronounced dead:* "Happenings of the World Tersely Told," *Riverdale* (IL) *Pointer*, April 15, 1921, 3, and also "Plunges Headlong to Death in the Theater Auditorium," *San Antonio* (TX) *Light*, January 4, 1928, 74.

172 *"Well, look at you":* Anita Codona.

173 *"absolutely charming":* Ibid.

175 *"Because he treated Clara so shamefully":* Ibid.

176 *"No married woman would trust her":* Parkinson citing a Marilyn Parkinson interview with Victoria Codona in Palm Springs, CA, 1974.

176 *"When he and Alfredo were arguing":* Anita Codona.

177 *She had started engaging in a nightly ritual:* Austen Lake, "Doping to Win: Humans and Horses," *The American Weekly*, April 15, 1948.

178 *"A fighter steps into the ring":* McCloskey.

178 *"Why don't you let go?":* Codona, Cooper, 76.

179 *"The mind seems to let go":* Ibid.

179 *"She could have had the life":* McCloskey.

CHAPTER 17

180 *The party, a fete, really:* "Impressed by the Circus," *New York Times*, October 30, 1927, sect. IX, 9.

181 *For much of the day and night:* Evans.

182 *"The circus":* F. W. Murnau quoted in "Impressed by the Circus," *New York Times*, October 20, 1927, sect. ix, 9.

182 *"If I had remained another day":* Ibid.

184 *The final straw:* Petition for divorce filed December 10, 1927, in Hamilton County Court, Cincinnati, OH.

184 *Clara did not identify:* Ibid.

185 *After traveling to 119 cities:* www.circushistory.org/Routes/Route.htm. Circus routes page at CircusHistory.org, online site maintained by the Circus Historical Society.

185 *Clara did not accompany:* James L. Adams, "She Flew through the Air . . . with Tragedy," *Cincinnati* (OH) *Post and Times,* May 23, 1964.

186 *It was January 3, 1928:* Bergstrom, "Murnau in America," 439.

186 *"We expected to see":* Anita Codona.

187 *Because the narrative:* Janet Bergstrom in e-mail to author, February 20, 2009.

188 *"This is impossible, Mr. Murnau":* "Reminiscences of Janet Gaynor," Oral History Department, Columbia University, New York, 1956.

189 *"This is the way":* Ibid.

CHAPTER 18

193 *"Because Leitzel and Alfredo":* Freeman.

195 *"Her dressing tent," said Bradna:* Bradna, 190.

195 *"We'd be drinking coffee":* Evans.

196 *One Chicago writer:* Bradna, 192.

198 *"I hadn't seen Uncle Adolph":* Pelikan.

198 *Finally she did appear:* Ibid.

199 *Colonel Howard took a seat:* Ibid.

200 *"You see anything of Mrs. Codona?":* Taylor, "Star II," 66.

201 *"The resultant tantrum":* Bradna, 193.

CHAPTER 19

203 *"Probably every woman":* McCloskey.

203 *McCloskey remembered an afternoon:* Ibid.

204 *Said Merle Evans:* Evans.

NOTES

204 *The fights between Leitzel and Alfredo:* Bradna, 191.

206 *"I don't care how much":* Concello.

206 *"I got goose bumps":* Ibid.

206 *"Alfredo was not only the greatest flyer":* Ibid.

207 *"You heinie sons of bitches":* Wallenda.

208 *"Maybe you heinies":* Ibid.

208 *"Ladies and gentlemen, the sensations":* "Detailed Review of Display and Features of the R-B Circus," *Billboard*, April 21, 1928, 56, 58.

209 *"Well, we really stunk up the place":* Wallenda.

210 *"I shall never forget their debut":* Bradna, 265.

210 *"She never really seemed":* McCloskey.

212 *"Sometimes Leitzel's temper":* Bruce, 58.

CHAPTER 20

214 *After years of being gnawed at:* Cooper, *Literary Digest*, 4.

214 *Leitzel likely smiled wryly:* Bull, 2.

215 *"Easily," she said:* Cooper, *Literary Digest*, 4.

215 *"Then it seems to me":* Ibid.

215 *"All right":* Ibid.

215 *"I understand . . . but you don't":* Ibid.

216 *While the circus had been playing Boston:* Alfredo letter to Pat Valdo, Ringling personnel manager, in Circus World Museum collection.

216 *It was also far more:* Data from Brookings Institute, Washington, D.C.

218 *In all, the Great Codona Circus:* *Billboard*, July 29 and August 3, 1929.

219 *"'Laugh, clown, laugh'":* Burlington (IA) *Hawkeye*, November 13, 1929.

220 *"Miss Leitzel, The Queen of the Air":* Illustrated advertisement in *Laredo* (TX) *Morning Times*, November 19, 1929.

220 *"It was a disaster"*: Antes.

221 *A* Billboard *correspondent*: *Billboard*, November 16, 1929.

221 *"We had four or five clowns"*: Antes.

222 *"Alfredo was my brother-in-law"*: Anita Codona.

222 *"The train was nothing like"*: Ibid.

222 *"All the time we moved"*: Anita Codona.

223 *"We were afraid"*: Arley.

223 *"Dear Sir"*: Original letter in Paul Arley collection.

224 *"We were home again"*: McCloskey.

225 *The Great Codona Circus, "The Show Beautiful"*: Laredo (TX) Morning
     Times, January 1, 1930.

CHAPTER 21

229 *"My sister never told me"*: Pelikan.

232 *He slammed into Carl:* "Circus Acrobat Killed at Bronx in Pole-
     Balancing Act," *New York Times*, March 30, 1931, 1.

233 *Leitzel embraced Gretchen:* Gretchen Jahn and Dolly Copeland (née
     Jahn).

233 *"What could have happened?"*: Ibid.

233 *"Why don't you let go?"*: Codona, Cooper, 76.

234 *"Some mornings"*: Copeland.

236 *It was during these partings:* Bruce, 38.

236 *"Vera was always scrupulously honest"*: Ibid.

236 *"My sister had taken in Vera"*: Pelikan.

237 *"Someday," she remarked:* Beal, George Brinton, *Boston* (MA) *Sunday
     Post*, March 3, 1931.

CHAPTER 22

241 *"I never before had a chance"*: Nellie in letter to Melba Pelikan, dated March 9, 1931, from author's collection.

242 *"She loved Alfredo perhaps too much"*: Ibid.

242 *"It was a bad wish"*: Ibid.

242 *"Do you know who this woman is?"*: Pelikan.

243 *He said he had been miserable*: Ibid.

243 *"I still remember the Tivoli Gardens"*: Milde.

244 *Milde joked with Leitzel*: Ibid.

244 *"Well, for a while it was diamonds"*: Ibid.

244 *"What are you interested in at the moment"*: Ibid.

244 *"Only my husband"*: Ibid.

244 *"Are you ever nervous?"*: Ibid.

244 *"I can wake up"*: Ibid.

244 *"And then what?"*: Ibid.

244 *"A wonderful house in California"*: Ibid.

249 *She rasped, "It's what I told you"*: Fanny McCloskey, quoting her husband, Frank.

249 *"I'm all right"*: North, 158.

249 *McCloskey and Mabel laced their arms*: McCloskey.

250 *A doctor injected Nellie*: Nellie in a letter to Alfred and Melba Pelikan, dated March 9, 1931.

250 *"Poor Leitzel hardly recognized me"*: Ibid.

250 *"My doll." He wept*: Fanny McCloskey, quoting Frank.

250 *By the afternoon*: Ibid.

251 *"Why hadn't I been with her"*: Ibid.

251 *The hospital rang up*: Ibid.

252 *She was wearing the same crème de menthe:* Saxburger, *Verden.*

252 *Before the start of a hockey game:* "Garden Crowd That Once Cheered Bows in Silence for Lillian Leitzel," *New York Times*, February 18, 1931.

252 *"To the memory of Lillian Leitzel":* Ibid.

252 *As the rope was slowly drawn upward:* Ibid.

253 *"I AM BARREN OF WORDS":* Colonel Howard in telegram to Alfred Pelikan. Copy of wire in collection of Circus World Museum.

254 *Heinz Saxburger, a Danish magician:* Saxburger in phone interview at his home in Copenhagen with author, December 10, 2002, and also in his book, *Verden rundt med flagrende kjoleskøder* (*Around the World in a Fluttering Frock Coat*).

254 *"It was a night sometime around 1960 or 1961":* Saxburger interview with author.

254 *"You saw her, Heinz":* Ibid.

255 *The Valencia Music Hall was razed:* Ole Simonsen, Danish circus scholar in Copenhagen, in e-mail to author.

CHAPTER 23

256 *Alfredo saw it in a dream the first time: New York Journal-American*, August 29, 1937.

256 *Someone told him of Professor Escoli:* Ibid.

257 *It bore a $38,000 price tag:* Pelikan.

257 *The wood-crated monument:* "Leitzel Monument to Reach Harbor Tuesday," *Long Beach Press-Telegram*, December 1, 1931, 1.

259 *"Nothing on but a fig leaf":* Alfredo in a letter to Pat Valdo, Ringling personnel director, the original of which is in Circus World Museum collection.

259 *"Dad and I":* Ibid.

259 *All the time: Long Beach Press-Telegram*, date unknown.

260 *Not surprisingly:* "Final Tribute Paid Lillian Leitzel," *Long Beach Press-Telegram*, December 10, 1931, 1.

260 *After the services:* Ibid.

CHAPTER 24

263 *"Mother, Alfredo wants to marry me":* Bruce, 60.

263 *On these occasions:* Ibid.

264 *"The more she practices":* Alfredo in a letter to Frank McCloskey, dated February 4, 1931, from Fanny McCloskey collection.

264 *Like numerous great artists before him:* Jensen, 25, 26.

264 *Through arrangements made by Alfredo:* Junker, 157.

266 *"You did something that was strange":* Donovan.

266 *"I saw Leitzel's hands":* Ibid.

267 *Alfredo went to see Paul Arley:* Arley.

267 *He massaged Alfredo's back daily:* Ibid.

267 *By November of 1933:* "Codona Clan Meets Crisis/Father Takes Command as Family Starts Training to Aid Alfredo in Comeback Effort," *Los Angeles* (CA) *Times*, November 18, 1933.

267 *Alfredo damned the gods:* Ibid.

269 *Even there:* Hagenbeck-Wallace Circus official program, 1935.

270 *The "King of the Cowboys":* Pfening, Jr., 17–20.

271 *Years earlier:* H. D. Sterling, "A Wayside Garage That Draws 'Em," *Motor Maintenance*, June 1932, 22–23.

272 *"Maybe in another year":* Anita Codona, quoting Vera.

272 *Alfredo begged Vera not to leave:* Ibid.

273 *"Dear Wife Vera":* Bruce, 64.

273 *In another letter:* Ibid.

CHAPTER 25

274 *He had just finished:* Fanny McCloskey, based on her conversation with Clary Bruce.

275 *"Alfredo," she said firmly:* Ibid.

276 *"during the past year":* Copy of divorce petition, filed in Los Angeles County Court, June 28, 1937.

276 *In petitioning the court:* Ibid.

278 *"He was a man living in the past":* George Lait, "Loved Her as Pupil—Killed Her as Star," *Sunday Mirror Magazine,* September 5, 1937, 5.

278 *"He seemed to resent":* Ibid.

278 *She pushed the curtain:* McCloskey.

279 *"Frank, Am in plenty of trouble":* Note from Vera, author's collection.

280 *"Mexicali Rose":* music by Jack B. Tenney, with lyrics by Helen Stone, M. M. Cole Publishing Co., Chicago, 1923.

281 *His talks with his brother and sister:* Anita Codona.

281 *"Those were the days":* Ibid.

282 *"Hello, Mother":* Ibid.

283 *"Vera," he said:* Ibid.

284 *"Are you all right, Mother?":* Bruce, 64.

284 *A minister said a few words about Alfredo:* Anita Codona.

ʃELECTED BIBLIOGRAPHY

Accosta, Theresa Paloma. "Mexican Circuses." *Handbook of Texas Online*. Texas State Historical Association.

Bang, Herman. *Four Devils*, in *Great Short Novels of the World*. Edited by Barrett H. Clark. Translated from Danish to English by Marie Heyl. New York: Robert M. McBade & Company, 1927.

Barnum & Bailey Circus official programs, 1909–1912.

Beal, George Brinton, *Through the Back Door of the Circus*. Springfield, MA: McLoughlin Bros., 1938.

Beekman, Bernice. "La Belle Victoria." *Palm Springs Villager*, April 1956.

Bergstrom, Janet. "Murnau in America: Chronicle of Lost Films." *Film History* 14 (2002): 2. Copyright John Libbey, 2002.

Bradna, Fred, and Hartzell Spence. *The Big Top: My Forty Years with the Greatest Show on Earth*. New York: Simon & Schuster, 1952.

Bruce, Annie. "The Mad Love of Alfredo Codona." *True Story Magazine*, May 1938.

Bull, Los. "Leitzel, Famed Aerialist, Hurls Her Body from Illness to Health." *New York Evening Graphic Magazine*, April 27, 1929.

Burke, Billie. *With a Feather on My Nose*. New York: Appleton-Century, 1946.

Codona, Alfredo, as told to Courtney Ryley Cooper. "Split Seconds." *Saturday Evening Post*, December 6, 1930.

Cooper, Courtney Ryley. "Little Lily Leitzel." *Literary Digest*, April 14, 1931.

Cosmopolite. "Alfredo Codona and the Art of Aerial Acrobatics." *The Sawdust Ring*, official periodical of Circus Fans Association of England. Winter 1937–38.

Davis, Charles Belmont. "Vanishing Day at the Circus." *Metropolitan Magazine*, June 1910.

Donovan, Fitzpatrick. "The Flying Codonas." *Argosy*, September 1957.

Eisner, Lotte H. *Murnau.* Berkeley: University of California Press, 1973.

Farmer, Patsi. "Codona at the Coliseum." *Shreveport* (LA) *Magazine*, August 1958.

Fellows, Dexter. *This Way to the Big Show.* New York: Viking Press, 1936.

Forbes, Camille F. *Introducing Bert Williams: Burnt Cork, Broadway and the Story of America's First Black Star.* New York: Basic Civitas Books, 2008.

Foster, Frank. *Pink Coat, Spangles and Sawdust: Reminiscenes with Sanger's Bertram Mills and Other Circuses.* London: Stanley Paul & Co., 1948.

Fox, Charles Philip. *A Ticket to the Circus: A Pictorial History of the Incredible Ringlings.* New York: Bramhall House, 1959.

Hayter-Menzies, Grant, and Erik Myers. *Mrs. Ziegfeld: The Public and Private Lives of Billie Burke.* Jefferson, NC: McFarland, 2009.

Hillenbrand, Laura. *Seabiscuit: The True Story of Three Men and a Racehorse.* New York: HarperCollins, 2002.

Jando, Dominque, with Noel Daniel, Fred Dahlinger Jr., and Linda Granfield. *The Circus Book, 1870–1950.* Taschen, 2010.

Jensen, Dean. *Center Ring: The Artist; Two Centuries of Circus Art.* Milwaukee: Milwaukee Art Museum, 1981. Published in conjunction with the exhibitions shown at the Corcoran Gallery, Washington, D.C., Columbus (Ohio) Museum of Art, and the New York State Museum, Albany.

Junker, Patricia. *John Steuart Curry: Inventing the Middle West.* New York: Hudson Hills Press, 1998.

Kelley, F. Beverly. *It Was Better Than Work*. Gerald, MO: Patrice Press, 1982.

Liebling, A. J. "Here Comes the Clown." *New Yorker*, April 15, 1938. Profile of Bluch Landolf.

"Lillian Leitzel." *Saturday Evening Post*, July 17, 1920.

Milde, Erna. "Mistress of the Air, Abolisher of Gravitation." *Ekstra-Bladet*, Copenhagen, Denmark, February 13, 1931. Translated from Danish by Ole Simonsen, Copenhagen.

Moffet, Cleveland. *Careers of Danger and Daring*. New York: The Century Co., 1926.

Murnau, F. W. "Films of the Future." *McCall's*, September 1925.

_____. *Sunrise: A Song of Two Humans (Limited Edition)*, a 2012 20th Century Fox DVD release of the 1927 F. W. Murnau film, which also includes a forty-minute featurette on Murnau's *4 Devils*, for which Alfredo Codona did the trapeze sequences. The featurette is narrated by Janet Bergstrom and was brilliantly assembled by her from parts of the original script, along with production drawings, photographs, and advertising materials. No copies of *4 Devils* exist in Fox's archives today, nor are any known to exist anywhere in the world. Because it was a motion picture by Murnau, and also because it included flying scenes by Codona, its disappearance is lamented today by film and circus scholars alike.

National Cyclopedia of American Biography. Chicago: Stanley Paul & Co., Ltd., ca. 1930s.

North, Henry Ringling, with Alden Hatch. *The Circus Kings*. New York: Dell Publishing Co., 1960.

Parkinson, Greg. "Poster Princess—Victoria Codona." *Bandwagon*, vol. 29 (Dec./Jan.) 1980–81, 11–14.

Pfening Jr., Fred D. "Sisters La Rague," *Bandwagon*, vol. 3 (May–June): 1969.

_____. "Tom Mix: His Life, His Movies, and His Circus." *Bandwagon*, November–December, 2002.

Ringling Circus official programs, 1915–1918.

Ringling Bros. and Barnum & Bailey Circus official programs, 1919–1930.

Russell, Stephen Mims, and Gayle Moran. *The Birds of Sonora*. Tucson: Arizona University Press, 1998. Illustrated by Ray Harm.

St. Leon, Mark. *The Circus in Australia*. Richmond, Victoria, Australia: Greenhouse Publications, 1983.

Saxburger, Heinz. *Verden rundt med flagrende kjoleskoder/[Around the world in a fluttering frock coat]*. Denmark: Toptryk Grafisk, 2002.

Scholl, Walter C. "Mrs. Hortense Buislay Codona." *The White Tops*, November 31, 1931. Obituary.

Sells-Floto Circus official programs, 1919–1922.

Sheean, Victor. *Oscar Hammerstein I: The Life and Exploits of an Impresario*. New York: Simon & Schuster, 1956.

Slout, William. "Olympians of the Circus." *Bandwagon* online. Circus Historical Society.

Sturtevant, C. G. "The Clarke Family." *The White Tops*, December 1938.

Tait, Peta. "Re/Membering Muscular Circus Bodies: Triple Somersaults, The Flying Jordans and Clarke Brothers." *Nineteenth Century Theatre and Film* (Manchester University Press) 33, no. 1 (June 2006): 26–38.

Taylor, Robert Lewis. *Center Ring: The People of the Circus*. Garden City, NY: Doubleday, 1956.

———. "Profiles, Star I (Leitzel)." *New Yorker*, April 21, 1956, 45–66.

———. "Profiles, Star II" (Leitzel). *New Yorker*, April 28, 1956, 47–69.

Weeks, David C. *Ringling: The Florida Years*. Gainesville, FL: University Press of Florida, 1993.

Willett, Philip. "Blackpool Tower: The Dream of John Bickerstaff." http://ezinearticles.com/?Blackpool-Tower---The-Dream-of-John-Bickerstaffe&id=3031042.

Willson, Dixie. *Where the World Folds up at Night*. New York: D. Appleton & Co., 1932.

∫ELECTED INTERVIEW∫

Antes, Edna, by phone to her home in DeLand, FL, the date of which was not recorded but is believed to have occurred in the 1980s when she was secretary-treasurer of Universal Circuses, Inc., a production company in Sarasota, FL.

Arley, Paul, at his home in Sarasota, FL, March 1977.

Brann, Francis "Butch," at his home in Sarasota, FL, February 1977.

Codona, Anita, at her home in Long Beach, CA, July 1 and 2, 1976.

Codona, Victoria, by phone to her home in Palm Springs, CA, July, August, October 1976.

Copeland, Dolly Jahn, at her home in Sarasota, FL, February 1977.

Concello, Art M., at John Ringling Towers Hotel in Sarasota, FL, March 17, 1977.

Evans, Merle, with contributions from his wife, Neva, at their Sarasota, FL, home, March 1975; also at the Circus World Museum in Baraboo, WI, spring of 1977.

Feld, Irwin, by phone to Ringling Bros. and Barnum & Bailey Circus corporate offices in Washington, D.C., August 27, 1974.

Fox, Charles Philip. Dozens of times, sometimes by phone, but mostly in face-to-face either at the Circus World Museum in Baraboo, WI, where he was director from 1960 to 1972, or at his home in Baraboo, where he died in 2003.

SELECTED INTERVIEWS

Freeman, Freddie, at his home, and also the Brann home in Sarasota, FL, February 1977.

Jahn, Gretchen, at the home of her daughter, Dolly Jahn Copeland, in Sarasota, FL, February 1977.

Kelley, F. Beverly "Bev," conducted mostly by phone to his home in Philadelphia, but also at the Circus World Museum, in the 1980s.

Kelly, Emmett, at his home in Sarasota, FL, March 3, 1978.

Leontini, Jack, at the Sarasota (FL) Nursing Home, March 17, 1978.

McCloskey, Fanny, at her home in Sarasota, FL, in March 1977 and 1978, and also occasionally by phone during this same period.

Pelikan, Alfred, numerous interviews, all of them at his Milwaukee home, the first of them April 18, 1976, and continuing into the 1980s.

Rosen, Lew, at John Ringling Towers Hotel, Sarasota, FL, March 17, 1977.

Saxburger, Heinz, by phone to his home in Copenhagen, Denmark, December 2011.

Scaperlanda, Georgia, by phone to her home in San Antonio, TX, February 25, 1975.

Shives, Charlotte, at her home St. Petersburg, FL, March 21, 1978.

Siegrest, Joe, at Brann home in Sarasota, FL, February 1976.

Wallenda, Karl, by phone, July 2, 1974, and at his home in Sarasota, FL, March 1975.

Wirth, May, at her home in Sarasota, FL, March 1975.

INDEX

INDEX

INDEX

ABOUT THE AUTHOR

Dean Jensen is the author of *The Lives and Loves of Daisy and Violet Hilton: A True Story of Conjoined Twins,* published in 2006. He has been a dealer of contemporary art for twenty-five years and is the operator of the Dean Jensen Gallery in Milwaukee, Wisconsin, where he and his wife also make their home. Previously, he was an art critic and feature writer for the *Milwaukee Sentinel* (now the *Milwaukee Journal-Sentinel*). He has received numerous writing awards.